Revolution
at the Grassroots

SUNY Series in Urban Public Policy
Richard Rich, Editor

Revolution at the Grassroots

Community Organizations in the Portuguese Revolution

CHARLES DOWNS

State University of New York Press

DP
681
D68
1989

Published by
State University of New York Press, Albany

© 1989 State University of New York

For information, address State University of New York
Press, State University Plaza, Albany, N.Y., 12246

Library of Congress Cataloging-in-Publication Data

Downs, Charles, 1950-
    Revolution at the grassroots: community organizations in the
Portuguese revolution/Charles Downs.
        p.   cm.—(SUNY series in urban public policy)
    Bibliography: p.
    Includes index.
    ISBN-0-7914-0066-2.   ISBN 0-7914-0067-0 (pbk.)
    1. Portugal—History—Revolution, 1974—Social aspects.
2. Portugal—Politics and government—1974.   3. Setubal (Portugal—
Social Conditions.   4. Social movements—Portugal—History—20th
century.   5. Sociology, Urban—Portugal—History—20th century.
6. Community organization—Portugal—History—20th century.
7. Political participation—Portugal—History—20th century.
I. Title.   II. Series: SUNY series on urban public policy.
DP681.D68   1989
946.9'043—dc19   88-31217
                                                         CIP

10 9 8 7 6 5 4 3 2 1

This book is dedicated to
my parents,
Mary Ann and William T. Downs,
who taught us to fight
for democracy, equality and justice

Contents

ACKNOWLEDGMENTS ix

One   Introduction 1

Two   A Short History of the Portuguese Revolution:
The Dialectic of Popular Mobilization 15

Three   The Revolution in One City 34

Four   Neither Spontaneity Nor Manipulation:
Roots of Urban Social Movements 66

Five   Transforming City and Society:
The Impact of Urban Social Movements 87

Six   Theory and Practice of Urban Social Movements:
Implications of the Portuguese Revolution 108

Appendices   A. Case Histories of Selected CMs 138

            B. Guidelines to the Alliance Between
the People and the MFA 162

            C. Statutes of the Conselho de Moradores 170

            D. COPS: Proposal for Popular Organization 173

            E. Occupational Composition of Neighborhoods 177

            F. Complete List of CM Demands 179

            G. Complete List of CM Accomplishments 182

            H. SAAL Projects in Setubal 185

            I. Communique from the Setenave
Housing Group 186

ABBREVIATIONS USED 188

NOTES 192

BIBLIOGRAPHY 201

INDICES 209

Acknowledgments

This book is the result of a unique opportunity to observe firsthand the development of the Portuguese revolution at the grassroots and the impact of massive popular involvement on that revolutionary process. Throughout the work I have benefitted from the support, friendship, and criticism of many people. Without ignoring the assistance of many who will go unmentioned here, I would like to give a special thanks to a few whose help has been especially important.

In early 1975, I decided to go to Portugal, where I lived for the next three years. News coverage of the changes following the overthrow of the authoritarian Caetano regime was incomplete and tended to attribute events to personalities and manueverings of political parties (especially the Communist Party) and the military. But reading between the lines, one could see that much more was occurring, that important issues of equity, democracy, development, and social change were being debated in the streets by ordinary citizens rather than just among a politically organized or educated elite. I went to Portugal to see and learn what I could from that unusual opportunity. The basic lesson developed in this book is that the period of political transition—when the alliances, institutions, and programs of the next period are established—is largely shaped by the interaction between national government and local citizen pressure around specific problems. Thus, my first thanks go to those many people who were actors in the drama that underlies these pages and who shared and discussed their lives and experience with me and my collegues.

This study began as part of a project of the Curso de Estudos Urbanos e Regionais of the Instituto Superior de Ciencias Sociais e Políticas in Lisbon. Everyone in the program contributed in one way or another to the basic concerns and early phases of this study. My thanks to all of them, but especially to Helena Gonçalves, Fernando Nunes da Silva, and Isabel Seabra, with whom most of the interviews that went into this study were conducted. I am sure they will recognize the large contribution they made, and I hope they will not find the result in great disagreement with our common work.

I would like to express my gratitude, to many others in Portugal particularly: Nuno Portas, Manuel Salgado, Isabel Guerra, and Bruno Soares, all of whom were very helpful both as friends and in the material support they provided.

Over the years since leaving Portugal in 1978, I have worked on this material for extended periods. During this time, I have benefitted from the comments of many people who shared my enthusiasm for the study and whose interest and effort have resulted in clearer arguments and fewer errors. This is especially true of Sy Adler, Steve Downs, Jack Hammond, Mimi Keck, Erica Schoenberger, and Marla Tepper.

I cannot possibly express my gratitude in these few lines, neither to the people named above, nor to the many others who have contributed to this study in one way or another. I would like to thank all of them for their support, without holding any of them responsible for the arguments, conclusions, or any deficiencies of this study.

ONE

Introduction

A t certain moments in history, large numbers of ordinary people seek to directly transform their society through participation in mass movements. The opportunity to do so does not depend on their volition or that of political organizers, but on the development of broader social and class struggles, to which their own involvement contributes. Such opportunities are not frequent, but when they occur they reveal the possibilities and dynamics of massive participation in social change latent in other times and places. The 1974 to 1975 Portuguese revolution was one such moment, with mass movements focusing on issues of concern to people in factories, farms, military barracks, and urban neighborhoods. This book focuses on the last of these—neighborhood based movements—the one which best represents the potential and limits of participation by the majority in changing both their immediate conditions and the broader society.

Urban social movements have been recognized as actors on the stage of history since the late 1960s. Community organizing and protest against urban renewal have longer histories, but neighborhood-based direct action movements gained a new prominence with ghetto uprisings in U. S. cities, grassroots pressure from the Brazilian *favelas*, Peruvian *barriadas*, and Chilean *campamentos*, and rent strikes in the United States, France, Italy, and elsewhere. Often associated with broader political crises and transformations of society, these movements have played a very important role in national and local development. Initially, a direct expression of grassroots protest and desire for change, over time, as they began to change the way cities operate and the way decisions were made, they became a concrete source of hope of broader democracy for some and of fear of anarchy for others.

Much debate—rarely very analytical—has focused on questions of urban social movements' origin, nature, significance for society and participants, and potential for producing change. Serious discussion often falls victim to the limited number of cases of urban social movements, leading some authors to apply the term to all forms of community-based movements and organizations (e.g., Lowe, 1986). But it is used more narrowly—as in this book—for those urban movements that are capable of qualitatively transforming the city and society. All authors recognize a multiplicity of factors shaping the

1

development and impact of urban social movements, but there is great variation regarding which they consider to be the most critical; some focus on organizers' strategies regarding choice of demands or links to other movements, others on the specific distribution of problems among social groups, while others concentrate on the political-institutional context, or on the process of political-economic modernization.

These movements share characteristics with other types of mass political movements, but essential elements are necessary to understand them and their dynamics, which can only be acquired by analyzing their specifically "urban" aspects. Not only do they arise in cities, but the issues they confront and their base of organization are specifically urban: they focus on problems of government organized and/or provided goods and services, such as housing, transportation, and social services, and community control over quality of neighborhood life. In addition, these movements are based primarily in groups defined by place of residence rather than place of work, that is, they are neighborhood—rather than factory—based. These two factors mean that the urban social movements' issues, potential social base, and immediacy of antagonism with the state are all distinct from the experience of other movements, differences which have important implications for theory and analysis, for strategy and tactics.

There is, moreover, a qualitative difference between urban social movements—which typically have much greater grassroots participation and the potential for profound change of the urban and political systems—and other types of urban organization and protest. But that difference is not a product of the intrinsic characteristics of the respective movements. The central argument of this book is that change in the *political conjuncture*—the balance of forces between social classes—is the critical element in creating the various characteristics of urban social movements.

The political conjuncture has two principal components: the situation of offensive or defensive of the popular classes; and the relationship of the state to the popular movements. The conjuncture is more than simply a "context" for understanding or developing urban movements—it is an important element determining who (members of which classes) participates, when they do so, what their concerns are, how they act to find solutions to their problems, what response they receive, what political attitudes they develop, the probable effects of their actions, and, finally, their structural impact.

This book is a detailed study of an exemplary case of urban social movements that developed in one city in a country undergoing a political and social revolution. The often-ignored story of the way ordinary people are affected by important events, attempt to be a part of them and take control of their own destiny and that of their country and city, as well as their perception of the process and the impact of their actions, is important and interesting in its own right. Moreover, examining the relatively rare cases of urban social movements, such as their little-known but advanced development and role in the Portuguese revolution, is important not only for the history and detailed understanding of the specific process involved, but also for its contribution to understanding the potentials, limitations, and dynamics only hoped for or feared with other movements.

For two years, from 1974 to 1976, the Portuguese revolution was a topic of frequent debate and commentary in Western media and political circles.[1] A nearly bloodless coup had brought the oldest and longest lasting authoritarian regime in Europe to an end in a matter of hours, unleashing a process of class conflict which began to develop into a social revolution. Political parties, foreign governments, and the Portuguese people each struggled to develop and implement their model for the new Portugal. During nineteen months of revolutionary development, Portugal had six provisional governments with significant variations in policies and party composition held power. They faced internal and external pressures including petitions, demonstrations, strikes, capital flight, sabotage, and coup attempts as different groups sought to gain control over the state and society in general and the economy and workplace in particular. Struggles over conditions of life in the neighborhoods paralleled the struggles over control of the state and economy. The resulting urban movement, actually composed of specific submovements involved in different struggles, included several waves of housing occupations, demands to change regulations in government housing, demands for the removal of fascist administrators, for physical infrastructure and social services, for housing programs, for lower rents and more favorable terms on loans, for changes in other government policies and personnel, for an end to the colonial wars, against capitalism and for popular power.

From the beginning, the *comissão de moradores* (neighborhood commission or CM) developed as the basic organizational structure of the urban movements. The CMs developed in all types of neighborhoods: in *Popular* neighborhoods with a majority of manual workers; in *Interclass* neighborhoods with a substantial percentage of manual workers together with many white-collar and service employees; and even in *Elite* neighborhoods with few manual workers and many white-collar professionals and businessmen. (This classification is discussed further in Chapter Four.) CMs cooperated extensively among themselves and with the workers' commissions that also developed during this period, forming various coordinating bodies that experienced qualitative advances in composition, analysis, and program. These organizations became a significant political force in their own right, with many viewing them as the cornerstone for building a democratic and socialist society. But this possibility passed as another military coup brought the development of the popular movement to a halt. Neither the community organizations nor the popular gains they had been instrumental in making were immediately eliminated, however, and a long period of defensive struggles ensued.

The development of grassroots organizations in this period stimulated much political debate as it demonstrated the practical possibility of ordinary people organizing and acting directly and democratically to deal with the problems they faced. The CMs saw themselves as "popular organizations" representing the people of their neighborhoods and maintained three specific political principles of operation: autonomy, unity, and nonpartisanship. All three principles developed from early CM experience and took into consideration some of the problems that had threatened to restrict the effectiveness and development of the urban movements.

In response to the perceived attempt of local government officials to mobilize some commissions to denounce the activities of others, the CMs were to be *autonomous* from the state apparatus, not in any way dependent upon or subservient to it. In response to the sense that partisan debate was unproductive and drove people away from movement activities, they were to be completely *nonpartisan*, that is, neither the tools of any party, nor a forum for interparty political debates, nor were they to take positions in such debates. Instead, they were to be open to all people interested in their neighborhood and revolution, regardless of party affiliation or ideology. Finally, in response to attempts to splinter or establish competing neighborhood commissions, the CMs were to be *unitary*; only one commission was to be established in each neighborhood, and all the residents of that neighborhood had an equal right to participate in it. The three principles were generally fiercely and successfully defended during the period of most intense popular mobilization, and they helped maintain the CMs as representatives of the local community and popular movement rather than of any individual actor.

The strength and self-identification of the popular movement as a whole came from the struggle and support of the working-class movement. While the various specific struggles might have taken place anyway, they would have been weaker, more isolated, and could not have had so great an impact. Urban movements were a key to building a majoritarian popular movement, reaching beyond those who could be organized at the workplace to include unemployed men and women, young people, employees of small and large factories and offices, professionals, and small shopkeepers. The urban movements made three important contributions: they had a role in changing the relation between different fractions of capital, thereby altering the operation of the (still

4

capitalist) city; they broadened the base of the popular movement to include those from other classes who faced the same problems; and they developed a more complete social and political program for the popular movement.

The CMs and their activities became part of a general process and consciousness of the residents that they were making the city their own. A woman from a fishermen's public housing neighborhood described one impact of the neighborhood commissions in transforming the city from the grassroots: "they didn't want to hear anything about the fisherman before, but the CM changed all that." This reclaiming of the city—the fact that ordinary residents of the city began to feel they could affect it, that it was *their* city—could be seen in the attitudes of people in the neighborhoods, streets, cafes, workplaces, and, of course, in meetings. The change was visible in other very striking ways: in the posters and slogans painted on walls everywhere adding a feeling of life and current events to every building; in the demonstrations occurring in the streets; and in the constant use of the main public spaces (such as the local government offices, central plaza, schools and other public buildings, as well as streets and open spaces) as formal and informal meeting places. New public spaces were also created as CM headquarters were established in occupied and other buildings, playgrounds were created, and open spaces in neighborhoods were cleaned up. People began to use all these spaces for daily activities, with banners in all these spaces proudly proclaiming that they had been "occupied by the neighborhood commission" and were now "at the service of the people."

These changes were part of the struggle against the previously dominant class forces fighting to regain the power they had lost. This struggle in the realm of symbols was not merely symbolic. The expression "occupied by the neighborhood commission" was a concrete proposal as to how the people of the city should act, by organizing and directly appropriating those unutilized resources which could help to serve their needs. It was a sign of the presence of the CMs and an indication of a solution to collective problems within reach of all. Similarly, the slogans on the walls were not simply slogans. They had a concrete content, which was a call to some, a threat to others, and a suggestion of possible solutions to still others. They reflected the struggle between class forces in the society and represented an attempt by one side to gain dominance and to garner support in intermediate as well as popular strata. They demonstrated the presence of the popular forces, what they were doing, and the outlines of the society they hoped to build.

The intense development of urban social movements during this period highlights many of their basic characteristics, permitting a clearer assessment of their dynamics, effects, and significance. This provides the possibility of empirically testing relevant theoretical arguments and common beliefs, generating new hypotheses about the sources of urban social movements and their relationship to structural change, and responding to basic questions regarding such movements' potential. A rapid review of the most influential general theories related to urban movements puts this work in a broader context and illustrates some of the conclusions that can be drawn from the Portuguese experience; Chapter Six examines the most relevant specific conclusions drawn from other theories and experience and compares them to conclusions from this study.

Explanation of the origin of social movements commonly focuses on broad historical forces often associated with urbanization and economic development which transform a country's economy, social organization, and demographics. Early discussions of mass political movements treated them as largely irrational behavior, based in the strains of modern life and the breakdown of the controlling socializing institutions of traditional society (see Smelser, 1962; Kornhauser, 1959; Johnson, 1966). This view has been soundly critiqued theoretically, empirically and politically by several authors.[2] Later discussions focused on the way these broad historical shifts create concrete problems, new social sectors interested in change, and population concentrations able to organize and act politically. Although these explanations remained far too general to specify when movements arise, the factors they consider often underlie movements. Thus, in Portugal, the main issues of concern to the urban movements were, in part, the product of economic growth during the preceding decade, which brought rapid urban growth without the provision of adequate housing and community facilities. But the existence of urban problems was not sufficient to produce movements.

Ted Gurr (1970) used the concept of "relative deprivation" as an intervening variable to explain when rebellion takes place, given the transformations resulting from a society's development. According to this theory, the critical factor is a significant disjunction between what one believes to be one's due from society and the reality of what one receives or expects to receive. Because directly measuring this sense of relative deprivation is nearly impossible, most studies that tried to test Gurr's theory (e.g., Gurr, 1968; Hibbs, 1973, 1974; Snyder and Tilly, 1972) instead measured change in the objective situation (e.g., economic fluctuations), with some studies finding an association between this indicator and rebellion and others finding none. Gurr's theory was an important antidote to the previously dominant conservative arguments, and the studies it inspired presented protest and revolt as attempts to resolve real problems and oppression; but it still left open the question of why relative deprivation increases and protest arises at some times and not others. Portuguese experience suggests that people generally believe they deserve equitable treatment, but that those denied equal access to society's basic goods will only act when they believe it will be effective. The most potent force for such a change is the shift in the relative power of classes at the national level to the benefit of the unemployed and employed poor, the disadvantaged and excluded. When that national change takes place, people's sense of relative deprivation and the right to improvement increases as they act.

Focusing on the options of the poor and powerless, Piven and Cloward (1977) argued that disruptive social movements are the only means the poor have to change their conditions. And, they continued, such movements do develop from time to time, but for reasons outside the control of those involved in them. They argued that the timing of movements is set by crises that disrupt the institutions and social relations of daily life.

> 'A revolution takes place' says Lefebvre (1971), 'when and only when, in such a society, people can no longer lead their everyday lives; so long as they can live their ordinary lives relations are constantly reestablished.'
>
> Ordinary life for most people is regulated by the rules of work and the rewards of work which pattern each day and week and season. Once cast out of that routine, people are cast out of the regulatory framework that it imposes. Work and the rewards of work underpin the stability of other social institutions as well (Piven and Cloward, 1977:11).

This breakdown of daily life may indeed be an important factor in many movements, including especially movements of the unemployed, such as those studied by Piven and Cloward. Nevertheless, as the case of Portugal shows, daily life may remain largely stable and strong movements for social change will develop with the specific breakdown of institutions of repression and social control.[3]

Political conflict theorists argue that social movements and collective violence are actually part of the normal politics of any country, manifestations of adjustments in the coalition of groups with political power produced by historical developments and shifts in the importance of the various groups. Tilly (1978) treats social movements—up to revolutions—as mobilization strategies rationally adopted by competing groups seeking to gain or retain political power. He argues further that two of the most important variables conditioning their action are the repression they expect to face and the opportunity they have for success. While this has some similarities with the approach suggested here, clarifying differences helps understand the role of the political conjuncture.

The tremendous reduction in repression resulting from the initial overthrow of fascism in Portugal, as well as further reductions later, was very important in the development of the urban social movements. But the reduction of repression alone did not produce the urban social movements; it only gave them more fertile conditions in which to develop. As the chapters below show, while some movement activities (e.g., housing occupations) developed immediately, the overall effect of reducing repression was to unleash the potential for mass activity, allowing social processes to develop more freely, eventually producing portions of the urban social movement. Similarly, the greater opportunity for affecting government actions during the entire nine-teen month period does not explain the specific development of the urban movements. Government responsiveness can be quite important, but, as illustrated by the Portuguese data, it too must be analyzed largely in terms of changing mobilization and shifting relations of class forces. Furthermore, while groups and parties jockeyed for position and sought to mobilize mass movements in Portugal, they had relatively little success at exercising the control they sought. Rather than following the mobilization strategies of spe-cific organizations, the development of the CMs was dependent upon shifts in the political conjuncture of relations between classes, and the CMs in turn were part of the process of class struggle taking place in the society as a whole.

Marxist discussion of social movements would generally accept Tilly's assertion that collective violence, protest, and revolution are natural out-growths of intergroup power struggles, rather than products of widespread discontent. But it would add that these groups are actually classes or frac-tions of classes whose interests are largely defined outside the urban realm, and whose relations are the result of the specific history of economic and political development of a given society. A large share of recent writing on urban social movements relies on this approach. Castells and others in this tradition have focused on the potential role of urban movements in resolving urban contradictions and in changing the general political relations between classes, according to the presence or absence of system-challenging demands, of political parties, and of connection to workplace struggles (Borja, 1974; Castells, 1973a, 1973b, 1977a, 1977b, and 1983).

Castells, whose work has shaped much of the debate, has been criti-cized for having an overly structural approach, paying too little attention to the consciousness of the actors, to the problems of developing a social force from a social base (with particular reference to the importance of resource differences among groups [Pickvance, 1976]), and to the broader political-institutional context within which movements develop (Dunleavy, 1979; Katznelson, 1981; Lowe, 1986; Pickvance, 1985). These authors have documented and analyzed the importance of community and consumption cleavages, organizational resources, bureaucratic contacts, and political and institutional context, with one attempt to integrate these contextual factors proposed by Pickvance (1985). While such factors are important in the specific history of each movement, this study argues that they are quite second-ary with regard to producing the qualitative shifts in the importance and character of the movements of concern to most analysts.

Most case studies examine the relationship between the social base of movements, the issue at stake, the actions carried out, and their impacts, all within a given political-institutional context.[4] The issue at stake is part of what characterizes these as specifically *urban* movements, because it focuses on altering the relationship between the population and some aspect of the urban collective resources. While most analysts argue that the issue deter-mines both the potential radicalness and probability for success of a move-ment, they differ as to whether the choice of issue is treated as a structural given (Borja, 1974) or an element of strategic choice by political parties and organizers (Ash, 1972). The social base is considered important first in order to characterize the relatively progressive or reactionary nature of the move-ment, and second because movements with different social bases will vary as to their available human and material resources, access to authority, modes of operation, and success (Pickvance, 1975, 1976). Finally, the political con-text is assumed to provide conditions that are more or less favorable to the development of the movement and to its receiving a positive response from the authorities (Lipsky, 1968; Lowe, 1986; Pickvance, 1985; Useem, 1975).[5] Their emphasis on individual factors varies, but they all assume the develop-ment and outcome of movements depend essentially on how well local lead-ers choose issues, mobilize the local community, and use outside political and institutional connections.

Most past discussions of urban social movements have ignored or given insufficient weight to the role of the relation of forces between classes in the society as a whole in the dynamics and effects of each specific movement. While some have considered aspects of the context in which the movements developed, this was usually viewed as a purely exogenous constraint. In con-trast, this study highlights the implication of drastic change in the "given political context," arguing that changes in the conjuncture do much more than simply produce "better" or "worse" external conditions for the move-ment; such changes are the essential factor for the qualitative transforma-tion of local protest into an urban social movement. The single most important conclusion from the Portuguese experience is that *the political relations of forces among social classes in the society as a whole is the dominant factor determining the origin and spread of urban movements, and estab-lishing limits on the essential qualities of their social base, issues, internal dynamics, history, and urban and political effects.*

This leads to theoretical and practical conclusions which differ from those of the existing literature, as illustrated by the answers to several important questions—rarely systematically addressed by past writers—concerning the origin, effects, and significance of urban social movements. Responses from examination of the Portuguese experience are summarized herein, developed in the case material in the next chapters, then compared at greater length in Chapter Six to the expectations derived from other approaches. The chief questions are:

1. What gives rise to urban social movements? What are the forces or dynamics that produce movements at one moment rather than another? Can they be created by organizers, political parties, or the state?

2. Once they have begun, what determines their subsequent evolution, radicalism, and political orientation? Are certain demands or social bases inherently more radical than others? Does the evolution of movements depend primarily on effective local organizing, on a "life cycle" of organizations, on party strategies, on state responsiveness, or on broader social conflicts?

3. What effects can urban movements have on a city? How deeply can these effects go? Can they go so far as to permanently alter the urban structure—the relationship between the various social classes of the population and the physical and social resources of the city? What conditions their ability to have a greater or lesser effect?

4. What is their relation to broader political movements? Specifically, how do they contribute to enlarging the base of support for and changing the demands of a workers' movement to develop the social base and program of a broader popular movement?

5. In a period of intense social conflict and change, to what extent do such movements cooperate closely or conflict with the state apparatus, especially with those parts under the relative control of progressive forces?

6. Finally, what can we project from this experience regarding alternative models of democratic society? What lessons can we draw for the debate on the relationship among democracy, grassroots participation, popular power, and socialism?

This book argues that urban movements are an element in the struggle between classes in a given society and a normal response of populations in times of popular advance and favorable conjuncture. Changes in the conjuncture directly affect specific movements and individuals to the extent they embody class positions represented in the general relation of forces. Insofar as a broad class offensive develops, urban movements based in those same class fractions become more likely as one expression of that struggle—

but an expression with its own dynamics and history once underway. Many aspects of this history, including internal dynamics, social base, and particularly qualitative advances in strategies, mobilization, the extent of effects, and the political significance and nature of the movements are, however, dependent upon the conjuncture and its changes, rather than on the internal characteristics of movements or on the strategies of individual actors.

The impact of the political conjuncture can be illustrated in the distinction among three general types of movements: protest, democratic reform, and revolutionary. Protest movements develop in a conjuncture of defensive or limited popular mobilization when the state is quite stable and completely outside the control of the popular classes. Piven and Cloward's (1977) "poor people's movements," which must act essentially through disruption, are a good example of such protest movements. Democratic reform movements require broader class offensive and the possibility of directly or indirectly influencing public action, often through alliance with part of the state to change its policies. Revolutionary urban movements require both a generalized class offensive and a crisis that puts control of the state at issue, allowing popular organizations to not only influence public action but to act directly to solve important problems. At any moment, there may be movements and actions that are very radical, individual organizations and movements may unify and coordinate their actions, they may articulate broad programs of change. Nonetheless, an urban movement cannot progress from one type to another through its own development or the strategies of its activists; it is change in the overall political conjuncture which modifies the character of the movement, not change in any aspects internal to the movements.[6]

Shifts in the relation of power among classes also alter access to the state and change the willingness and ability of the state to use repression against the movements. Other things being equal, a major reduction in repression will encourage development of movements. A similar situation can result from a split in the ruling bloc of classes which opens the possibility that other alliances will develop and compete for state power. Such a crisis of the ruling bloc often produces an inability to use repression, and may develop into a revolutionary situation in which urban movements may also become revolutionary.[7]

Urban movements can effectively broaden a working-class-led popular movement. They do so by involving other sectors of the population in specific struggles around issues of concern to them. Generally, even in a period of broad popular offensive, the main actors in social conflict are a small dominant class minority and a larger popular class minority, while a majority of the population may still be willing to align with either of the principal contending forces. Different segments of these classes may become involved

11

in or attracted to the popular movement through their participation in any of the specific struggles of which the urban movement is composed. The popular movement as a whole is actually built through the development and linking together of specific struggles and movements with differing constituencies and issues. Such struggles are thus one factor contributing to possible shifts in the overall relations of political forces. This process of involving new groups through relevant specific struggles serves at once to broaden the social base of the popular movement and potentially to increase the range of specific issues whose resolution becomes part of its program.

Different social and institutional positions allow different groups to deal with distinct issues—and, conceivably, for a joint movement to deal with all of them. In the same way, if certain issues are to be addressed then the appropriate groups must be involved in the struggle. The urban movements contribute to this popular movement the specificity of their concerns, thereby helping develop a broader and more articulated agenda. The urban movements bring to the popular movement not only a consciousness of urban housing and social service issues, but also a focus on local democracy: the transformation of the local organs of the state and of the populations' relationship to them. This transformation involves a much wider democratic participation and control of local political affairs and government, as well as a greater contribution of the population to the resolution of problems with which the government deals, increasing in turn the latter's ability to resolve them.

In summary, and as shown in the following chapters, urban movements are an embodiment of changes in the national relation of forces among classes, and their specific contributions result from the characteristics of the movements and those of their frequent antagonist—the state bureaucracy. This perspective attributes different roles to the social base and issue of the movement than does much of the existing literature. The development of a movement with a given social base becomes important primarily insofar as it contributes to changing the conjuncture by affecting the composition and strength of the alliance of the popular forces—as well as by affecting the state's willingness to respond positively or use repression. Even in periods of intense class struggle, the majority of people may have only a weak attachment to either of the principal contenders. A given movement may consolidate its initial social base, and expand or reduce the participation of other social sectors through their mobilization around the issue of the movement. Different segments of the population respond differentially according to the participation of their class in the broader offensives of the conjuncture, and according to the particular material problems they experience in their neighborhoods. The initial base for a movement will come from the sectors of the population whose mobilization is part of the new balance of class forces and who suffer from a given problem. Depending on the nature of these problems, some can be resolved through direct action, some produce at most isolated protest, and some lead to mass movements to pressure the state to act in ways that will bring about their resolution.

The multimovement and multiclass nature of the urban struggles helps expand the social base and concerns of the popular movement; their conflicts with the state bureaucracy and successful use of direct action lead to proposals for a new relationship to the state, and a new model of society. As part of the process of adjustment of class relations, urban social movements fade away when that readjustment is resolved, whether in victory or defeat. In the meantime, they are an element of change during a short but very important period of transition.

The research examined here documents the urban social movement that developed in Setubal, an industrial city some twenty-five miles south of Lisbon, which witnessed the most widespread and coordinated urban struggles and organizations of any city during the Portuguese revolution. It is based on extensive firsthand investigation which included interviews with every CM in the city (see Appendix A for selected case histories.) What we can learn as a result provides valuable insight into what grassroots organizations could do elsewhere. The situation during the Portuguese revolution is not representative of most other countries today, but it does indicate the possibility of similar processes and movements developing for reasons peculiar to the history of each country. As such movements arise, proper understanding of the processes involved will allow people to more effectively channel their energy, rather than "attempt to do what they cannot do, and forfeit the chance to do what they might do" (Piven and Cloward, 1978:xxii).

Chapters Two through Five examine the history and role of urban social movements in the Portuguese revolution, highlighting the effect of the changing conjuncture on the development and effects of the movements, of social base and issue on the specific history of the movements, and in turn of their impact on the conjuncture. Chapters Two and Three provide a journalistic, experiential history of the revolution at the national and local levels, giving the reader a sense of the events, dynamics and relationships as they might have appeared to a well-informed observer at the time. Chapters Four and Five analyze the factors which produced the movements, shaped their political orientations, determined the likelihood of their affecting the conditions of the people immediately involved, as well as altering the deeper relations between the class structure of the city and the city's resources. The final chapter directly addresses the significance of this experience for movements and societies elsewhere.

This study of grassroots activity in the Portuguese revolution shows that the full development of urban social movements depends not primarily on their own internal evolution, but rather on the general dynamics of the class struggle of which they are part. Given the opportunity, large numbers of ordinarily passive people will become actively involved in discussions and actions to solve the problems of their neighborhood and city—and, in so doing, they can resolve in a short time problems with which they had lived for years, while contributing to possible change in the society as a whole. The process is not a simple one, and understanding its dynamics will contribute to a better awareness of the possibilities, limitations, and conflicts involved in the process of struggling for and building a more democratic society.

TWO

A Short History of the Portuguese Revolution: The Dialectic of Popular Mobilization

Prologue

Although it rarely received more than occasional mention beyond the exile media, the Caetano regime in Portugal was facing a major crisis in 1973. Opposition candidates campaigned for the October national assembly elections and then dropped out en masse charging that the elections were rigged. An illegal strike wave began in October and continued for months. The twelve years of colonial war in Africa were producing political repercussions within the military. A December coup planned by an extreme right-wing group of high-level military officers, wanting a more vigorous war effort and more stringent domestic policies, was uncovered. Discontent was growing among younger career officers who objected to long tours of duty in a losing colonial war. The wars, they felt, provided no benefits to ordinary people, but did contribute to the mass emigration of the nearly 20 percent of the population abroad seeking work and escape from conscription. In addition, these career officers were losing status as they were blamed for the failure of the wars, and as men who had only been through a short Officer-Candidate-School-type program were promoted ahead of them.[1] Because the United States used the Azores' Lages Air Force Base to supply the Israelis in the 1973 War, Portugal felt the full brunt of the 1973-74 oil embargo, with gas prices rising 60 percent virtually overnight.

The crisis reached the top echelons of government. At the beginning of 1974, a complete reshuffling of ministerial positions occurred. In late February, General António de Spínola, Military Governor of Guine-Bissau and close personal friend of Marcelo Caetano, published a book calling for a political solution to the colonial wars through the formation of a "Lusitanian Commonwealth." A few days later, Caetano staged a meeting of all the members of the General Staff to affirm their support of his policies. Spínola and one other general, Costa Gomes, refused to take part in the show of the "geriatric generals." On March 16, a cavalry regiment loyal to Spínola attempted to march on Lisbon but was stopped. Reports of the incident were confused, but the government played down the significance of the events and assured itself and everyone else that all was under control.

Then, in the early morning hours of April 25, 1974, a prohibited song, "Grandola, Vila Morena," was played on the radio. It spoke of a town in a land of fraternity, where one had a friend on every corner and equality shown in every face; a land in which the people ruled supreme. With this signal, a well-coordinated movement of troops began.

In a matter of a few hours, the oldest and longest lasting fascist regime in Europe was brought to an end. Without minimizing its importance or difficulty, the military coup may have been the easiest decision the Movimento das Forças Armadas (Armed Forces Movement or MFA) was to make. Once the old regime was overthrown, much more difficult social and political questions came to the fore. Who was to rule? On what terms and with what base of support? What changes were to be made? Who was to benefit and how? These questions were disputed during six provisional governments; in factories, farms, and barracks; in neighborhoods, and in the streets over the next two years.

There were four main periods and several subperiods in the conjuncture during the two years considered: April to September 1974; October 1974 to March 1975; March to November 1975; and November 1975 to June 1976. The main issues of concern for political debate, mass struggles and government policies were different in each period, as were the relationships among the mass movements, the military, the parties, and the state. Each period ended with major changes in the governing coalition embodying a significant shift in the relation of class forces, the partial resolution of some major problems, and the development of new ones.

April to September 1974

From the very beginning, conflicts existed between the leaders of the coup and those who assumed control of the new government. During the first five months following April 25, political debate centered around three basic issues: an end to the colonial war, improvements in the wages and the material and social conditions of those worst off under the old regime, and the purging from positions of responsibility of those associated with the old regime. The three were clearly interrelated, but those in different situations gave more direct emphasis to one or another. All were components of the basic theme that dominated this period: resolving the major problems inherited from fascism. In large measure, this was a period of struggles over the implementation of an antifascist program. The old regime had been top-pled, but people were not against it simply because of its name. They were against its many concrete features, and changing the top layer of the govern-ment did not automatically change these; specific struggles were necessary to do so. Many movements of workers and residents formed to force the government to resolve their specific problems and recognize democratic and social rights.

In the weeks following April 25, the strike wave which had begun in October 1973 spread and deepened. Where before strikes had focused pri-marily on wages (inflation in 1973 was 20 percent), now they included many other economic demands, as well as demands for purging fascists and others associated with the old regime, especially in government and com-pany administrations. Where before strikes were illegal and lasted at most a few hours before the secret police or National Guard were brought in,[2] now they often lasted days or weeks until management compromised.[3]

Economic demands, won relatively quickly in most cases, spread rapidly.[4] In late May, a national minimum wage was decreed. It was set at 3300 escudos per month ($135 U. S. equivalent),[5] providing increases for about 50 percent of all workers, including 65 percent of public sector employ-ees (Rodrigues, et al., 1976:59). Many unions also demanded and won a shorter work week, four weeks' annual vacation and other benefits. It soon became obvious that while economic improvements were gained relatively easily, the demand that fascist administrators be purged (*saneamento*) was much more sensitive for management and very serious for the workers. Many strikes continued even after the economic issues were settled where such *saneamento* remained the main or only issue.

The two institutions most thoroughly purged of fascist elements were the unions and local government. The unions were taken over by opposition groups often tied to the previously illegal Intersindical, organized some four years earlier.[6] Local government was generally taken over by members of the Movimento Democrático Português (Portuguese Democratic Movement or MDP/CDE), the antifascist opposition electoral front from the October 1973 elections.[7] Foreshadowing future party conflicts over control of the government and mass organizations, in mid-May 1974 the Partido Socialista (Socialist Party or PS) demanded that municipal elections be held in Octo-ber to reduce the influence of the MDP/CDE, and the Intersindical called a June 1 demonstration to "repudiate strikes for the sake of strikes" and tried to bring rank-and-file activities under its control.

Workers' initiatives soon produced experiments in economic organiza-tion. The first nationalization took place in early May, demanded by workers occupying the headquarters of the private Lisbon Water Company. After establishing a minimum wage, foreign companies began threatening to close down and leave the country. In response to this threat, workers occupied a French textile company and established the first self-managed company in late May 1974. While this was to become a common form of struggle against the threat of layoffs in textiles, construction, commerce, and other small production units, it was rare in larger firms, and arose only as a response to foreign economic boycott in certain sectors. It was not effective when U. S. electronics assembly companies falsely claimed bankruptcy and closed down.[8]

Demands for improved conditions also immediately arose in the poorer neighborhoods (*barrios*) around the country. On April 29, 1974, more than 100 families living in a Lisbon shantytown occupied housing in a new government housing project. It was the first indication that masses of people were going to be actively involved in the changes to come, as well as of the importance urban struggles were to have. In all some 2,500 units of housing were occupied around the country in the first fifteen days after the coup. These occupations focused mainly on large blocks of new public housing that had never been lived in—some of it not yet completed—and ended when there was no more new government housing to occupy. In a communique of May 14, the ruling Junta de Salvação Nacional (Junta of National Salvation or JSN) recognized that this "undisciplined occupation of houses [is a] reflex action against the ineffectiveness of official departments which never found a solution to problems." However, the JSN refused to legalize the occupations en bloc, but rather insisted this be done on a case-by-case basis through the occupiers' forming neighborhood committees and negotiating with the local administration. This served as an impulse to form local committees, although no reviews ever took place and almost all the occupiers remained in their new housing.

People living in shantytowns organized throughout the country and began to demand basic infrastructure and decent housing. CMs appeared in all major cities and began pressuring the government to respond to their needs with some type of housing program. While many only demanded housing and basic services, others included broader demands dealing with the most pressing national issue: the colonial war. For example, when the barrio of Liberdade, in Lisbon, decided to form a CM at the end of May, it demanded "decent houses to which the people have a right; ... [and] the immediate and complete independence of the people of the colonies."

Organization and demands for improvements also spread through the armed forces, and here, too, the demands often went beyond a concern with their immediate situation. For example, the Representative Commission of the soldiers at the military base in Torres Novas sent a statement of its support to the MFA in June 1974, and included among its demands: increased monthly pay; the right to wear civilian clothing; free use of public transportation; medical assistance for family members; revision of the Uniform Code of Military Justice; the right to wear shoes [instead of boots] with the uniform; and an end to the colonial war (Rodrigues, et al., 1976:25).

The three issues that constituted the antifascist program for change were also the critical issues dividing the highest levels of government. In the first months, the colonial question was clearly central.[9] The coup had been carried out by two factions: on one hand, Spínola and his allies wanted to negotiate a political solution to the colonial wars that would lead to a commonwealth, with the liberation movements excluded from effective power; on the other, the core of the MFA, which had planned and executed the coup, recognized the "right of the peoples of the colonies to self-determination."[10]

The first ten weeks after the April 25 coup were occupied with maneuvering and struggles within the government as Spínola tried to gain dominance. This phase ended with Spínola's clear defeat as the First Provisional Government was brought down by opposition from public sector workers and the MFA; the MFA imposed Vasco Gonçalves as prime minister of the Second Provisional Government. Spínola remained as president, but the MFA strengthened its position and the government began to take several decisive steps. One of its first actions was to guarantee direct control of the armed forces by the leaders of the MFA. On July 12, the Continental Operational Command (COPCON), was established to coordinate the use of troops in the country, under the direct authority of the military commander of the April 25 coup, Major Otelo Saraiva de Carvalho.

Efforts began to resolve the worst housing problems, with assistance focusing on barrios in bad conditions but with "internal organization that would permit their immediate involvement in 'self-help' solutions." On July 31, *Serviço Ambulatório de Apoio Local* (Mobile Local Support Service or SAAL) was created to support local "initiatives of the poorly housed population to cooperate in the transformation of the barrios, investing their own latent—and perhaps monetary—resources . . . ."[11] The program demanded that the population be organized in an association or cooperative. It offered technical help and a basic investment fund, which the population was to complement by either borrowing the rest of the money or using its own labor to build the housing. While the initial intention was to run a few demonstration projects, the CMs of the shantytowns refused to accept these limits and insisted that all shantytowns be included. By early September 1974, brigades were active in some barrios in Lisbon, and they eventually expanded to include virtually all shantytowns and severely run-down areas in all major cities.

The large number of vacant housing units being kept off the market was another focus of government concern. Even though only government housing had been occupied in the first weeks following the coup, both large and small property owners felt insecure—a problem which was aggravated by a few scattered occupations of old private homes during the summer. On September 12, the government passed a decree-law intended to reassure owners of private housing that their property would not be forcibly seized, at the same time it required that if habitable it would not be kept off the market. It required that all habitable vacant housing be rented within 120 days or turned over to the local government to be rented. It furthermore prohibited demolition of housing until adequate legislation could be enacted,[12] and specified that as new housing was completed it, too, would fall under the new legal restrictions. The law was attacked by the right as an infringement on private property, and by the left for defending it and giving too long a waiting period. Very few landlords cooperated: many did not report housing, and many owners of new housing refused to "complete" it—by leaving off a minor finish, such as a lightswitch.

Unemployment increased with layoffs in construction, textiles and other labor-intensive industries in the summer of 1974. High labor costs was the reason normally given, even though Portugal still had by far the lowest labor costs throughout Europe. In an attempt to reassure businessmen and prevent a recurrence of the radical strike activity of the previous months, in late August 1974, the government passed a Strike Law, which recognized but severely limited the right to strike. It met extremely strong protest and was soon a dead letter (for one and one-half years). One of the protests was a march on September 12 by several thousand workers from the Lisnave shipyards. This march was declared illegal by the government, and troops were sent to prevent it, but in the midst of the incident there was a dramatic shift. After a long discussion in which the officers and soldiers considered the workers' reasons for demonstrating, they decided the workers had a right to make their position known and let them pass. The turning point came when a worker declared: "Major, I know very well what your orders are; your mission is to prohibit and kill, if necessary. And our mission is to go on and die, if necessary" (Rodrigues, et al., 1976:59).

During September, there was increasing polarization of social forces, with a confrontation clearly coming. The MFA went ahead with its decolonization plans, and an agreement was signed in Lusaka on September 7, setting Mozambican independence for June 25, 1975. On September 10, Spínola, still the president, made a speech calling for the "silent majority" not to let the country fall into chaos. He and other right-wing forces began organizing to stop the destruction of the *Pátria* before it went any further, and they scheduled a march on Lisbon for September 28. On September 11, the first anniversary of the bloody coup that ended the Unidad Popular gov-

20

ernment and Chilean democracy, workers in many factories around the country observed a moment of silence in memory of Salvador Allende and other antifascists killed in struggle. On September 16, the workers of the large Setenave shipyard in Setubal adopted a motion in which they affirmed their solidarity with workers demanding high-level purges and denounced the strike law. On September 22, the workers of the *Jornal do Comércio* went on strike demanding purges of the administration and editorial board. The right, meanwhile, held meetings and published inflammatory statements calling on people to go to the September 28 demonstration to support the president's taking decisive steps and prevent the installation of a communist dictatorship.

The demonstration never took place. Grassroots factory and neighborhood groups established checkpoints to look for arms on all the major access routes to Lisbon on the day before the demonstration was to take place; they were soon joined by the military. That night, the MFA banned the demonstration. Spínola resigned on September 30 and was replaced by General Costa Gomes, the man who had been the MFA's original choice for president. Vasco Gonçalves remained prime minister and the Third Provisional Government was formed.

September 28 was a turning point. The right learned it could not return to power peacefully, and, in January, the first communiques of an extreme right-wing guerrilla group based in Spain appeared. Many owners of capital became more concerned with the situation, stopped investing, and began taking money out of the country. The MFA and the left learned that, while they had a large base of support, many still supported the right, in part because they had still seen no positive effects of the changes of April 25; furthermore, the economic situation showed clearly that the distribution of economic power had not changed.

October 1974 to March 1975

Many concluded from these events that the only secure way to avoid a return of the old regime was to develop democratic participation involving more people and to spread the material benefits of the political changes initiated April 25. The key to all of this was breaking the centers of economic power which had been the main beneficiaries of the old regime and remained largely intact. Political events and their effects on the economy (and vice versa) underlined the importance of the MFA program's call for:

> a new economic policy, at the service of the Portuguese People, in particular of the sectors of the population up to now most underprivileged, with an immediate focus on the struggle against inflation and the successive increases in the

cost of living, which will necessarily imply an antimonopoly policy. (Rodrigues, et al., 1976:104)

In order to successfully implement and secure their antifascist political program, the MFA and others realized they would have to adopt an antimonopoly program.

In mid-October, a group was formed to develop a socioeconomic plan and guidelines (the Melo Antunes Plan) to deal with the economic crisis in the economy and indicate steps toward an economy at the service of the people. On November 12, the *Boletim do MFA* published an article entitled "From Politics to Economics" which argued:

> One could say that political power is now in the hands of the progressive forces of Portuguese society. However, we must not forget that in a society with characteristics like ours, in which capitalist structures predominate, the economic element is determinant, and this is now, as it was on April 24th, in the power of the large capitalist groups (finance capital) and of the rural proprietors, who have caused some perturbations in the democratization process now underway. . . . Economic power continues in the hands of those who were the grand beneficiaries of the regime deposed on April 25th. . . . We must recognize that the consolidation of democracy in Portugal necessarily requires measures which immediately aim for an economic democratization. (Rodrigues, et al., 1976:105)

The MFA Assembly, three weeks later, affirmed its agreement with the need to advance rapidly in the direction of an "anti-monopoly policy at the service of the working classes."

A significant step in this antimonopoly policy came in late November, with the decree of a law allowing the state to intervene "in cases in which the enterprises are not functioning normally."[13] This provided a vehicle for the state to act against firms guilty of economic sabotage, as well as to aid companies on the verge of bankruptcy by providing loans in exchange for the right to nominate the board of directors. Another step was taken on December 13, when the chief administrators and owners of several banks and major financial institutions were arrested and accused of economic sabotage. But neither of these were structural measures, and the government did little more while awaiting the report of the Melo Antunes Group to propose socioeconomic guidelines. However, in some factories (e.g., Siderurgia Nacional Steelworks), workers took the initiative and imposed "complete control over production," seeking neither self-management nor to remove the administration, but rather to eliminate privileges and waste.

Between October and January, virtually all political parties held conventions, reaffirmed or adopted programs appropriate to the postfascist period, and began preparing for the constituent assembly elections planned for March or April. Obviously, many important differences existed in the platforms adopted, but, given the mood of the times, all from center to left included antimonopoly positions and declarations favoring some kind of socialism. The other noteworthy result of the conventions was the internal clarification of positions and hardening of political lines, producing increased interparty frictions especially between the Socialists and Communists.

Increasing tension between parties convinced those in grassroots organizations that they needed to remain nonpartisan and advance their own interests whether in neighborhoods, factories, or countryside. This attitude was supported by the MFA, which in November had begun carrying out "cultural dynamization campaigns" to motivate people—especially in rural areas—to examine their situations and decide what could be done about them. One officer explained the rationale of the campaign to the people of a small village:

> On April 25th the military carried out a coup d'etat, which could only be done by force and had to be prepared in secret in the barracks. But on the 26th, or perhaps already on the afternoon of the 25th, when the people went into the streets is when the Revolution began. Because only the people can make a revolution. Now it's up to you: if you want it we will have a Revolution; if you don't, we will only have had a coup d'etat. (Rodrigues, et al., 1976:9)

Once they began organizing, the shantytown CMs involved in the SAAL program quickly found themselves involved in political disputes, even over supposedly technical and bureaucratic issues. They struggled with the local governments whose approval was required for all operations and which were intermediaries in both the expropriation of land and the allocation of funds for the projects. They argued with the central government, which determined the ground rules of the program and interest rates, as well as with the state bureaucracy that employed the technical help and provided funds. The Intercommissions (the coordinating body) of the CMs from Lisbon shanty-towns was created, and, under the banners of "Houses Yes, Shacks No!" and "Decent Housing for All," presented the government with a list of demands including that the new barrios be built in the same places as the old ones; that residents know when construction would begin; that the maximum rate of interest be 2 percent; that the control of the distribution of all public housing rest with representatives of the poorly housed; and, in the meantime, that all vacant housing be occupied by those in greatest need. It then went on to reject self-help construction; the rehabilitation of the existing shantytowns; and aspects of the law regulating the formation of housing cooperatives. In February, a similar Intercommission was created in Setubal, and the two began meeting at the beginning of March.

On February 7, the workers' commissions of Lisbon held a large demonstration against unemployment and the North Atlantic Treaty Organization (NATO), with part of the NATO fleet then in port. The government prohibited the demonstration, which nevertheless attracted approximately 80,000 workers. This demonstration saw the second dramatic shift in position by lower-ranking military personnel: the demonstrators were allowed to pass the U. S. Embassy after convincing the commandos guarding it that they had a right to peacefully demonstrate and, when they arrived at the Ministry of Labor, soldiers guarding it raised their fists in solidarity with the demonstration.

Also in February, the occupation of uncultivated agricultural land began as unemployed agricultural workers and tractor drivers occupied unused land or the land they had traditionally worked but which the owners refused to plant. Finally, in addition to problems the right faced with urban and rural workers, soldiers, and shantytown dwellers, the grace period in the September rental law expired on February 17, and over the next few days an estimated 2,500 units of private housing were occupied in Lisbon alone.[14] The law which had sought to avoid the attack on private property helped to create the conditions that legitimated it. These occupations were considerably more organized than the first wave had been, benefitting from the earlier experience and knowledge of when the waiting period was to expire. Both the Secretary of State for Housing and Urbanism and the Prime Minister spoke out against the occupations, attacking their "opportunism" and "lack of organization," arguing they did not help consolidate democracy and served only to increase unemployment in the construction industry. The military frequently intervened in the occupations, but often sided with the occupiers and the justness of their cause. There were some evictions, but occupations continued, although at a slower rate.

Then, in the midst of growing rumors of an impending right-wing coup, the *Partido Popular Democrático* (Popular Democratic Party or PPD), whose leaders came primarily from the liberal opposition during the fascist regime, held a preelection rally in Setubal on March 7. Police were called in and opened fire on the counterdemonstrators outside the hall where the rally was being held, killing one and wounding eighteen. The police headquarters was then surrounded by the demonstrators, and the police were only able to leave under military escort several hours later. A demonstration the next day took place without incident, and the following days saw a wave of housing occupations in Setubal.

This situation was too much for the right: land and housing were being taken over; workers were calling for basic changes in economic and political policies; bank workers were calling for the nationalization of the banks and were interfering in attempts to transfer funds abroad; the colonies were being handed over to "terrorists";[15] right-wing parties faced demonstrations when they tried to campaign; and the military not only did not act to repress these moves, but even showed signs of supporting them. The base of support for the revolution was on the offensive and growing, with no one prepared to stop it. In desperation, the right wing within the military attempted a coup on March 11. While they detained some MFA leaders and occupied communications centers, the only military action was a paratroopers' attack against an artillery base on the outskirts of Lisbon. The leadership of the coup apparently believed this would act as a spark and the rest of the military would join them. They were wrong. The paratroopers denounced their officers for having tricked them into attacking supporters of the revolution,[16] and Spínola and the other leaders of the coup fled to Spain where some began working with clandestine right-wing paramilitary groups in Spain, Portugal, and Angola, and others continued on to exile in Brazil.

March to November, 1975

In the aftermath of the March 11 coup attempt, antimonopoly structural reforms of the economy began to be implemented. The domestically owned banks and insurance companies were nationalized within the first days after the coup. Given the preexisting debt structure, this gave potential state control over an even larger share of the economy. Over the next few months, virtually all of the large, domestic companies in all major economic sectors were nationalized.[17]

Once this was in process, the base of support for these progressive changes began to break down. Three principal positions became increasingly evident during the following months.[18] First, there were those who sought to develop a strong state sector of the economy, along with institutions of mass integration into the political process, along lines close to those of Eastern Europe. Second, there were those who had been concerned with breaking the power of the monopolies, in order to allow smaller scale private enterprise to operate freely and develop as the base of the economy. Thus, they did not want a strong centralized state economic mechanism. Third, there were those who opposed the consolidation of a centralized economic machine for other reasons. They wanted to use the elimination of private property as the basis for building democratic control over production and distribution decisions by those directly involved. Supporters of these three views, represented approximately in the Communist Party, the Socialist and Popular Democratic Parties, and the revolutionary left respectively, had united in support of the antimonopoly project. Once underway, their differences came to the surface. The history of the spring, summer, and autumn of 1975 is in large part the history of failed attempts to create a working agreement for revolutionary advance, under increasing pressure from a developing popular movement impatient for rapid advances and from an ever more active right-wing opposition. Only when the Communist Party and revolutionary left remained disunited and the Socialist Party and PPD aligned themselves openly and strongly with those who opposed the entire revolutionary process was the second position able eventually to defeat the other two.

There were more occupations of land and housing in March and April, together with strikes and factory occupations and expulsions of owners. The vast majority of housing occupations were for the use of individual families in need, but many were also made to provide buildings for community facilities—especially day-care and health centers—as well as for party headquarters. The government discussed various laws to legalize the situations created, and in early April 1975, the media began speaking of a forthcoming "revolutionary law" on housing that would finally establish the legal basis of landlord-tenant relations.

Actually, two proposals were being discussed at the time. Both began by referring to the housing crisis, and both said that it was not acceptable to have "houses without people as long as there are people without houses."[19] Both were concerned with justice and began by legalizing the occupations made up to that time. But there the similarities ended, for they were concerned with very different kinds of justice. The COPCON proposal[20] was concerned with justice for those who desperately needed housing, when good vacant housing was available. It defined housing subject to occupation or distribution as "all uninhabited housing that does not endanger human life." It effectively legalized all occupations, with only a very few exceptions. In contrast, the law adopted on April 14 was concerned with justice for the landlords and private property owners. It began by legalizing the exiting occupations, and then provided exceptions that effectively made 80 percent or more of them illegal.

Two weeks later, the Socialist Party obtained a plurality in the elections for the Constituent Assembly with 38 percent of the vote, followed by the right-wing PPD with 26 percent and the Communist Party with 12 percent. The Socialists claimed victory and the right to a greater role in the government. In the following weeks, relations between the Socialist and Communist Parties deteriorated further.

At the same time, a number of specific struggles of national significance developed as the popular movement sought to advance the revolutionary process through direct democracy and mutual solidarity. Throughout April and May, CMs throughout the country presented a series of demands to the government. On May 17, large demonstrations in Lisbon and Oporto were called by the CMs of those cities. Under the slogan of "Houses for All—Against Capitalism," they demanded revocation of the law on housing occupations, the legalization of all occupations, a response to the demands previously presented by the SAAL barrios, the recognition of the CMs by the government, and, in Oporto, purging the Administrative Commission of the Camara. Then, in Setubal, residents of many of the newer barrios decided to impose an upper limit on the level of rent per room. On May 28, the Administrative Commission of the Camara of Oporto resigned and was replaced by a group of military officers who pledged to work with local CMs, "true representatives of the workers of this city," and created a "Municipal Council" toward this end.[21] In response, the CMs of the city—mostly from shantytowns (SAAL) and public housing barrios—formed the Conselho Revolucionário de Moradores do Porto (Revolutionary Council of Moradores of Oporto or CRMP) to coordinate and direct the participation of the CMs' delegates to the Municipal Council.

On May 19, the workers of the independent newspaper *República* occupied the newspaper building, accusing the editorial board of becoming a partisan voice of the Socialist Party rather than serving the workers' movement as a whole. In early June, the workers of the Catholic Church-owned Rádio Renascença similarly took over that establishment, putting it "at the service of the working people." Both occupations were to bring about a greater polarization of attitudes inside the country and were exploited by the Socialist Party internationally to attack the Communists for limiting freedom of speech—even though in Portugal the Communist Party was against both the occupations, and the occupiers (who were generally closer to the revolutionary left) included Socialist Party members as well (Milkman, 1979).

But at the formal political level, the period was dominated by (often acrimonious) debate about what should follow. The decolonization process continued and Mozambique became independent on June 25, 1975, followed by Guinea-Bissau and the Cape Verde Islands a week later. In the meantime, the principal financial and industrial monopolies had been nationalized and brought into the realm of political control and debate. Thus, the antimonopoly coalition lost its raison d'etre, and debate now focused almost solely on the questions of what type of new society was to be built and what the respective powers and roles of the different classes and institutions in it would be.

A rather indecisive direction was offered by the Political Action Plan (PAP) adopted by the MFA Assembly on June 21, 1975. The PAP defined the MFA as

> the liberation movement of the Portuguese people, above parties, with the principal objective of national independence. National independence requires a

process of internal decolonization, which can only be achieved through the
construction of a socialist society, . . . a society without classes, obtained through
the collectivization of the means of production. (Neves, 1975:17)

It recognized the existence and usefulness of various political parties and
emphasized that socialism would be built by following a "pluralist" and "democratic" path. At the same time, it called for the development of "links with
all the unitary grassroots organizations," which will constitute "the embryo
of an experimental system of direct democracy." But all of this required
"strengthened, firm revolutionary authority" on the part of the MFA and the
state, and "determination that all laws shall be firmly carried out." While it
included many contradictory elements, the PAP's principal concern was to
halt the turmoil of the revolutionary process and rapidly develop a state
and political structures to direct a nationalized economy and more democratic society.

But both outside and inside the MFA, others were more concerned
with taking the revolutionary process further and continuing to transform
society and state. Workers in many nationalized companies quickly found
that little had changed in their workplaces, and they began (or continued)
calling for *socialization* of the company through democratic workers' control, various forms of which were imposed in many enterprises during these
months. SAAL programs to rehouse the poor faced many problems in the
bureaucracies, as did other attempts to gain improved social services. There
were large numbers of unemployed agricultural workers and large amounts
of unused land in the countryside, as well as vacant houses in the cities, all
kept idle by the existing laws. Experience during the previous year indicated
that advances came through the actions of those at the grassroots and that
the government would follow. Finally, signs of growing division in the leadership of the MFA were evidenced, exacerbated by interparty conflicts, and
there was reason to doubt that the parties victorious in the April elections
would continue to carry out the necessary actions toward major social and
economic changes. In order to achieve social, economic, and political equality for working people, implementing antimonopoly policies had to continue,
but had to be suplemented by anticapitalist democratic policies to develop
workers' control over the workplace and citizens' control over the government.

Two weeks after the PAP, the MFA Assembly adopted another document entitled "Guidelines to the Alliance between the People and the MFA"
(see Appendix B), which focused on the need to develop the revolutionary
process generally and "a new state apparatus with a popular base," through
direct democracy and support to and links with the grassroots organizations, especially CMs and comissões de Trabalhadores (workers' commis-

sions or CTs), with the "final and ultimate objective the construction of the socialist society." It described a system of local, regional, and national popular assemblies, composed of delegates of grassroots organizations, government, and the military. These popular assemblies were to:

- transmit the aspirations, opinions, and demands of the population to the competent authorities;
- intervene in local, regional, and national planning, through the competent agency, as the delegates (*mandatorios*) of the local population; and
- examine and control the activity of the administrative organs, and of their ability and rate of response to the necessities of the population.

A graphic indication of what this could mean was given by the decision immediately afterward to allow the *República* to be published under the editorial control of its workers' commission. In addition, during the preceding fortnight, the first meetings of a Popular Assembly of workers' commissions, CMs, and soldiers took place at a military base near Lisbon, and the Municipal Council of Oporto had already begun to function along similar lines.

The popular organizations and left parties generally strongly supported the Guidelines, and the center and right parties vigorously opposed them. The Fourth Provisional Government ended as the Socialist Party attacked the document as "antipluralist" and "antidemocratic" and resigned from the government in protest on July 10th, with the PPD following a week later. The following days saw demonstrations for and against the document. Revolutionary left and grassroots organizations held one that called for an end to the Constituent Assembly, the formation of a revolutionary government, and power to the workers. In the middle of the demonstration, several tanks from an artillery base on the outskirts of Lisbon rumbled up a main thoroughfare and into the midst of the crowd, because "we had an assembly of the barracks and decided we agreed with the demands of the demonstration, so here we are to show our solidarity." The Socialist Party opened its campaign in the streets against the government with a demonstration in Lisbon to oppose the Guidelines and the role of the Communist Party in the government. The Communist Party fed the growing sectarian conflict by denouncing the Socialist demonstration as equivalent to such counterrevolutionary attacks as the September 28 "march of the silent majority," and the March 11 right-wing coup attempt.

During the following months, organizations of the popular movement continued to struggle for workers' control, occupy agricultural land to form cooperatives, organize around their local concerns, demonstrate in favor of the "Alliance between the People and the MFA" and "Popular Power," and debate how best to implement it. This process involved much greater contact between grassroots organizations and rank-and-file soldiers than had previously been the case. During this period, the Fifth Provisional Government passed a number of major laws that had been promised for some time, including an Agrarian Reform law and more nationalizations.

During July and August, the Socialist Party joined with the right to carry out a domestic and international campaign to identify the revolutionary process with the Communist Party in order to isolate both (Milkman, 1979). Articles appeared in the international media expressing concern about the threat to liberty and free speech in Portugal, and many demonstrations were held, often ending by burning left party headquarters. Center-right opposition was strong and developed bases of support and agreement. Following a period of intense internal mobilization and struggle, the center and right forces won out in the MFA Assembly of September 5, and reorganized the MFA to reduce the influence of progressive officers. The Sixth Provisional Government was formed two weeks later.

The popular movement was also faced with a new situation. Through August, the governments had consistently—even if not always smoothly—moved to the left, following the actions of the popular movement and validating its moves. But, the PS and PPD had made "the return of occupied housing, *República* and Rádio Renascença to their rightful owners" a condition for their participation in the Sixth Provisional Government. The movement was no longer simply a little ahead of the government, but was now in opposition. In their efforts to defend and further gains already made, grassroots organizations began developing greater base level contacts, specific policies,[22] and alternative centers of decisionmaking and power.[23]

During the Fifth Provisional Government, the state was relatively immobilized due to the isolation of those at the top resulting from the opposition of the other principle parties (Socialist Party and PPD). With the installation of the Sixth Provisional Government, the center-right coalition regained control of the top state positions, but found itself nearly powerless to act. The major bureaucracies were filled with people largely sympathetic to the popular movement. More important, large numbers of military officers and enlisted men—and COPCON specifically—supported the popular movement and refused to repress it. As a result, many government orders were simply ignored. The center-right alliance headed the government, but it was unable to govern.

The government tried hard to regain control. In its first weeks, it began purging left-wing officers, made it illegal to publish news about military affairs, resumed eviction trials, and closed down Rádio Renascença, all to little avail as the grassroots challenges spread within the military itself.[24] When rank-and-file soldiers saw the right regaining control of the military hierarchy, they received much stronger support than even they expected when they began to organize independently, demanding improvements in pay and conditions, an end to purging of the left, unity with the workers, and a revolutionary government. The possibility of a massive challenge from the ranks came on the heels of the refusal of members of the elite Military Police to embark for Angola, insisting they must remain in Portugal to defend and further the revolution. Two weeks later, members of the Associação dos Deficientes das Forças Armadas (Association of Disabled Veterans or ADFA) occupied the bridge connecting Lisbon with the southern shore of the Tagus river—contributing the bridge tolls collected to help the *República*—and demanded training to become productive members of society and that the revolution go forward. When two soldiers distributing leaflets for a September 25 Lisbon *Soldados Unidos Vencerão* (Soldiers United Will Win or SUV) demonstration were arrested, at least 5,000 people of the more than 40,000 that eventually came to the demonstration commandeered seventy buses, drove fifteen miles to the military prison, and successfully demanded their release. When a leftist military base in Oporto was ordered demobilized, the soldiers went to a nearby artillery base and occupied it until the order was rescinded. For one week, the base was run collectively without regard to rank, and when the regional military command threatened to bomb them, they trained their artillery on the command headquarters.

When troops were sent into the Lisbon radio and TV stations to prevent reporting of military news (because the law prohibiting such coverage was being ignored), those sent to Rádio Renascença, after long discussions, declared they were there to defend the workers from any threat. The government then sent commandos to seal off the transmitter, which renewed broadcasting three weeks later when it was reopened by a large demonstration. Each time the government tried to hold a housing eviction trial, occupiers filled the courtroom preventing the trial from taking place and holding "popular tribunals" absolving the defendant. Twice as much agricultural land was occupied in September and October than had been during the previous seven months.

In these and other confrontations with the popular movement, the government was continually forced to retreat, but it began carrying out military and civilian reorganizations to provide itself with better control and improved conditions for a future confrontation. Nonetheless, the popular movement took the offensive and directly challenged the government in many areas, and the Communist Party began to throw its weight behind the movement and call for a new government, much as the Socialist Party had earlier done during the Fifth Provisional Government. During the first week of November, two ministries were occupied (one by the ministry's own workers) with demands for the removal of a minister and a secretary of state. They were met by police armed with automatic military weapons for the first time in months. At the same time, the government blew up the Rádio Renascença transmitter because its workers refused to go off the air. The paratroopers responsible for its destruction unexpectedly said they had been tricked again, repudiated their officers (who then left the base), and put themselves under the command of the left-oriented COPCON. A few days later, some 100,000 striking construction workers surrounded the main governmental building, sequestering the Constituent Assembly for some hours and holding the prime minister until he acceded to their demands nearly two days later. COPCON was called upon but refused to intervene against the workers, saying they were acting nonviolently and within their rights to make themselves heard.

It was apparent that the conjuncture would soon change again: the working-class and popular movement could not continue to take increasing amounts of effective power in the economy and society while the bourgeoisie was reestablishing control over the state and the forces of repression. A more stable relation of forces would have to be achieved, and this required the clear dominance of one bloc of classes or the other. Faced with a growing popular movement and the complete inability of the Sixth Provisional Government to govern, the center-right alliance decided this was the moment for a crucial confrontation, while they still had the government. They began to speak of civil war and of moving the capital to Oporto. Rather than resign, the government went "on strike" on November 20, demanding the military provide "the conditions for the full exercise of power." Beginning on November 25, the right-wing of the military successfully used the occupation of Air Force bases by the paratroopers as the opportunity they had been waiting for to carry out a coup.[25]

November 25, 1975 to July 1976

Discussion over the direction and manner of advancing toward socialism was now closed as the issue became one of defending what had been gained. In the following weeks, many factories, farms, CMs, and other popular organizations were searched by the commandos and police; officers and soldiers sympathetic to the popular movement were demobilized and some imprisoned; among the workers who lost their jobs were approximately 120 journalists fired from the major newspapers; all wage increases were cancelled; and both *República* and Rádio Renascença were returned to their owners. In one of the demonstrations to free those detained after November 25, four people were killed and seven wounded. Demonstrations were held against price increases and about other political issues; but these were all defensive actions. The right was on the offensive, demanding the return of national-ized banks and factories, an end to the Agrarian Reform, and carrying out many bomb attacks against leftist targets. The popular movement was very much on the defensive, and even those in the government expressed fear of a coup from the far-right.

But the April legislative elections showed that public opinion had not shifted far to the right. The Socialist Party and the PPD fell slightly to 35 percent and 24 percent, respectively, while the Communist Party increased its vote to 15 percent, and the rightist Centro Democrático Social (Demo-cratic Social Center or CDS) nudged the Communists out of third place by doubling their share to 16 percent. In mid-May, attempts were made to remobilize the popular movement around the presidential candidacy of Otelo Saraiva de Carvalho (the military leader of the April 25 coup and head of the now-extinct COPCON), with a campaign focusing on defending the "con-quests of April." Out of four candidates, he came in a distant second (with 17 percent of the vote, compared to 62 percent for Ramalho Eanes, the military leader of the November 25 coup). But his campaign demonstrated continu-ing strong and militant support for the previous gains, and the new Constitu-tion, which entered into effect with the elections, legally codified many of those gains. Portugal thus entered a period of unstable equilibrium with the popular movement on the defensive and none of the basic economic or political problems of the country resolved.

THREE

The Revolution in One City

April to September 1974

In the first months after the overthrow of Caetano, the dynamics in Setubal were a microcosm of national developments. The issues underlying the struggle for power centered on the resolution of the critical problems inherited from the fascist regime, that is, (1) improving the most severe working and physical conditions; (2) purging the institutions of control and repression; and (3) ending the colonial war. These were critical issues not only for the competing political elites but also at the grassroots level where neighborhood and workplace struggles developed to improve the basic conditions of the population and install democratic rights. This period is composed of two subperiods, separated by the shift in the national conjuncture in July. In both, right-wing opposition movements were turned back; during the second subperiod, grassroots' organizing and struggles spread and intensified.

In the first two weeks after the military coup, the population of Casal das Figueiras shantytown, threatened with eviction by the landowner seeking a speculative profit on the property,[1] sent a delegation to demand the local government guarantee their right to remain on the land.[2] Residents of the fishermen's public housing barrio expelled the directors of the *Casa dos Pescadores* (Fishermen's Benevolent Association) and replaced them with a new committee to run the social services and defend their interests. Residents of three different shantytowns occupied housing in as many public housing barrios. While all of the apartments "had been vacant for some time, and some of them had never been inhabited," the occupiers were forced by the military to abandon two of the three barrios (*O Setubalense*, May 10, 1974).

Purging fascist elements often required rank-and-file initiative and was an important issue in both the public and private sectors. Demands made by local groups included the removal of some primary school teachers, demanded by a Teachers' Provisional Representative Commission; removal of the head of the Fire Department, demanded by a general meeting of firefighters; payment of back wages together with the complete replacement of the administration of a yeast and bread factory (Propam); and salary increases and purging of administrators in a large paper products factory (Socel). Workers' commissions sprang up throughout the city demanding salary increases, improvements in working conditions, and some purges.[3] In cases where the demands (especially for purging fascists) still had not been met by late June, workers began occupying their factories to exert further pressure.[4]

During the dictatorship, the *Câmara Municipal* (City Administration) was not elected by the local population; it was appointed by the central state. Following the overthrow of the fascist regime, meetings were organized in most cities to purge the old officials and nominate a new Administrative Commission which, subject to approval by the new government, would hold office until elections could be held. According to one local official:

> At that time the MDP/CDE was the only united anti-fascist force that existed, and it carried out the organizational process throughout the country. Thus, the MDP consulted people who had earned a certain amount of political credit for their work and honesty.
>
> In this way it brought together the seven people necessary for the Administration of the *Câmara*, and presented them to an assembly of the population, full of people, which unanimously approved our coming. The JSN sanctioned the proposal, and we were put in office by their dispatch [on May 16].[5]

The new *Câmara* was composed of people respected locally for past democratic work as well as for illegal union and other political activity. Once empowered, it began to try to familiarize itself with the problems of the different parts of the city, and

> encouraged people to create local organizations, to discuss their problems, present them to us, and participate in the work of the *Juntas de Freguesia*.[6] Without really knowing what a CM was, [we told them] 'Organize yourselves, create CMs, see what you need most, present these needs and the contribution you can make to solving them'. (in Downs, et al., 1978:135)

As part of this work the MDP tried to create *freguesia* level democratic consultative commissions as early as late May.[7]

The old leadership of the local government had been replaced by people much more concerned with responding to the problems of the city's people and limiting the power of those who had caused the problems in the past. The bureaucracy, laws, and financial structures from the time of fascism, however, remained unchanged. As a result, the new leadership's capabilities were quite limited, both legally and financially. Furthermore, no clear plan was found to guide them in responding to the problems of the city or charting a new course. Thus, in this period officials here and elsewhere began to call for a *Lei das Autarquias Locais* (Local Government Law), revision of the fascist Administrative Code, expanded revenues and independent sources of financing and planning for local governments.

In mid-June, as Spínola began to campaign publicly to halt the advances of the young revolutionary process, the *Câmara* faced one of the first right-wing demonstrations to take place in the country since the coup. Several thousand small builders and construction workers demonstrated with the slogans: No to anarchy!; No to unemployment!; Builders are sons of the people!; We want a competent *Câmara*!; Down with the slogan painters!; and Down with the false Portugueses! The *Câmara* had done nothing more than enforce the already existing laws regulating urban development. A demonstration a week later supported it, but all had been warned of the danger of workers being pitted against each other, especially by demagogic appeals to the threat of unemployment.

In the first major showdown between Spínola and the MFA, in Setubal as elsewhere in the country, government employees demonstrated on July 8 in opposition to the limited salary increases and improvements proposed by the First Provisional Government. These demonstrations were a major factor in the downfall the following day of Prime Minister Palma Carlos and the First Provisional Government.

During the following weeks, workplace struggles became more intense as workers continued to press for basic reforms, and factory owners responded with layoffs and plant closures. These struggles were seen as a test of whether the new government and the revolution were going to extend to all the new rights won by some, stop where they were, or go even further. In mid-July, the Propam workers' commission reassured the stockholders that their ownership was not in question and that the occupation of the plant would continue only until management satisfied their demands (for back pay and removing fascists). The Socel management fired a group of farmworkers who had demanded the same forty-four-hour workweek the urban workers enjoyed. A public employees' committee presented demands to the government, including purging of fascists, reduction of salary differentials, standardization of work schedules, a minimum wage and benefits (*O Setubalense*, July 19, 1974).

In August, the first local threat of mass layoffs appeared as the administration of the electronics firm Signetics tried to lay off 900 of 1,300 employees and remove equipment from the factory at a time when most workers were away on vacation. Pickets supported by workers from other companies forcibly stopped the removal of equipment. The workers' commission then proposed a 50 percent reduction in work with no layoffs; purging two administrators; equal salaries for all; and that the workers would forgo their Christmas bonus of an extra month's pay (*O Setubalense,* August 16, 1974). The Ministry of Labor adopted a similar position calling for a 50 percent reduction in work at 60 percent pay, with a floor of 3300 escudos per month (the minimum wage—about $135 U.S. equivalent; the Ministry would subsidize the difference when necessary); no layoffs before the end of 1974; forgoing the Christmas bonus; and a reduction in supervisory personnel. The Ministry postponed any decision on the purges, which had been refused by management. This provided a temporary resolution of the conflict.

Throughout these months, the local government in conjunction with the MDP continued to try to establish citizens' advisory commissions to work with the *juntas de freguesia.* By mid-July, at least one other political organization, the *Grupo de Acção Popular Socialista* (Socialist Popular Action Group or GAPS)[8] began initiating the formation of CMs in some of the older and poorer parts of the city. In their meetings, discussion ranged from local problems to national ones, from improving housing conditions to ending the colonial war. With the creation of SAAL to provide technical and financial assistance to house shantytown residents, many other poor barrios created CMs to participate in the program.

While GAPS and the MDP were the principal political organizations seeking to create community organizations, all of the political parties busily held rallies and educational meetings in neighborhoods and factories. These meetings were especially frequent in the weeks immediately following the end of the First Provisional Government and then again in September as the next major confrontation approached. The right-wing concern with workplace struggles and their apparent government support was reinforced when the far right-wing *Partido Liberal* (Liberal Party)[9] was prevented from holding a rally in Setubal by a counterdemonstration at the beginning of September.

A governor was finally named for the Setubal District in September, while organizing and struggles continued in shantytowns and workplaces. In the middle of the month, a plenary of the workers in the new Setenave shipyard approved a motion in which they

> express solidarity with workers who carry out the purging of fascists to the highest level; denounce the recently approved strike law as contrary to workers' interests; repudiate all divisionist manipulations; demand the strike law be revised and lockouts banned; and demand an *Intersindical* which defends only the interests of the workers.

Attention focused on the developing confrontation at the national level. When the date set for Spinola's "march of the silent majority" arrived, hundreds of people in Setubal, as elsewhere in the country, set up barricades on

37

the main highway to prevent the flow of arms and people to the right-wing mobilization, picket teams protected factories, and a crowd destroyed the local headquarters of the Liberal and another extreme right-wing party, *Partido do Progresso* (Progress Party) whose national leaders were implicated in plans for a coup. The new government was then greeted locally by a demonstration of thousands of people who came out to "show their solidarity with the MFA" (*O Setubalense*, October 2,1974).

October 1974 to March 1975

The successful repelling of the first major right-wing assault on the revolutionary process did not have much immediate effect on the daily activities and struggles of grassroots organizations. It did create awareness that deeper structural changes were necessary to implement and secure their democratic goals, and the conviction that "the masses" were a key element in those changes. Shantytown CMs continued organizing and pressuring for participation in the SAAL process, and citizens' advisory councils continued meeting with the *juntas de freguesia.*

The economic situation worsened as the year ended and new forms of worker and government intervention were tried. At the beginning of October, just prior to the national "day of voluntary labor for the economic reconstruction of the country," workers and stockholders of Propam requested government financial assistance. While they awaited a response, other workers once again showed their solidarity, organizing a benefit concert, and loaning or donating the proceeds of the "day of voluntary labor" to Propam rather than sending them to the Ministry of Labor. The electronics assembly firm Signetics announced it would begin substantial layoffs in January. Many workers of other firms found themselves without the Christmas bonus to which they were entitled and some strikes were called in response. At the end of December, the government finally agreed to name a new management for Propam and provide it financial aid. Within a month, the local governments of the district were debating how best to use the partially idled labor force of a major construction company administered by the government since its owners were arrested for economic sabotage.

While the first pragmatic steps were being taken toward an "antimonopoly economic policy at the service of the people," the most visible change following the September 28 events was the dramatic increase in public activities of increasingly polarized political parties. During the last months of 1974, in addition to purely political rallies, meetings were held to discuss housing, labor unions, health, condition of women, sports, current events, the Russian revolution, workers' struggles, alliance between workers, soldiers and sailors, and other topics. Calls that "all strikes are just" (*O Setubalense*, November 20,1974), that "a factory works just as well without a boss, but without the workers it doesn't work at all" (*O Setubalense*, November 29, 1974), and "the land to those who till it" (*O Setubalense*, December 11, 1974), were heard. In the process, interparty debate became more heated, with the PPD denounced by the revolutionary left groups as right-wing, and the Socialist and Communists as reformist and not representing the interests of the workers, while the latter parties accused the revolutionary left groups of having no base and even "objectively serving reactionary interests." Throughout this period, the MFA sought to maintain its distance from these disputes, holding only one educational meeting in late November on the "current situation" (*O Setubalense*, November 27, 1974), while its *Comissão de Bem-Estar* (the Welfare Commission established during the Cultural Dynamization Campaign) continued to function as a kind of ombudsman.

The *Câmara* continued to try to develop grassroots participation in government. In early February, it began organizing the First General Assembly of the County of Setubal. This was to be a meeting of local government with all the organizations of the people—unions, sports clubs, CMs, firemen's association, etc.—to discuss the problems of the area and set priorities for their solution. Toward this end, the *Câmara* encouraged both urban neighborhoods and rural communities to organize themselves, and for all to consider the local and national problems. Some felt that while such a meeting was a good idea, the *Câmara* was not unbiased, seeking to bring all these organizations under its wing perhaps with a view toward the upcoming elections.

In February, the Intercomissões dos Barrios de Barracas (Shantytown Coordinating Commission or ICBB) was created to coordinate the shantytowns, with leadership from the first two *Associações de Moradores* (AMs), which were CMs for SAAL, legalized.[10] The ICBB, which included all the shantytowns of the city, was formed to coordinate their struggle for decent housing and their relations with SAAL, develop their grassroots organizations taking part in local negotiations with SAAL and the *Câmara*, and pressure the relevant bureaucracies at the national level to expedite land expropriations, construction, and other activities.[11] Relations between the *Câmara* and the ICBB were necessarily somewhat conflictual; the strong presence in the ICBB of a revolutionary left group (Frente Eleitoral Comunista/ Marxista Leninista; Communist Electoral Front/Marxist Leninist or FEC/ML) generally in disagreement with the *Câmara* and central government augmented the tension. As the first coordinating body formed in Setubal, the ICBB's leading members later participated in the leadership of other coordinating organs, and it continued as a group concerned especially with problems of the SAAL process, and in debates both with the government and with the other CMs.[12]

Revolutionary conflicts reached from the society directly into the government bureaucracies. The *Instituto da Família e Assistência Social* (Institute of Family and Social Assistance or IFAS)—the other main government institution with which the population and neighborhood organizations had most dealings—is illustrative. IFAS, charged with basic social welfare programs for the young and old (orphans, food programs, subsidized day-care, and old-age homes, as well as some other social and cultural programs), was created under fascism and entered a prolonged phase of reorganization after its overthrow. The 1975 Work Plan, written in February, indicates the local social workers' frustration with the slow pace of reorganization and their own orientation:

> Immediate central action has become indispensable to effectively (and not just financially) decentralize the Institute, in order to carry out a revolution in the Services.

> The force of change is in the people and not the Services; either these accompany and dynamize the popular process, or they will be left behind and become counter-revolutionary.

> Mobilizing and organizing the population of the barrios to resolve the problems of lack of housing and community facilities is the most important area of our action in that it creates the agent of change (the organized population) and transforms the existing structure of the Services. (IFAS, 1975)

While this was taking place, the second national wave of housing occupations began. During the first few days of widespread housing occupations in Lisbon,[13] there were actually only a few in Setubal, all in old housing in older parts of town. The occupations nonetheless became a heated topic of debate, defended by most of the revolutionary left organizations, and denounced by the Socialist Party, Communist Party, and the *Câmara* as a measure which could not solve the housing problem, but did cause disruption that could only benefit the reactionary opposition. As an alternative, the Administrative Commission of the *Câmara* proposed to the 1,500 attendees of the First County Assembly that the CMs conduct surveys in their own areas to determine which houses were unoccupied. The *Câmara* would collect a list of those in need of housing, and then distribute the available housing to them, acting in the place of landlords who refused to sign a lease, and setting the rent, "correcting, when necessary, the criteria of the law with more general social criteria." While there were those who wanted to simply go ahead and occupy, the CMs did generally begin a survey of available housing and people in desperate need.

Then, a few days later, on March 7, the situation changed. That night a number of left groups organized a protest demonstration outside the meeting hall where the right-wing PPD was holding an election rally. The police were called in and suddenly opened fire on the unarmed demonstrators, killing one and wounding eighteen others. The police stations were then beseiged by the demonstrators, and the Army was finally called in to control the situation. One of the police posts was then closed down completely, and the main one stopped functioning for several days (the chief of police was subsequently replaced).

The election rally and police actions were seen as a clear right-wing attack against the direction of the revolutionary process. That attack called for an offensive response, for which there was now greater possibility given the removal of the main repressive force from the city. In the ensuing days, a wave of occupations was openly carried out. According to one participant in the occupations,

> You could walk out in the street and see people with all their belongings on their backs, looking for a house to put them into.[14] People even took the luxury of choosing their house, considering each one and saying, 'this one is too big', or 'this one is too small', and they'd leave the door half open for the next one to come along. (Downs, et al., 1978:48)

Occupations were also undertaken to provide office space for political parties and community facilities. Many parties, including the Communist Party, obtained offices in this way. The only one forced to vacate was the FEC/ML which had occupied a public building. This wave of occupations was reinforced by the failure of the attempted right-wing military coup on March 11, and the ensuing atmosphere of demands for nationalizations and decisive revolutionary advances.

March 11, 1975 to November 25, 1975

During the period leading up to summer 1975, the existing mass struggles (SAAL and occupations) developed further and a struggle began on a third front, focussed on reducing high rents. All three struggles, but especially the occupations, were sources of conflict and tension in relations with the *Câmara*, and all contributed to internal struggles to transform other state agencies. While some tension also developed among the different movements, this was a secondary aspect within a growing popular unity which produced greater coordination between CMs and agreement among left parties to support their further development. While the summer was filled with

41

debates over models of coordination and the type of new society sought, at the grassroots level, all movements continued to advance. As individual CMs saw how successfully mass direct action had advanced the struggles they began carrying out direct actions of their own to solve local problems. When the rightward move of the central government in September began to threaten the revolution and popular movements, a pragmatic form of defensive coordination was established, a council that linked together organizations of residents, workers, and soldiers. As the next confrontation over state power approached, this council began to function as an alternative to the government, not only as a center of political opposition, but also as the distributor of government and economic resources.

In the days following the March 11 coup attempt, there were many demonstrations and statements of support for the MFA and the new Fourth Provisional Government as well as for their action of nationalizing the banking system. These support activities were often lead by the Communist Party, MDP, and Intersindical, but also by the Coordinating Commission of the First County Assembly.

Housing occupations increased. The *Câmara* said that people should have more patience and that the occupations were a deliberate challenge to its authority. But, according to one participant, "the occupations were all quite disorganized; that is, there was no way of organizing such a thing." The occupations themselves may have been unorganized, but the *Câmara* actually contributed to them by its proposal to the Assembly, which had legitimated the distribution of vacant housing to people, and focused attention on the need to keep track of all empty housing. All the houses occupied in the first days after March 11 were old houses, not new ones, and there were no evictions.

Discussion became much more acrimonious with the first occupations of new housing:

> On Sunday morning, the 16th of March, several families living in shanties in the area of Quatro Caminhos and Nova Sintra, with the support of the CM, occupied two buildings.
>
> These families were evaluated according to their family situation and their living situation, as well as by the courage they showed in their effort to leave the terrible conditions in which they lived. After these occupations, other families from the area of Pinheirinhos followed their example and occupied other housing, also with the support of the Commission of Quatro Caminhos and Nova Sintra.

Thus began the communique to the population of the city issued by the CM Quatro Caminhos (quoted in Downs, et al., 1978:185-187, emphasis in original), which went on to explain that people were occupying housing because they were no longer willing to live in paper and wood scraps when there were more than enough vacant new apartments in the city to house all those living in shanties. It should make no difference that rents for those apartments were too high for them to pay, they argued, because "they were built by workers from barrios like ours, with money stolen from the work of other comrades."

Then the communique argued that those opposed to the occupations are "bourgeois," "with comfortable houses who don't know what it is like to live in a shanty lacking even minimal hygenic conditions and feeling exploitation in your skin."

They asked what the *Câmara* has done about this issue—"the *Câmara* that says it is the defender of the people of Setubal."

The Administrative Commission [C.A.] of the Câmara speaks of laws, saying the occupation is illegal and Bosh [the landlord] is right. *But what laws are these?*

They are laws that defend the capitalist. They are laws made before the 25th of April, like the inspection law, and others made after April 25th, like the law of 120 days—but they all defend the capitalists.

After all, just what is it that is illegal?

Is it people living in shanties or the exploitation by Bosh and others like him which gives them enough profit that they can build buildings?

On the night of Tuesday the 18th, the commissions and population of Pinheirinhos, Castelo Velho and Liberdade concentrated in the Câmara in support of the just struggle of the occupiers of the buildings in Quatro Caminhos. In a meeting with the C.A. the people of these barrios demanded the C.A. support the struggle of these families for the right to housing, and that it do so publicly.

The position of the C.A. was not to support the occupation saying it could not defend the interests of the occupying families because it didn't have sufficient power. We answered that if the Administrative Commission does not feel it has the ability to defend the people's interests, which it already considered just, then it would do better to resign and stop claiming that the Câmara belongs to the people.

After the population had been in the Câmara six hours, the C.A. gave in, and signed a document stating the position it promised to take in support of the occupying families. It was about 4am on Wednesday the 19th when people returned home.

What lessons can we draw from this struggle?

1. *Our country has still not seen the day in which "THE PEOPLE ARE IN CHARGE."* Worse than that: the authorities who say they represent the

43

interests of the people, like the C.A. of the Câmara, continue at the service of the capitalists.

2. We learned that when the people unite and struggle for a just cause, they gain enormous strength and can go over all the laws which exist and are against the people. *Then, the people themselves make the law.*

3. We also learned that *only organized will we be able to win,* as was proven on the night of the 18th to the 19th of March. That is why the CM of Nova Sintra and Quatro Caminhos calls on all the shantytowns that are not yet organized or just beginning to support unity of all in a struggle which concerns us all:

THE RIGHT TO HOUSING!

This excerpt from the communique of the occupiers reflects their outlook at the time, and suggests some of the conflicts that were developing, both with other citizens of the city, and with the *Câmara.* This particular occupation both symbolizes and was at the root of some of the specific tensions that were to continue to exist between the CMs of the shantytowns and the *Câmara.*

At about the same time as these occupations were occurring, another set of new apartments in barrio São Gabriel were occupied. Parts of the barrio were still under construction, and the builder was able to set the construction workers on the project against the occupiers with the argument that if the houses were occupied he could not sell them, and in that case he could not finish them, and they could be out of work. The events were described a few months later by a member of the CM:

> The houses belonged to a builder, and it seems they were already sold or promised. The builder said to the construction workers: "If I build houses to be occupied by the first one who comes along and if we don't receive money we will all be unemployed. As of tomorrow there will be no more work." He was able to mobilize workers against other workers who had occupied the houses. We're beaten there. From the moment we have to struggle against other workers we're automatically defeated and the person up on top of the heap just laughs to himself. That was a defeat for the CM and for everyone else. And the Army came and evicted the occupiers. (Personal interview with CM leader.)

Later discussion of what to do with vacant new construction in the city focused on the need to work closely with the construction workers and their organizations.

The *Câmara* and the military called a March 21 public meeting to try to resolve the situation stating:

> In the past few days there has been a wave of wildcat occupations, but those who most need housing are not the ones getting it. Occupations are part of a

reactionary plan to destabilize the country. There is a plan worked out to distribute housing to the most needy, and a list of empty housing to be distributed. In order to put this plan into practice, all occupied housing must be vacated by March 24th. (*O Setubalense*, March 24, 1975)

When the *Câmara* insisted that it "will not be marginalized and will not legalize the situation that has been created" [*Minutes*, 75-11], a speaker from the shantytown CM Barrio Liberdade responded with: "The Fundo de Fomento de Habitação [Housing Development Fund or FFH] and the *Câmara* have promised a lot but haven't done anything. There is no such thing as a revolution by legal means." (*O Setubalense*, March 24, 1975)

Commenting later on this meeting and the occupation of the new building that had led up to it, a local social worker said:

> They occupied the building in an organized way, then the entire barrio discussed who would move in, according to two criteria: first, not being afraid, and secondly, being in need, because there were those who needed housing but wouldn't take the risk. They filled up the whole building that way, and held meetings and decided they would pay a percentage of family income as rent. This all created quite a scene, and forced the Câmara to convoke a plenary with the local MFA people, ... completely full ... in which they made all sorts of incredible statements such as that the occupiers had taken a donkey to the third floor and were making fires on the carpet, none of which was true. The occupation was carried out by gypsies. I went there several times and they wouldn't even let me smoke in the house for fear I'd burn the carpet. So, you can imagine the care they took there, they only let me smoke in the kitchen. ... The carpets were all covered with plastic—they really took all that care to an absurd point! They ended up being forced out by the MFA, by the local regiment, who showed up with a lot of military hardware. (Downs, et al., 1978:47)

Others continued occupying old housing, and the *Câmara* did in fact distribute some vacant housing to people on a waiting list, although in one shantytown only three of the thirty-three people on the list received housing.

Overall, it was clear that there were ways of occupying old housing, but it was not possible to occupy new housing, at least under existing conditions. The military, the state, the middle class, and the right all reacted more strongly to the threat of occupations of new construction. Thus, all the new construction, sufficient to house nearly all those in the city needing housing, remained empty.

The IFAS social workers, working in the shantytowns, seeing vacant housing available and encountering what appeared to be bureaucratic obstacles to the better use of community resources, often sympathized with the direct action of the local population. A few months later, IFAS would supply financial resources and personnel to maintain community services established by the CMs. But those initiatives had not yet begun, and IFAS was still operating through its old structure, tightly controlled from Lisbon. On April 22, the IFAS social workers went on strike to correct the job classifications of some people, and improve conditions to better serve the population through the reorganization of their service, increased funding, and decentralized decisionmaking. They argued that,

> The professionals of this Service continue without any knowledge of or partici-
> pation in its reorganization; without any possibility, on the other hand, of actively
> participating in the revolutionary process taking place in our country. The
> force of change is in the people and not the Services; either these accompany
> and develop the popular process, or they will be passèd by and become coun-
> terrevolutionary. (IFAS, 1975)

The strike resulted in greater practical autonomy for the regional office, but the formal reorganization still was not completed.

Three days later, national elections were held for a Constituent Assem-
bly. While local results gave the Socialist Party a plurality (as in the rest of the country), the Communist Party came in a strong second. Together with the other left parties they polled more than 80 percent of the vote, a much stronger left showing than in most of the rest of the country (see Table 3.1).

Table 3.1: Elections for Constituent Assembly (April 1975)

	National	Setubal (Concelho)
PS	37.9%	50.6%
PPD	26.4%	8.0%
PCP	12.5%	27.8%
CDS	7.6%	2.4%
MDP	4.2%	4.8%

The large May 17 demonstrations in Lisbon and Oporto had been organ-
ized by the CM coordinating organs from those cities, and the CMs in Setubal thought they, too, would be stronger if they had an organization of all the CMs of the city. Thus, three of the CMs who had taken part in the Lisbon demonstration called a meeting when they returned to Setubal, arguing that the organization and focus of the struggle should be broadened.[15] The meeting was attended by most of the shantytown CMs as well as by three public housing CMs from barrios composed partially of people who had lived in shanties until a few years earlier, and who wanted to support the struggle of those trying to obtain better housing. They decided that the "Comissões de Moradores should deal with all aspects of the city: housing, playgrounds and

other community facilities, transportation, etc." They invited all the commissions of the city to a May 31 meeting to discuss the objectives and formation of an Intercommission for the entire city; the *Conselho de Moradores* (Council of CMs) came out of this meeting.

The importance of the housing problem was emphasized in a meeting called by the *Câmara* a few days before the first meeting of the *Conselho*. In a public meeting to discuss housing, the *Câmara* pointed out that there were at that time

> fifty-eight occupations that had been legalized or were on the way to being legalized; 840 shanties of which 200 were not yet involved in SAAL; two months earlier there had been 3300 units under construction and another 520 completed but empty because of prohibitive rents. In addition, there are landlords who own empty apartments in different *freguesias*, and are thus able to evade the requirement to rent them out. (*O Setubalense*, May 30, 1975)

The *Câmara* then concluded calling upon the CMs to take a more active role in the solution of the housing problem, an encouraging sign for the *Conselho*. In the words of the local government spokesperson, "the *Câmara* is unable to control this situation; it must be done by the CMs."

Three days later, CMs from newer Interclass barrios that had not previously been particularly visible began to try to bring part of this situation under control, although in a way the *Câmara* certainly did not expect.[16] The housing crisis was not only a problem for the poor who lacked decent housing. There were many others from all classes who had decent housing, but had to pay 25 percent to 40 percent or more of their income for it. The CMs considered two ways to deal with the problem of very high rents for otherwise decent housing: a maximum limit tied to the conditions of the housing unit (i.e., a ceiling on the rent per unit or per room) and basing rent on the income of the tenants. The first, as a political project, responded to the effort required and the indignation felt by those struggling to pay a rent much higher than the average. But its disadvantage was that potential active participation was limited to that 10 percent or 15 percent of the population whose housing was much more expensive than average and who normally had higher-than-average income. For everyone else, this seemed an irrelevant struggle; or worse yet, a struggle of the privileged few. The second proposal—rent as a percentage of income—would presumably benefit shantytown dwellers as well as the better-paid workers and professionals.[17] But it posed other problems related to the public declaration and policing of income. The CMs decided that "rent should be 10 percent of family income [but] due to the lack of conditions to carry out this proposal . . . we approve the payment of 500 escudos per room (and 300 escudos per room in basements) as a first step." (*O Setubalense*, June 2, 1975)

This decision soon lead to the development of an important part of the urban social movement in Setubal; furthermore, it proved to be a way of extending and expanding the base of the previously existing urban movement to new sections of the population, although generating some conflicts in the process. At the time the proposal was made, it would have directly affected less than 10 percent of the housing units in the city.[18] While it thus was not a demand which would directly appeal to most of the population, it did spread quite rapidly amongst all those who were affected by high rents.[19] Simply put, it spread to all barrios with rents greater that 500 escudos per room, and it was strongest in those barrios where high-rental units were concentrated.

The "struggle for 500 escudos per room," as it was called, was quite successful in immediately reducing rents to that level, but that was not the only or even the principal objective of those who began the struggle. They had a three-part goal. First, the struggle was a means to attack urban specu-lation, with the hope that it would lead to a new national housing policy, based on the idea of housing as a social service and right, available to all at a reasonable price. Second, it was a way of "challenging the reformist CMs and local governments."[20] Finally, it was a way to reach "large numbers of people who had not yet been motivated by a revolutionary process which directly affected them, [by] bringing them together around one problem—housing—over which they could have a large objective effect." (*Revolução*, July 1975)

Nevertheless, many people, especially those living in shantytowns, were not sure what benefit could be expected from this struggle. While some felt it was simply "irrelevant," others initially judged it more harshly. A slightly misinformed member of one shantytown CM commented: "we can't sup-port this 500 escudos thing—we can't even afford 150 escudos." Another said:

> That's a struggle of those who want swimming pools [one of the CMs involved had previously demanded heating for a public pool]. It's more important to build houses than swimming pools. We'll help them in their struggle, if they'll trade houses with us in the winter when our barrio is full of swimming pools. (Personal interview with CM leader.)

The first meeting of what was to become the *Conselho de Moradores* took place in this context of highly mobilized shantytown CMs and other long-standing CMs joined by recently formed militant CMs from newer more expensive barrios. The *Conselho* was started "in order to have an organized struggle for the resolution of the problems of the city's barrios," spreading popular organization and supporting each CM in its own struggles, as well as broadening their focus to issues not previously at stake. Those in the 500 escudos struggle saw this as a way of gaining legitimacy in their broader struggle, as well as showing that they were not only concerned with the high rents for those better off, but also with the lack of housing and supporting the principle of unified struggle.

Those in the ICBB also saw benefits in uniting into one organized struggle, but they were somewhat wary about those in the 500 escudos struggle, suspecting that it was a struggle of those who were better off. While they joined out of a belief in the political importance of unity, it was with the understanding that the goal of that stronger front should be primarily the provision of decent housing for those living in shanties. As a member of one shantytown CM said at the time, "We're going to put together a Council of the Commissions, and the first thing we are going to do is house the most needy." (*O Setubalense*, June 6, 1975)

The difference in priorities brought out a number of divisions, in particular that between the shantytown CMs and the others. In the second meeting of the group in June,

> the barrios were informed by a member of the CM of Quatro Caminhos that, in a meeting that afternoon, the shantytowns had decided to continue for the time being to work together, but separate from the other barrios. Nevertheless, they would ask for the help of the other barrios when necessary. The justification for this attitude was the similarity of their problems at the present time, and the need to accelerate the construction work.[21]

This attitude was not well-accepted by the other CMs attending. To some, this seemed to promise the early end of the *Conselho*, while others felt that "the struggle for housing is the highest priority, and such a division between shantytowns and the other barrios was not just." Given no other choice, however, the decision of the shantytown CMs was finally accepted in a tense meeting. The *Conselho* as a whole then reaffirmed the principle that

> it [*Conselho de Moradores*] would only deal with the general problems of the city, or problems common to many barrios, or to support a specific barrio, when so requested by the CM. The specific problems of each barrio would continue to be dealt with by the respective CM without any interference from the *Conselho*.[22]

Discussion then turned to the problem of long, wandering, inconclusive meetings, which had prompted people to walk out of the first meeting complaining. As a result, the convocation for the next meeting requested that each CM bring in a written proposal for the objectives, functioning, and immediate tasks of the *Conselho*. Discussion of proposals continued throughout June.

In the meantime, important changes were occurring in workplace struggles and in local cooperation between left political parties. While there continued to be some short strikes and factory occupations as pressure for payment of back salaries, or for other traditional reasons, workplace direct actions began imposing alternatives to management decisions for running the factories. The workers at the Movauto automobile assembly plant decided to convert one production line from expensive Peugots to producing refrigerators because "in an economy at the service of the workers there is no reason to produce cars a worker could never buy," and nobody else was buying them either (*O Setubalense*, June 13, 1975). When the owner of a private nursery school decided to close the school for lack of clientele, the teachers decided to run it themselves, lowering fees and opening it to families that could not afford the former scale. The workers at the Belgian-owned chemical plant, Sapec, occupied the installations to demand not only state intervention and purging of the administration, but also a halt to transferring of nearly $500,000 in profits out of the country and reducing superfluous expenses. Following successful cooperation in a June 21 rally in support of the Movimento Popular para a Libertação de Angola (Popular Movement for the Liberation of Angola or MPLA), and after the MFA's June PAP, seven left parties that previously had often competed met together to analyze the significance of the PAP, the role of grassroots organizations, and concrete proposals for united (*unitária*) action.[23] The decisions included common action to:

1. push forward the popular movement of the masses around the economic and political problems they feel most strongly;
2. go beyond the old structure of the bourgeois state, strengthening and creating unitary organs in the factories, fields, and barracks; and
3. push forward the creation of Popular Assemblies of the unitary organs, assemblies that should hold real power within their area.

After a period of sometimes heated and sometimes boring debate, statutes were finally adopted for the *Conselho* at the beginning of July, in a meeting with 200 people representing more than twenty CMs (see Appendix C). They specified that it:

1. shall be the union of all the CMs of the city of Setubal, oriented toward organized struggle around the resolution of the problems of the barrios and of the city (housing, community facilities, health, transportation, etc.);

50

2. shall be unitary and nonpartisan (*apartidária*);
3. shall place itself in the vanguard of the struggle of the people for their rights; thus, it shall be autonomous and independent of all bodies before which it may appear;
4. shall, in its actions, always be based in assemblies or plenaries of the respective barrios, and should be submitted to the criticism of the popular masses;
5. shall always act collectively, repudiating all individualistic and egoistic actions; and
6. shall always try to link the struggle of the barrios with that of the factories.

The *Conselho* began to pass from a focus primarily on discussions of what its structure and priorities should be to actively supporting different struggles. Among the first actions it supported was the occupation of a religious home for the aged (Asilo Dr. Paula Borba) by the workers of the home. The *Conselho* showed the people of the city the conditions of the home in a public people's trial, purged the old administration, and began helping the workers to improve conditions. A few days later, the *Conselho* participated in the occupation of a large country estate at the edge of the city for a recreation center and to better house the worker-run nursery school mentioned above. Soon after they began to function there (in August), however, COPCON evicted them from the property and returned it to its French owner. These first actions of the *Conselho* were important in its development, but were viewed somewhat warily by the shantytown CMs, who did not see how this contributed to getting housing:

> For us it was very important to expel the nuns from the old-age home; but for the shantytown dwellers it was much more important that they have houses. While they were struggling to get a house we were already in a much more advanced phase, struggling for the complements to that house: better rents, electricity, sewers, a whole series of things the shantytown residents weren't struggling for. There began to be a bit of a shock between the two groups.[24]

A conflict was averted by unity in response to legal action threatened against participants in the rent reduction struggle. The first relatively widespread refusal to pay more than 500 escudos per room had been in June. In early July, the *Ministério de Equipamento Social e do Ambiente* (Ministry of Community Facilities and the Environment or MESA) stated officially that it considered the struggle "illegal and subject to penalties." When challenged the *Câmara* refused to take any position, saying "the problem transcended" its authority. But the tenants in the struggle responded with a mass assembly where they called upon all CMs to support them and to come to the first announced trial of a participant. They also scheduled a demonstration in Lisbon to demand purging the MESA minister; immediate closing of the Constituent Assembly; houses, not shacks; and immediate nationalization of the construction industry.

At the next meeting of the *Conselho*, the approximately one dozen CMs present agreed that the immediate tasks were to:

1. support the struggle of the shantytowns;
2. support the struggle for lower rents; and
3. support the struggle of the peripheral barrios for infrastructure (sanitation, electricity, water, etc.). (*O Setubalense*, July 11, 1975)

Furthermore, they decided that the *Conselho* would comprise three members of each CM, with membership barred only to "landlords, builders, and all others that profit from the exploitation of man." (*O Setubalense*, July 11, 1975)

A few days later, they countered the first attempt to bring anyone to trial for participation in the struggle with a demonstration of 3,000 people outside the courthouse. The court workers expressed their solidarity, and the judge presiding suspended all legal proceedings against anyone involved in the struggle. Saying he was unable to dictate a final verdict, he sent the case to the Ministry of Justice, recommending that the defendant be absolved and all similar cases dropped. The government suspended all further proceedings.

Following the court case, the movement spread rapidly throughout the city, and began changing conditions that impeded occupations of new housing. Previously occupations had been a way to get access to housing that the landlord wished to keep vacant, but still paying a rent that provided a fair market return to the landlord. As one occupant put it: "we want to pay; we aren't here to rob anyone." But if they were to occupy new housing, the rent would be far out of the reach of most of those living in the city. The gypsies who occupied a new building in March had responded to this problem by proposing to set their rents at a percentage of their incomes; in its proposal to the First County Assembly, the *Câmara* had already made a similar suggestion to adjust rents on this basis for the old housing it was going to distribute. But no such principle was yet widely accepted for new housing. The struggle to "reduce speculative rents" was a step in this direction. The ceiling on the highest rents opened this housing to a group of people who could not previously afford it. Because direct action seemed able to impose this limit, this struggle was a step in the direction of "housing as a social right," and instrumental in the development of occupations of new housing beginning in July 1975.

This third wave of occupations was less intense than the previous ones, but it was a qualitatively new phase. Occupations were well-organized and concentrated particularly in the barrio Liceu, one of the barrios leading the struggle against speculative rents, and also one in which rents were highest and where there were the most vacant new apartments. Most occupiers immediately entered into the struggle for 500 escudos per room, and could not otherwise have afforded to live there. They were frequently spurred on by groups from the revolutionary left, and sometimes by groups of refugees returning from Africa during the decolonization process. Those involved in the struggle became active in other questions of housing policy, maintaining their concern with the issue of rent as a share of income. Mass direct action taken to begin and defend the struggle was thus strongly vindicated.

By mid-July, the *Conselho* had grown to include almost all of the CMs of the city, representing considerable broadening of the social base and issues involved in coordination. Several of the shantytowns continued to attend its meetings, and the ICBB, represented on the secretariat (whose eight CMs included three shantytowns), was maintained as an independent caucus within the *Conselho*, as well as dealing with specifically SAAL related questions on its own. Just as the *Conselho* was beginning to function effectively as an autonomous coordinator and supporter of the struggles of the CMs of the city, conditions changed to apparently create the possibility for a quantum leap in popular coordination.

Given an ideology of direct action, there was much that should have been possible through direct coordination with workers' organizations. While many benefits had been gained from organizing all of the CMs together, participants were aware of two structural limitations to the *Conselho*. First, it had no real authority and the government was not required to respond to its decisions. Second, it could neither speak for the popular movement as a whole nor address critical issues outside of urban consumption because it did not include the workers' organizations, the other main component of the popular movement. Working together would give each the power and legitimacy to do much more than they could do separately. The MFA Guidelines, unity among left parties locally behind the development of grassroots organization and popular assemblies, and particularly the Communist Party effort to create a mass base of support for the new Fifth Provisional Government and against the Socialist Party and right-wing opposition combined to create the conditions for a general coordinating body.

The left parties all generally supported some kind of entity that would link different popular organizations. But the organizations included were very different, as were the roles each wanted fulfilled. The revolutionary left parties generally believed that such 'councils' or 'assemblies' should have legislative and executive power, and that they should be based in the CMs, workers' commissions (CTs) and soldiers' commissions (CSs). This, the revolutionary left believed, would make them the basis for a revolutionary transformation of the state, and aid the advance toward socialist revolution. The Communist Party viewed these groups as potentially very similar to the Cuban Committees for the Defense of the Revolution, and felt they would be a more representative form of vigilance to keep the state and production under the democratic control of the people, as well as act in support of their representatives in the state. The PCP believed this was a way to solidify and defend the gains won until then—both those made by the Portuguese workers in the society as a whole and by the PCP within the state. This was especially important when boycotts from within and without the state were becoming more pronounced, and the relative hegemony of the PCP within the state was being increasingly challenged. Still others saw such a form of grassroots coordination as an alternative to a state and political system continually divided by political infighting. Various formal proposals to develop such an organization were being considered by the MFA and political parties during the latter part of June and July 1975.

The hegemonic political influence in the *Consejo de Moradores* was that of the revolutionary left. In the political crisis of mid-July, the PCP saw a way to try to replace the *Conselho* with an organization better serving its interests. While the PCP nationally began to mobilize against the July 17 PS demonstration, in Setubal it convoked a meeting to encourage action to prevent the "reactionary advance" and called for a "revolutionary government that would push the general line of the politics of the MFA," as outlined in its Guidelines Document. Out of this meeting came the Comité dos Organismos Populares de Setúbal (Committee of the Popular Organizations of Setubal or COPS), with its first meeting on July 25th described by the press at the time as "very polemical and not very productive."

The presence of some fifty CTs and thirty CMs at the next meeting showed that people were interested in developing an organization that would bring together workers' and residents' organizations; nonetheless, a member of the MFA in attendance challenged the representativeness of COPS. More meetings were held, but the stillborn nature of the organization was manifest in their level of rhetoric and reinforced by the fact that it found no concrete functions to execute. Many who had been most active in the CMs and CTs saw it as a conscious attempt to destroy the autonomous organizations, burying them among a wide variety of other organizations and bringing them under the influence of less politicized groups and the control of the PCP. Afterward, a participant commented:

Many sessions were used up discussing statutes. Who has the right to vote? Who doesn't? Do the trade unions vote? Sports clubs? Who has more votes? Who has fewer? Meetings were used up that way on the objectives also: for a popular democratic revolution; for a socialist revolution; to defend democratic liberties. . . . No one ever reached agreement on anything. The problems were so theoretical, and at the same time so bureaucratic. (Interview in Downs, et al., 1978:54)

As an organization to coordinate local struggles, COPS had little positive effect and interrupted the development of the Conselho. Its one useful product was a proposal for popular coordination, based on the ideas of popular assemblies and armed vigilance, which was eventually circulated widely (see Appendix D). Otherwise, its effects were basically to make people much more wary about spending time in coordinating bodies, and to demonstrate the destructiveness of sectarian discussion and manipulation within popular organizations. One of the things that those in the *Conselho* learned from the process was the importance of maintaining ongoing work paralleling the discussions in coordinators—and that this work could best be carried out by specialized subgroups, much as with CMs. But this conclusion was to be drawn and applied only after somewhat more extensive operation of the *Conselho* itself.

In mid-August, the first of a series of housing occupations to provide community facilities took place. An assembly of the barrio Salgado discussed at length the need for day-care and cultural facilities and decided to check on the conditions of a large abandoned building belonging to a religious order as a possible location for some community activities. This building was occupied by the CM the next day. According to CM members interviewed by the local newspaper at the time, the residents of the barrio viewed very favorably the occupation of the building to use as a day-care center.

But there are many here who are petty bourgeois and are not at all interested in this because they have money to put their children in daycare centers that are more or less bourgeois. . . . But there are also others who live here who are quite well off who have actively cooperated with us. (*O Setubalense*, August 20, 1975)

Before much time had passed, twelve CMs obtained their headquarters through occupations, and nine provided some type of community facilities—usually a day-care or social center, often in the same building as the headquarters. These occupations did more than provide social facilities lacking in the city and now available to the working people of the city. They also helped characterize the political and social nature of the occupations and of the

CMs as institutions that could act *directly* to resolve some of the problems of the working people of the city.

A nucleus of the *Conselho* began meeting again, trying to redevelop the *Conselho* and debate problems of the city's CMs. Its discussions continued to focus mainly on housing related problems and continued to show the division of priorities between shantytowns and newer barrio CMs mentioned earlier. In its first meeting after the end of COPS (August 22), the *Conselho* analyzed the struggle for 500 escudos per room. After a long and heated debate, they decided it was a reformist struggle, agreed to seek a more advanced alternative, and voted to support the families involved.

A plenary assembly with some 700 people present on September 1, just after the fall of the Fifth Provisional Government, opened with information on the current political situation, and then discussed a proposal of the COPCON Document which states:

> A housing policy must be defined which directly attacks the large speculative landlords and their way of life, while defending small landlords who with an acceptable level of income would be able to assume the support of their families. Limits on rent in accordance with location, type of construction, etc., should be established. Neighborhood Commissions have a decisive role to play in establishing these criteria. (*Documento COPCON*, Part III, Article #6)

The assembly adopted a proposal calling for:

1. Nationalization or municipalization of urban land and nationalization with socialization of the large- and medium-sized construction companies. These nationalizations shall be carried out without compensation.
2. Complete elimination of all new licenses for luxury construction.
3. Immediate development of public construction.
4. Immediate socialization of all housing, with the exception of owner-occupied units. [*O Setubalense*, September 5, 1975]

Three alternative proposals to link rent to family income and housing characteristics were sent "back to the bases for further discussion," and were further debated in citywide meetings, with falling attendance, on September 8 and 15. At the next meeting on this issue, the majority of the twelve CMs present were from shantytowns, and

> the agenda was altered [at their insistance]. There is no point in discussing the question of a percentage [of income to rent]—the people of Setubal should force the nationalization of housing. There are 3,000 empty housing units; why shouldn't they be occupied by the inhabitants of the shantytowns?

Those in shantytowns don't want to occupy, since they have been integrated into the SAAL process. But other people in rundown housing, or refugees from the ex-colonies have every reason to occupy those houses. We should prepare these occupations. (*O Setubalense*, September 22, 1975)

While COPS did not take root, the idea of government based on direct democracy expressed in grassroots organizations did. Popular power became an alternative project for local organization and an alternative to the rightward shift of the national government. A September 8 demonstration in favor of Popular Power called by the CMs and CTs of the city brought out many thousands of supporters calling:

1. for the development and strengthening of Popular Power;
2. for the worker-peasant alliance;
3. against imperialism;
4. against the fascist offensive;
5. for the satisfaction of social demands of the workers (health, housing, daycare, etc.); and
6. for the arming of the workers.[25] (*O Setubalense*, September 8, 1975)

The *Câmara* became more concerned with the need to develop and institutionalize popular power as well as with the step backward represented by the Sixth Provisional Government.[26] It published its own document calling for Popular Power and began calling meetings of the CMs to elect delegates to a residents' assembly to work with the *junta de freguesias* as well as to a local Popular Assembly to be formed according to the outlines of the Documento-Guia. It also began calling meetings to form citywide task forces to work with it on the main problems of the city. One *freguesia* meeting with ten CMs and the *junta* present decided in favor of:

1. demanding the authorities repress the reactionaries and purge fascists;
2. popular vigilance;
3. solidarity with the Municipal Council of Oporto which had been attacked by the police under the orders of the Civil Governor of Oporto; and an immediate purge of that Civil Governor;
4. support to the struggle of progressive soldiers;
5. support to the struggle of the war wounded (ADFA);
6. support to the struggle of Rádio Renascença and *República*; and
7. demanding publication of the report of inquiry into the events of March 7 in Setubal.

The *Câmara* also cosigned a leaflet put out by most of the CMs and the regional union confederation calling upon the people of Setubal to join in the September 25 Lisbon SUV demonstration, which was to gather more than 10,000 soldiers and several times that number of workers and residents (*O Setubalense*, September 26, 1975).

The *Câmara* insisted that its initiatives were intended to help develop popular organization, but many of those in the *Conselho* were suspicious that it was an attempt to undercut their independent reorganization. This wariness increased when the *Câmara* continued to criticize the direct action movements of the CMs, for example, when it insisted that "a large share of occupations are done by opportunists; the people living in shanty-towns are still in their shacks." Nonetheless, the *Câmara* was cooperating, taking initiatives, offering its facilities, and not insisting upon control. A meeting of the *Conselho* in the latter part of September, with more than twenty CMs present as well as a representative from the *Câmara* agreed to the "urgent need to reorganize the *Conselho de Moradores* since the political situation of the country demands a strengthening of popular organization and since the problems the barrios now face can only be solved by their joint action."

The need for concrete work was emphasized "in order that popular power will exist not only on paper, but will truly exist in practice." The creation of several different work groups was discussed, and meetings were scheduled for September 29 to form two of them: a housing work group "that will discuss the problem of rents, vacant housing, shanties, and construction"; and a consumer cooperative work group, which "through contacts already begun with the agricultural cooperatives, will bring the city and country closer together in the same struggle." A second meeting to form other groups was scheduled for October 1, in the *Câmara*. Strong coordinated work programs were finally developing, but dramatic shifts in the national political situation intervened almost immediately.

Following the September 29 occupation of the radio and television stations in Lisbon by government troops, a meeting of CMs of the *Conselho de Moradores*, workers commissions and soldiers was held. They formed a Committee of Struggle to coordinate activities in case of further rightward moves by the government, as well as to coordinate and further their individual struggles. A meeting was convened for October 6, to which all CMs and CTs were called in order to broaden and formalize its formation.

Nearly all the CMs were represented at that meeting, and a mixed secretariat was elected, composed of six delegates from CTs, four from CMs (of which two were from shantytowns), and five members of the soldiers commission of the local barracks. (The numbers reflect the relative importance which each was believed to have.) It was further decided not to spend time on the discussion of principles, statutes, and structure—the experience of COPS and other such debates had convinced everyone that such discussion was sterile and divisive. Thus,

> from the beginning emphasis was given to the need to carry out work oriented to the concrete problems of the city and factories, enabling unity of the workers in practice and not the theoretical definition of principles that would bring to the fore sectarian differences. Thus the structure which was maintained up to November 25th consisted of weekly plenaries of Workers Commissions and Residents Commissions (unions and other popular organizations could participate in discussions but had no right to vote), and there were mixed work groups for specific problems. (Fatima Brinca, "Setúbal e o Poder Popular," March 1976)

The members of the *Conselho de Moradores* insisted strongly on the importance of work groups with concrete themes, and the ones created at the October 6 meeting were housing, health, infancy, city-country link, and organizing (*dinamização*). Other discussion focused on the current political-military situation: announcements were made of an October 9 SUV demonstration in Coimbra and of attempted purges of the left at a military base in Oporto (CICAP) and in an Air Force base in Beja; the Socialist Party was accused of acting divisively and of having sought to provoke a counter-revolutionary coup on the night of October 1; and support was voted for a demonstration called by the metalworkers' union for the next day. That demonstration became the largest in Setubal up to that time.

While the lack of debate on structure did reduce the number of divisive problems that arose and was perhaps necessary for a rapid beginning of the Committee of Struggle, it had drawbacks. It meant that no formal channels of communication and control between the coordinating body and the grassroots existed, and it simply avoided some debates over real political differences. This was a conscious decision, in the belief that unity in struggle would keep differences in perspective and eventually overcome them. Participants agreed that only later would they decide on a more complete structure based on the practical experience of work groups and political developments.

The October 13 meeting of the Committee of Struggle was attended by 300, although two of the four CMs and two of the six CTs on the secretariat were not present. Discussion focused on four points: (1) members of the soldiers commission of the Setubal Infantry Regiment (RIS) warned of attempts to purge leftist soldiers in Setubal; (2) representatives of one factory informed that management was purging their union committee; (3) CM Liceu announced that it was preparing to occupy and distribute all vacant housing "to avoid opportunism";[27] and (4) all were called to participate in a local demonstration of support to progressive soldiers on October 16 (*O Setubalense*, October 15, 1975).

Thousands of people participated in the demonstration. Speeches, prepared under the collective responsibility of the secretariat of the Committee of Struggle and presented by a representative of the CMs, another for the CTs, a soldier from RIS, and a soldier from RASP (the heavy artillery base in Oporto occupied by soldiers from CICAP when their base was closed down), focused on opposition to fascism, militarism, the purging of the left, and the Sixth Provisional Government; and support to the development of popular power, the agrarian reform, developing the broad progressive alliance, and defending the democratic and social conquests of the workers.[28] An unexpected result came the next day when three leading reporters for the local newspaper, *O Setubalense*, were fired for their sympathy to the demonstration.

In the next days, more public debates and plenaries were held on the housing question, focusing on the crisis of the construction industry as well as how to best use vacant housing to meet the needs of the population. Then, in the October 20 session of the Committee of Struggle, with 500 attendees, a meeting was scheduled between construction workers, union delegates, and officials, as well as representatives of the CMs to produce a proposal for the occupation of the remaining vacant housing in a way that would avoid opportunism. Then, the possibility of occupying *O Setubalense* and reinstating the fired reporters was discussed, and the assembly affirmed its support to the struggle of Rádio Renascença. At that point, a representative of the soldiers commission spoke up saying:

> We are not here representing the MFA. The MFA ended many months ago if it ever existed. Nevertheless, we are here on the side of the working class of Setubal (...) we are here to defend the democratic liberties on the side of the People. The working class must liberate itself. (*O Setubalense*, October 27, 1975)

When the meeting ended at 2 a. m., the Committee of Struggle went with the workers of *O Setubalense* to occupy the newspaper and purge its director and owner. With the next issue, the paper began selling 10,000 copies per day instead of its prior average of 3,000.

The next session of the Committee of Struggle was convened in the *Câmara* on October 27 with 300 attendees. The agenda included a self-criticism and evaluation of the functioning and lack of expansion of the base of the Committee, consideration of a proposal from the housing work group, discussion of support to the organs of mass media aligned with the popular movement (*República*, Rádio Renascença, *Setubalense*), and the March 7 inquiry. But the meeting was suspended to go to a nearby town and stand picket duty in support of the occupation of a latifundist's house for an agrarian reform center, following the destruction of the previous center by a bomb.

A general housing strategy was finally adopted in meetings on November 2 and 3 between the Committee of Struggle, the *Câmara*, construction unions, the local planning office (Gabinete de Planeamento de Setúbal or GPS) and the FFH. This strategy called for:

- support for the completion of existing SAAL projects, under the control of the CMs, but without initiating any more projects;
- occupation of all vacant housing, new and old;
- distribution of housing according to need, with rent tied to family income, and taking into consideration the age of the building, its location and size, family size and other factors [first proposed in the *Conselho de Moradores* on Septbember 1];
- rent to be paid to the Committee of Struggle rather than to the landlord;
- occupation of necessary land and beginning of construction of infrastructures for a public housing project first planned four year earlier; this work would be carried out by a construction company whose CT was a member of the Committee of Struggle, with large numbers of workers facing imminent unemployment; other work would be carried out by nationalized companies or small enterprises working under workers control;
- political orientation would be provided by the Committee of Struggle;
- economic orientation and supervision by the construction union; and
- technical orientation by GPS and FFH.

After hearing reports on the purging of the left from the RIS, the nearby Montijo air force base, and the Elvas Agrarian Reform Center, the Committee gave its support to a demonstration planned for Montijo one week later. In addition, the Committee criticized the insufficient work done by its member commissions in developing organization at the grassroots level. The Committee of Struggle postponed its next meeting, recognizing the lack of representativity of those present (virtually all of the major CTs were absent[29]) and a new assembly was called for the November 17, in the *Câmara*, to reorganize the Committee.

About 300 people attended that meeting of the Committee of Struggle where they evaluated its past work and considered reorganization proposals. One week later, the meeting began with a discussion of the political-military situation to determine "what we do not want from the next government" (workers at Movauto had already repudiated the Sixth Government's suspension of functions). Discussion then turned to drawing practical conclusions from the organizational proposals made one week earlier, including the link between CMs and agricultural cooperatives through the direct marketing of products began in some barrios a few days earlier.

It is not possible to know what might have happened had the revolutionary process continued to develop. The November 25 coup met with some organized resistance locally, but because the resistance did not get support from elsewhere, it could do little. The final issue of *O Setubalense* was published on November 26, in defiance of martial law, under the headline "Arm the Workers Now!", before it was occupied and closed down by the military on November 27. Warrants were sent out for the arrest of many members of the Committee of Struggle, many leading political militants went into hiding, and progressive soldiers at RIS were furloughed and a few arrested.

November 25, 1975 to June 27, 1976

The ensuing weeks saw a general sense of apprehension and demobilization. It soon became clear that while the popular advance had been ended, the repression and move to the right was less pronounced than many had anticipated. It thus was both necessary and possible to seek to defend and institutionalize as many of the "conquests of the revolution" as possible. At the beginning of January 1976, the first issue of the newspaper *A Nova Vida* appeared, published from the same facilities and with the same staff as *O Setubalense*. Meetings were held in factories and neighborhoods to evaluate the past and orient the future work of their respective commissions.[30] The direct sale of agricultural goods (the so-called city-country link) was extended to more and more neighborhoods. The president of the *Câmara* spoke out saying, "The CMs have done very noteworthy work and must continue to participate in public life."

Throughout the first months of 1976 one or more CMs met virtually every night in addition to weekly meetings of the housing, infancy, and city-country link work groups. Without the popular mobilization and participation of the earlier period, however, the commissions were held less accountable to their grassroots and the political parties came to exert a more dominant role (Downs, et al., 1978:130). By mid-1976, nearly all CMs were much less active than they had been previously.

In mid-January, general assemblies of CMs and CTs met to analyze the experience of citywide coordination. Evaluations of the Committee of Struggle varied widely. Among the CMs, some people felt it "did very little," or "was only for talking and arguing," and even those who made favorable comments remained critical of certain aspects. "The Committee of Struggle was an important link in the strengthening of popular power and the alliance between the working class, peasants, and soldiers ... in spite of its functioning somewhat as an isolated elite." The CTs concluded that during a time before November 25 it had suffered from sectarianism, but then carried out useful work, and that there was an insufficient flow of information and representativity from the CTs and their bases. Both groups decided that on the basis of the experience of the *Conselho de Moradores,* COPS and the Committee of Struggle, "it is extremely difficult to conduct a process of struggle involving the combined organization of factory [CT] and neighborhood [CM] commissions," rather it would be better to have two secretariats, one for the CMs and one for the CTs. They further decided that the Committee of Struggle as a whole should meet when necessary to deal with joint problems, and each secretariat should develop its own sector. "The CMs have the moral and revolutionary obligation to solve the problems of the people at the barrio level," and should develop the city-country link through the direct sale of agricultural products in the barrios. Similarly, "the CTs should solve the problems of the factories and their workers," and should take their products to the cooperatives. The two secretariats were elected and began meeting separately; and the only time they met together was at the end of March, when a general assembly of CMs and CTs called at the initiative of the latters' secretariat eliminated the name *Committee of Struggle.*

All three of the principal urban struggles continued, although in greatly changed circumstances. By January 1976, the number of people in the struggle to limit rents to 500 escudos per room had dropped from its high point of more than 1,500 to about 1,200. Court eviction proceedings had begun once again, and the coordinating body met with the Minister of Justice to stop them. The people in the struggle decided to accept the recommendation of the local judge that they try to negotiate agreements with the landlords. The landlords, in turn, had their expectations concerning legal proceedings reduced by at least one case in this period in which the judge ruled the rent should be higher than the 1,500 escudos the tenant was paying for the three-room apartment—but at the same time ruling that the entryway should be counted as a room (making four rooms), establishing the rent at 2,000 escudos (rather than the 2,700 escudos the landlord had demanded).

Some tenants settled with their landlords, paying back rent, and in some cases buying the apartment involved. Some others were able to negotiate favorable collective settlements.[31] But many landlords refused to negotiate any agreement, and in late February, a plenary of participants decided to refuse any further conciliation. In March, the coordinating group of the struggle began publishing the results of a survey which showed that the average family income of those in the struggle was 7,000 escudos per month, with the average monthly rent for the same group at 3,000 escudos; that is, at this rate, 43 percent of income would be going to their official rent. In May, a large demonstration was held before the district civil governor, and in June, 400 to 600 families remained involved.

Housing occupations generally ended with the right-wing coup of November 25. But there were still a few isolated occupations in the first months of 1976, including two cases in which several buildings of new public housing nearing completion were occupied by the construction workers of the project. The construction workers' CT then invited all the CMs of the city to a meeting to discuss the distribution of the apartments.[32] After two meetings, the basic proposal of the workers' commission was adopted:

> The apartments should not be distributed by the *Caixa Nacional de Pensões* [the institution sponsoring the project], but rather there should be a study of the conditions of those workers of the project in need, and the first units completed should be given to these workers. After all their needs are taken care of, the CMs together should decide on the cases of those in greatest need, including those in the SAAL process, and rents should be established according to family income.

But the government saw this as no more than a "suggestion" for how it should act, and bureaucratic fighting over government attempts to establish rent levels and sell the apartments followed. These attempts would have put the housing beyond the means of those who had received an assignment from the CTs and CMs.

The shantytown struggles continued, now faced with greater bureaucratic obstacles. The ICBB continued to function sporadically, depending on the problems that developed, and in March 1976 it mobilized the AMs of the city to take part in a national demonstration in Lisbon to demand that the SAAL process be expedited.[33] As the April legislative elections approached, the CT secretariat and the district labor federation called for people to vote "for a government of the left, in defense of the conquests of the revolution" (the campaign slogans of the Communist Party). While the local election results still gave the left parties (including the Socialist Party) 80 percent of the votes, significant shifts were still evident compared to one year earlier, with a major loss of votes by the Socialists and most of the revolutionary left groups, and a significant increase in votes to the Communists on one hand and the right-wing PPD and CDS on the other.

Because results were better than expected for the left, both locally and nationally, spirits improved considerably, and some flagging activities were renewed. In June, more local meetings were held, but most attention turned to the upcoming presidential elections. Newspaper reports of the rallies held in Setubal by three of the candidates one week before the elections indicate that Eanes (the national front runner) was met by "700 people", Pato (PCP) by "thousands," and Otelo (GDUP) by "thousands and thousands." Returns showed the strength of the popular movement and left in Setubal, giving Otelo a strong lead with 47 percent of the vote to Eanes' 35 percent, a dramatic reversal of their national pollings of 17 percent and 62 percent respectively.

FOUR

Neither Spontaneity Nor Manipulation: Roots of Urban Social Movements

M ass movements focusing on the conditions and control of the work-place and neighborhoods were very important during the Portuguese revolution, but their genesis and role were often disputed. Much debate focused on whether the popular movement was essentially "spontaneous" or "manipulated." Most advocates of the "spontaneity" position had a revolutionary left political perspective and considered this spontaneity a positive feature of the movement. They insisted that they were not responsible for it, and argued that, given the opportunity, popular movements and organizations directly expressing the democratic will of the people—unmediated by political parties—would necessarily arise everywhere. In those situations where the Communist Party recognized that these organizations were not under the control of the revolutionary left, it also considered them spontaneous but argued that meant they were uncontrollable and unreliable allies. Partisans of the "manipulation" position generally opposed these movements, argued they were directed by one or another left political party, and were significant only because of party strategies.

This chapter provides an empirical response to the questions underlying the polemics regarding the extent of "spontaneity" or "manipulation" of the popular movement during the Portuguese revolution. Was it essentially organized and directed by outside political forces, or did it essentially develop according to a logic specific to the movement and outside the control of any political organizations? If it is the latter, does this result in relatively random and unpredictable behavior, as a simple view of spontaneity might suggest, or in consistent behavior that is largely determined by identifiable structural factors, and which should be differentiated from traditional "spontaneity?" Finally, if the structural model is supported, what does that imply for the role of political parties and their organizing strategies?

The preceding chapters have discussed the history at the national and local levels during the period between 1974 and 1976, highlighting the important role of neighborhood-based organizations and movements. In Setubal, the CMs mobilized tens of thousands of people for demonstrations, thousands in neighborhood assemblies, and hundreds in ongoing projects and work group activities. These organizations were critical elements in the development of a broad popular political movement; in the creation of an atmosphere of a city at the service of the vast majority of its residents, and in the struggle to make the nation as a whole correspond to these changes. They were instrumental in improving housing conditions for some 10,000 of the city's inhabitants; they created several low-cost day-care centers; and they helped direct local officials in the general improvement of city services. All of this was seen as part of the basis for a new, more democratic system of popular power.

But these movements arose neither randomly nor in response to a central decision. As analysis of the *comissões de moradores* of Setubal shows, the origin of urban movements, their actions, development and ultimate effects depend fundamentally on structural factors rather than on characteristics internal to the movements or on voluntaristic political will. The principal determinants of the dynamics and significance of urban social movements are the *political conjuncture* (i.e., the relation of forces between social classes in the society as a whole), the *social base* of the movements, and the *objective problems* suffered by the various sectors of the population. A clear test of the impact of these structural factors—as compared to that of spontaneity or political will—is provided by the origin of the CMs. As demonstrated below, alternative explanations may be relevant to the history of specific cases, but they explain much less than—and in fact are sharply conditioned by—these three fundamental variables. Nevertheless, even if CMs initially resulted from structural forces, one could argue that once they exist they come under the control of political parties. Thus, the second part of this chapter will analyze the CMs' political orientations and the factors producing them. Once again, the analysis will show that political orientations were determined primarily by those same objective factors rather than by the intervention of any political organization and that the presence of specific political parties was much more an adaptation to each CM's political orientation than a cause of it.

Before doing so, however, we need an appropriate operational classification of the city's neighborhoods to enable us to analyze the impact of similarities and differences of social base and objective problems among the CMs. Table 4.1 presents the neighborhoods grouped into three types of social base—Popular, Interclass and Elite—according to the occupational distribution of the employed population of the barrio, and indicates the relative weight of the different occupational groups in each barrio compared to their weight in the city as a whole.

Table 4.1

Classification of Barrios by Social Composition

Barrio	Occupational Group[a]						
	1	2	3	4	5	6	7
Elite							
Cinco de Outubro	--	##	##	##	--	##	##
Ferro de Engomar	--	--	##	#	--	##	--
Jose Maria da Silva	--	--	##	##	#	--	--
Liceu	--	0	0	##	##	-	--
Montalvào	--	--	#	##	0	##	0
Interclass							
Alves da Silva	-	--	-	##	##	##	-
Azeda	0	##	0	-	-	#	-
Baptista/Tebaida	-	##	--	0	--	##	0
Camilo C Branco	--	##	--	--	##	##	##
Centro Histórico	-	##	--	--	##	--	##
Est de Algeruz	-	0	##	##	##	--	--
Est dos Ciprestes	--	0	--	##	--	--	##
Inf D Henrique	0	0	--	#	##	--	--
Monte Belo	0	##	--	0	--	--	0
Na Sa da Conceição	-	--	-	##	--	--	--
Praça do Brasil	-	--	##	##	#	--	0
Salgado	-	##	-	#	--	--	#
Santa Ma Sul	-	##	##	-	--	0	#
Sào Domingos	0	##	0	--	##	--	##
Sào Gabriel	--	#	##	##	#	--	#
Zona Portuária	0	##	--	0	##	##	--
Popular							
Afonso Costa	##	-	0	--	--	--	--
Amoreiras	#	--	0	0	--	--	0
Areias	#	0	--	0	--	--	0
Az da Varzinha	#	--	##	--	##	--	--
Camarinha	#	0	-	--	##	0	--
Casal de Figueiras	##	--	--	--	--	--	--
Castelo Velho	##	-	#	--	#	--	--
Dias	##	-	##	--	0	--	0
Fonte da Lavra	##	#	--	--	--	##	--
Humberto Delgado	##	--	0	--	--	--	--
Liberdade	##	##	0	--	--	--	##
Maltalhados	##	--	--	--	0	--	--
Monarquina	##			--		--	
Pescadores	##	--	--	--	--	--	--
Pinheirinhos	##	-	--	--	--	--	##
Primeiro de Maio	#	0	0	0	-	--	--
Quatro Caminhos	#	--	--	0	#	--	##
Reboreda	#	##	0	--	--	--	--
Santos Nicolau	##	--	#	--	-	-	-
Terroa de Baixa	##			--		--	
Trindade	#	##	0	--	##	--	##
Troino	#	#	0	-	--	0	0
Vintecinco de Abril	##	0	--	--	0	--	--
Viso	##	0	#	--	##	--	--

The city's economically active population included 44.4 percent manual workers and 32.5 percent white collar and professional employees. The Popular barrios were those with 50 percent or more manual workers, and included twenty-four of the forth-five barrios of the city, with 50 percent of the city's population. On the whole, these barrios also had a much lower than average share of white-collar workers. The Interclass barrios had less than 50 percent manual workers, but this group still represented a substantial share of their inhabitants, with a minimum of 25 percent. Some of them had relatively more white-collar workers, and others had more personal service workers. These barrios included sixteen of the city's forty-five barrios, and 29 percent of its population. The Elite barrios had much more than the average share of white collar and professional employees, generally more than 55 percent, and fewer than 20 percent manual workers. (While the Elite barrios were the areas of residence of the economically better off and of the local political elite, they were not the residence of the nationally dominant economic elite, which generally lived in Lisbon or outside the country.) There were five such barrios, with 21 percent of the city's population.

In considering neighborhood housing conditions, we should distinguish between five basic types: shantytowns; old housing that often suffers from lack of running water, sewers, and other infrastructure; public housing; private modern apartments built before the late 1960s which provide generally decent conditions and much lower rents than later construction; and new apartment housing where high rents are common. Table 4.2 presents the barrios classified according to their social composition and housing conditions (see Appendix E for occupational data).

°Key to Table 4.1:

A:	1 — manual workers								
	2 — personal service workers								
	3 — commerce (owners and employees)								
	4 — business service workers/white collar professionals								
	5 — police and military								
	6 — owners								
	7 — rural and others								
B:	## — very high	(GE)	56.4	11.2	11.9	40.0	3.9	2.0	4.0
	# — high	(GE)	49.4	9.2	9.9	35.5	3.2	1.5	3.3
	0 — city average		44.4	8.0	8.9	32.5	2.7	1.0	2.8
	− − low	(LE)	39.4	6.8	7.7	29.5	2.2	0.5	2.3
	− − − very low	(LE)	32.4	4.8	5.5	25.0	1.5	0.0	1.5

Table 4.2

Barrios by Housing Conditions and Social Composition

	Elite (5)	Interclass (16)	Popular (24)
A. Modern expensive (11)	Liceu Montalvâo	Alves da Silva E de Algeruz I D Henrique Monte Belo P do Brasil Sâo Gabriel	Amoreiras Areias Fonte da Lavra
B. Modern inexpensive (8)	F de Engomar J Ma da Silva	Azeda B/Tebaida E d Ciprestes	A d Varzinha Camarinha Reboreda
C. Public housing (7)	–	NS Conceiçâo	Afonso Costa H Delgado Pescadores Primeiro de Maio Vintecinco de Abril Viso
D. Old (10)	Cinco de Outubro	CC Branco Centro Histórico Salgado SM Sul S Domingos Z Portuária	S Nicolau Trindade Troino
E. Shantytowns (9)	–	–	C Figueiras C Velho Dias Liberdade Maltalhados Monarquina Pinheirinhos Q Caminhos T da Baixa

Periods and Dynamics of CM Development

On April 25, 1974, no CMs existed in Setubal. By November 25, 1975, three-fourths of the Setubal barrios had CMs, including barrios of all social classes. The CMs did not all form in the same way, nor at the same time, nor in a more or less even progression over the period from April 25, 1974, to November 25, 1975. In particular, they did not all arise either "shortly after April 25th" or in the summer of 1975, as an immediate result of the overthrow of the fascist regime or of the adoption of the Guidelines document by the MFA. During the two years considered, there were many attempts and campaigns to develop CMs in the neighborhoods of the city. The local government, revolutionary and traditional left political parties, people already active in CMs, the local media, and the MFA were all involved in attempts to

70

get neighborhoods to form CMs. Their efforts sometimes focused on specific barrios, but often they were directed throughout the city, calling upon all barrios to form CMs. However, their impact was both less dramatic and more differentiated than might be expected, as a review of the systematic differences in CM formation in each period of the conjuncture shows (see Table 4.3[1]).

Table 4.3

Beginning of CMs

Group	Barrio	I:1974 4-6	I:1974 7-9	II	III:1975 3-6	III:1975 7-11	IV:1976	never
Elite								
A	Liceu		•					
	Montalvão		•					
B	Ferro de Engomar							•
	Jose Ma da Silva							•
D	Cinco de Outubro							•
Interclass								
A	Alves da Silva					•		
	Inf D Henrique							•
	Est de Algeruz							•
	Praça do Brasil					•		
	São Gabriel			•				
	Monte Belo				•			
B	Est dos Ciprestes		•					
	Azeda		•					
	Baptista/Tebaida			•				
C	Na Sa da Conceição							•
D	Salgado					•		
	Camilo C Branco							•
	Centro Histórico							•
	Santa Maria Sul					•		
	São Domingos			•				
	Zona Portuária							•
Popular								
A	Amoreiras		•					
	Fonte da Lavra						•	
	Areias							•
B	Az da Varzinha			•				
	Camarinha			•				
	Reboreda			•				
C	Afonso Costa	•						
	Humberto Delgado		•					
	Primeiro de Maio		•					
	Vintecinco de Abril			•				
	Viso				•			
	Pescadores	•						
D	Santos Nicolau						•	
	Trindade							•
	Troino			•				
E	Casal de Figueiras	•						
	Castelo Velho	•						
	Dias	•						
	Monarquina	•						
	Liberdade	•						
	Maltalhados		•					
	Pinheirinhos	•						
	Quatro Caminos		•					
	Terroa de Baixo		•					

April 25-September 28, 1974

The first period after the overthrow of fascism was characterized by attempts to resolve some of the most severe material and political problems inherited from the old regime, especially decolonization, improving living conditions of those worst off, and purging fascists from positions of authority. The CMs that began in this period arose in attempts to respond to these problems at the local level. Roughly one-half of the CMs formed in the first six months after April 25, but they did not represent a cross-section of the city's neighborhoods. Virtually all were formed in one of three types of neighborhoods. The first CMs were formed in the barrios with the worst physical conditions in order to demand government intervention to provide decent housing: two-thirds of the shantytowns had CMs by the time the government established the SAAL program to provide aid, and the remainder had CMs before September. Shortly after the shantytowns began forming CMs the public housing barrios did so too, in an effort—encouraged by the *Câmara*—to get neighborhood improvements and organize their relations with their public landlord. The *Câmara* also sought to promote organized citizen participation in local government throughout the city. However, aside from public housing barrios, it was successful only in two Elite neighborhoods, the only Elite barrios to form CMs during the entire two-year period.

Thus, social classes responded in distinct ways that reflected their position in the new political conjuncture, and the neighborhoods where they were preponderant acted accordingly. For example, some groups were overwhelmingly concerned with their severe material problems, and were not convinced that participation in local government would affect anything. The wealthy and professionals were concerned with the political stake of governing, and active community involvement was one part of their new, expanded participation in a wide range of social and political arenas. The problems of the majority of people were not as bad as those of the shantytowns, nor had they any reason to think class relations had shifted enough in society to give them any real power or influence. Finally, the two CMs resulting from efforts of a left party developed fitfully and ended a few months later. Thus, the impact of deliberate political strategies to promote CMs was strongly constrained by limits on political participation reflecting the national relation of class forces.

October 1974-March 1975

Following the second attempt by the right to regain power, this period was characterized nationally by the effort to develop antimonopoly economic

policies and to develop institutions of democratic participation. For the organization of CMs in Setubal, the single most important event during this period
was the holding of the first County Assembly of popular organizations at the
beginning of March. In preparation for the assembly, the *Câmara* pushed
the formation of CMs in all those areas where none had yet been established.
In all, eight new CMs formed in the period of preparation for the County
Assembly, five of them in Popular and three in Interclass barrios; one-half of
the new CMs were in the less expensive modern neighborhoods, with less
acute problems and little previous apparent interest in participating in local
affairs. Thus, at the end of this period there were a total of twenty-six barrios
with CMs—nineteen in Popular barrios, five in Interclass barrios, and two in
Elite barrios. The shantytowns had all formed CMs prior to this period, and
no new CMs formed in the Elite barrios. While all the less expensive modern
Interclass barrios had CMs, very few were found in either the older or more
expensive Interclass barrios. At the end of this period 80 percent of Popular
barrios were organized while only 30 percent and 40 percent respectively, of
the Interclass and Elite barrios were. Thus, the climate of the County Assembly was dominated by the Popular barrios while a majority of those living in
Interclass barrios were not represented.

March-November 1975

Nationalization of the banks, insurance, and heavy industries followed
the failed right-wing coup of March 11. As the fight for political power became
more intense nationally, the crisis and breakdown of the antimonopoly coalition was accompanied locally by the disintegration of most of the Interclass
CMs, representing barrios inhabited by the middle sectors, a key component
of the coalition. By July, as the different sides became more clearly drawn
and the MFA adopted contradictory policies of consolidation and advancing
the revolution, fighting intensified in a multisided conflict among those who
controlled the state, the parties on the outside, and a growing independent
popular working-class movement which sought its own path and prevented
the adoption of many compromise solutions. In this period of crisis, one of
the most crucial issues was whether the popular movement would be able
to incorporate new social sectors to broaden the revolutionary alliance or
instead would begin to lose influence—that is, in terms of urban struggles,
whether the popular movement would advance by drawing in participation
of the middle sectors who resided in the Interclass barrios or would become
more isolated.

While the *Câmara* and Communist Party tried unsuccessfully to promote further organizing through popular assemblies, the revolutionary left

in Setubal tried to broaden its base of support and to develop further the revolutionary process by extending organization and its benefits to people and areas not yet touched by it. This was done in two specific ways, the first of which was the struggle to reduce rents to a maximum of 500 escudos per room. In this effort, new CMs were formed in the modern expensive Interclass barrios and existing ones expanded to include additional people in other barrios. At the same time, specific attempts focusing on direct action in response to local social service problems were made to organize in some of the older Interclass neighborhoods in the center of town.

Thus, this period did see a significant expansion of the popular movement into the Interclass barrios, in large measure through the struggle against speculative rents. At the time of the right-wing coup on November 25, the city had thirty-two active CMs. Twenty of them covered 80 percent of the Popular barrios; ten of them concentrated in the modern neighborhoods covered 60 percent of the Interclass barrios; and there were CMs in the two (out of five) Elite barrios with modern expensive housing.

If, instead of considering the first CM in each barrio, we focus on the founding of the CMs active on November 25, then the expansion of the social base of the popular movement to include the Interclass barrios during the summer of 1975 is even more striking—eight of the ten Interclass CMs were formed during this period (see Table 4.4). While during the first two periods CM formation essentially consolidated the previous conjunctural changes, in the third period it clearly reflected the development of a specific alternative for further conjunctural change to resolve existing political instabilities. Table 4.4 also clearly demonstrates the close relationship between the periods of the political conjuncture and the formation of CMs in each type of barrio. It shows that CMs were more common among the Popular barrios than among the Interclass or Elite, and that they generally formed earlier in the Popular and Elite barrios. They were also most likely to form in shantytowns and public housing barrios and quite likely in barrios of modern housing.

December 1975-June 1976

One of the clearest demonstrations of the importance of a change in political conjuncture for the development of the CMs is the negative effects of the November 25 coup; in the seven-month period following the right-wing coup nearly all the CMs entered into crisis and some 20 percent effectively ended.[2] As the CMs tried to adapt to the new situation, the ones that continued the longest were generally those with specific responsibilities or work functions: SAAL (shantytown replacement), day-care, city-country

Table 4.4

Beginning of CMs Active in November 1975

Group	Barrio	4-6	7-9	10/74-3/75	3-6	7-11
Elite						
A	Liceu (w/Amoreiras)		•			
	Montalvão		•			
B	Ferro de Engomar					
	Jose Ma da Silva					
D	Cinco de Outubro					
Interclass						
A	Alves da Silva					•
	Inf D Henrique					
	Est de Algeruz					
	Praça do Brasil					•
	São Gabriel					•
	Monte Belo				•	
B	Est dos Ciprestes		•			
	Azeda				•	
	Baptista/Tebaida			•		
C	Na Sa da Conceição					
D	Salgado					•
	Camilo C Branco					
	Centro Histórico					
	Santa Maria Sul					•
	São Domingos					•
	Zona Portuária					
Popular						
A	Amoreiras (w/Liceu)		•			
	Fonte da Lavra					
	Areias					
B	Az da Varzinha			•		
	Camarinha			•		
	Reboreda			•		
C	Afonso Costa	•				
	Humberto Delgado		•			
	Primeiro de Maio					•
	Vintecinco de Abril			•		
	Viso				•	
	Pescadores	•				
D	Santos Nicolau					
	Trindade					
	Troino			•		
E	Casal de Figueiras	•				
	Castelo Velho	•				
	Dias	•				
	Monarquina	•				
	Liberdade	•				
	Maltalhados		•			
	Pinheirinhos	•				
	Quatro Caminos		•			
	Terroa de Baixo		•			

75

link (direct marketing arrangements with agricultural cooperatives), phar-macies, care of a mental patient. Once the city-country link ended in May, virtually all remaining activities were provided continuity and significant resources through the commitment of some government agency (primarily the *Câmara*, IFAS—the national social welfare agency, or FFH—the national housing agency responsible for SAAL). But all these activities were car-ried out by relatively small groups of people and not by larger democratic organs representing and involving the people of the barrio. Even the two CMs formed during 1976 did not get beyond the initial nucleus of people who had begun them during the national electoral campaigns. The CMs continued with the same name, but, after the end of the popular mobiliza-tion which had created them, they were no longer the same organs of mass participation and struggle.

Finally, let us consider the barrios that did not form CMs. Overall there were eleven barrios without CMs by the end of this two year period: three (out of five) Elite barrios; six (out of sixteen) Interclass barrios; and two (out of twenty-four) Popular barrios. These barrios represented about 14 percent of the population of the city (14 percent of the Elite; 23 percent of those in the Interclass barrios; and 5 percent of the Popular). The barrios that never formed CMs differed dramatically from the others in two critical respects: they did not include any with especially high-rent/income ratios; and they were much more often composed primarily of people born in Setubal.

The barrios involved fit into three large groups. First, the clearest case of underrepresentation is among the older barrios of the city. While these areas had significant problems of physical and social infrastructure, no move-ments ever developed to deal with these issues collectively, and individually their residents had little prospect of resolving their problems. If we add simi-lar barrios where organizing never advanced beyond the stage of a pre-CM or only developed after November 1975, this emerges as by far the least organized type of neighborhood. Second, those Elite and white-collar Inter-class barrios characterized by basically good physical conditions, high incomes, and low housing costs did not form CMs. The cause here is as much social composition as material problems because modern inexpensive areas with a significant working class population did form CMs. Third, areas that were not generally recognized as barrios did not form CMs. This case arose where there were a few large buildings together, with as many inhabit-ants as many barrios, but without the characteristics of a neighborhood, either as a geographic base for democratic representation or as a set of pub-lic facilities with problems.

The strong relation between the periods of formation of CMs and the class base of the barrios involved emerged partially from the correlation between class base and the material problems of different neighborhoods, as a result of the social segregation and development of the city. The two situations where CM formation seemed to reflect *primarily* a question of class base were the formation of the first two Elite CMs and the formation of several CMs for the First County Assembly, the effect of which was far stronger among Popular barrios because the working-class movement led the democratizing process around the country. Otherwise, the formation of CMs was largely a response to immediate problems and the possibility of resolving them, given the political conditions provided by the state and the popular movement. Once formed, they tended to expand the social base of the popular movement by including new groups as well as new problems. To the extent serious problems were affecting a large part of the population of the barrio, and to the extent that it seemed these problems could be remedied by pressure or actions of a CM, then a CM developed. Thus, while many agents were actively trying to form CMs, they generally did not have the impact they sought and could not cause CMs to develop whenever they wanted. The actual formation of the CMs was essentially a response to shifting political conditions in the society as a whole—mediated by the class composition of each neighborhood—and to the material problems of each barrio.

Political Orientation of the CMS

The CMs all saw themselves as "popular organizations" representing the people of the barrio. Members and supporters saw the CMs as part of an ongoing revolutionary process struggling for popular power and a new society (one older woman participated because "I like socialism, but I want a left socialism, not this socialism of the rich that we see today"), although not everyone would necessarily have agreed on the precise nature of that process. Furthermore, the people of the city agreed with this view of the CMs and saw them as left or "progressive" organizations. Throughout the city, a strong majority voted for the nominal left in the 1975 Constituent Assembly and 1976 National Assembly elections, and a near majority voted for the candidate of popular power (and the revolutionary left) in the presidential elections of 1976.

Actually, however, very significant differences were apparent in the political orientations of the CMs, with variations along two poles: (1) support for mass mobilization and direct action; and (2) emphasis on the relative dominance (or autonomy) of the popular movement with regard to the state. The specific experience of struggle of the various CMs produced three basic political orientations designated here as: *radical*, oriented toward mass direct action and transforming the state; *reformist*, oriented toward action through support of and cooperation with the *Câmara*; and *self-help*, that is, independent of the *Câmara* but not generally oriented toward direct mass action. Furthermore, while the orientation is often related to the political parties involved in the CM, it is not the same thing; the political orientation of the CM is based essentially in its grassroots activity, and is more a cause than result of the strength of the different parties. Table 4.5 presents the observed political orientation of each CM based on interpreting CM members' statements and actions according to the above two dimensions.

The *radical* group is composed of CMs oriented toward more radical tactics and solutions to problems. They were much more likely to favor mass mobilization and pressure, and direct action (coupled with negotiation), instead of relying only on negotiation and influence. They normally upheld an idea of "revolutionary legality." But more important for this analysis, these more radical barrios were those affected by severe problems that were not easily solved by simple administrative or "service" action. Specifically, they suffered from the worst housing conditions and the highest rents. Neither of these problems was immediately resolvable administratively, but solutions were forthcoming because of the pressure exerted by these CMs. These barrios tended to have a more radical approach not only toward solving their own problems, but also in their understanding of change in the society as a whole. Thus, this group strongly supported independent organization and mass action by others as part of a model of revolutionary legality and popular power. Their outlook is reflected in the call by one community leader that "the workers' and residents' commissions have to get off the ground to oversee the government, among other things"; and the argument of another that

> the state will never control the neighborhood commissions. This is something the bourgeoisie created against itself. Many people have already pointed out that when the bourgeoisie is born it carries within itself a microbe that will destroy it—the neighborhood commissions are part of that microbe.

Not surprisingly, conflicts arose between these CMs and different levels of the state. This was a result of their inclination toward direct action, which they found at least somewhat effective—whether for directly making some gains (e.g., lowering rents, getting headquarters) or for pressuring administrative organs to act (e.g., for expropriations, services). Their success in these conflicts with government, in turn, reinforced their orientation toward direct action and toward the need to radically transform the state apparatus.

Table 4.5

Political Orientation of the CMs

Group	Barrio	Radical	Reformist	Self-Help
Elite				
A	Liceu	•		
	Montalvão			•
B	Ferro de Engomar			
	Jose Ma da Silva			
D	Cinco de Outubro			
Interclass				
A	Alves da Silva	•		
	Inf D Henrique			
	Est de Algeruz			
	Praça do Brasil		•	
	São Gabriel	•		
	Monte Belo	•		
B	Est dos Ciprestes		•	
	Azeda	•		
	Baptista/Tebaida		•	
C	Na Sa da Conceição			
D	Salgado	•		
	Camilo C Branco			
	Centro Histórico			
	Santa Maria Sul	•		
	São Domingos		•	
	Zona Portuária			
Popular				
A	Amoreiras (w/Liceu)	•		
	Fonte da Lavra			
	Areias			
B	Az da Varzinha	•		
	Camarinha		•	
	Reboreda			•
C	Afonso Costa			•
	Humberto Delgado		•	
	Primeiro de Maio			•
	Vintecinco de Abril		•	
	Viso		•	
	Pescadores			•
D	Santos Nicolau			
	Trindade			
	Troino	•		
E	Casal de Figueiras	•		
	Castelo Velho	•		
	Dias		•	
	Monarquina		•	
	Liberdade	•		
	Maltalhados	•		
	Pinheirinhos	•		
	Quatro Caminos	•		
	Terroa de Baixo		•	

We can divide the group of more radical CMs into two subgroups in terms of their relations with the local government. The first subgroup, whose problems were all outside the capabilities of the *Câmara* to resolve, generally reported good (or neutral) relations with the *Câmara*. This subgroup is composed of eight CMs: six Interclass, one Elite, and one Popular. The second subgroup, whose material problems required some action of the *Câmara* for their resolution, often reported conflict with the *Câmara*, saying it was "trying," but did not fully respond to their needs, whether in repairs or political support.[3] All eight barrios in this category are Popular, and six of them are shantytowns.[4] The severity of the problems of these latter barrios, and the conflicts they had with parts of the state in attempting to resolve them, are reflected in the comment of a CM member from Casal de Figueiras that "we were not born revolutionaries; it was beaten into us."

The *reformist* group is composed of four Interclass and seven Popular CMs, more oriented toward institutional participation and cooperation with the local government. These CMs often saw themselves as intermediaries: much closer to the population than the local government (and thus able to understand the problems of the barrio better), but essentially working with it, rather than putting pressure on it. As one community leader stated:

> The CMs are not self-sufficient, rather they depend essentially on the local governments. The CM is the executive organ for the will of the moradores. Organized people have better access to the local government leaders; they can more easily present the problems of the moradores to them. . . . The people in the neighborhood are the ones who know best what they need; while the others in their offices may know in general that people need sewers, water, open space, etc., if they drew up the plans, they would be likely to put the park in a place where the residents didn't want it. Those who drive past from time to time can't know the neighborhood and its problems as well as those who face them in their daily life. . . . People ask for some things, but they give the rest for free; they give much more than they ask for, doing things the government has a responsibility to do for its citizens, which otherwise would cost more. But it is a two edged sword.

These barrios generally had neither the severe housing problems of the shantytowns, nor the high rents of the radical Interclass and Elite barrios. Nor did they have any other major problems that became an issue for mass mobilization, which meant they had no occasion to come into direct conflict with the state.[5] Finally, this group includes many of the CMs that began in response to initiatives of the *Câmara* (especially those formed in the context of the First County Assembly).

The *self-help* group are those CMs with a less radical (i.e., not direct mass action) approach to politics, but which were also quite concerned to maintain a clear independence from the *Câmara*. This group included four

Popular and one Elite CM. The reasons for their orientation are more diverse than for the previous groups. Overall, they did not have extreme problems, and the problems they did have provided little opportunity for involvement in mass direct action politics. This would seem to put them in the same category as the reformist CMs, but whether because the government was their landlord or for other individual reasons they stayed at arms' length from the *Câmara*.[6] They did not see themselves as a local more responsive arm of government and recognized the need for autonomous action to pressure the government to act. The differences in political orientation were based in the difference of problems and resulting experience of struggle.

Turning to the data from Setubal, Table 4.6 shows the extent of participation of the various barrios in the three principal mass struggles, according to the political orientations of the CMs. While there were housing occupations throughout the city, the four barrios with "many occupations" were all among the radical barrios. Because occupations were concentrated wherever there was vacant public or old private housing, this further supports the causal link going from involvement in mass direct action struggles to a more radical political orientation. It was also primarily the radical CMs that carried out occupations for community facilities, although three of the reformist CMs also did so.[7] Occupations for community facilities and services seem to have been a deliberate choice of the more radical CMs, perhaps reinforcing their orientations, but not causing them.

Table 4.6 also shows that while all three types of barrios had significant numbers of people in the struggle to lower rents to 500 escudos per room, a clear and strong tendency is found for participants to be in the more radical group, and they are least likely to be in the reformist group. Because the struggle developed most strongly in those barrios with the most apartments at the relevant prices, and because it developed in all such barrios, we can conclude that the development of this struggle was one of the roots of the greater radicalism in these barrios—a greater willingness to take mass direct action to solve problems and to see this as a politically viable approach.

Participation in mass struggles certainly did not always produce radicalization. That result also depended on the particular history of each CM's struggle. Nevertheless the tendency was very strong: fourteen of the sixteen radical CMs came from the twenty CMs with extensive participation in the major urban struggles (see Table 4.7). Conversely, while in theory lack of such participation was not an absolute barrier to the development of a mass direct action orientation, in fact only two of the twelve CMs not involved in mass struggles were among the radical CMs. The remaining CMs shared an orientation to local nonmass action, but differed in their views of

81

Table 4.6

Participation in Mass Struggles

Group and Type			Occupations			Rent Reductions	SAAL
			Housing	Headquarters	Community Center		
Radical							
A	E	Liceu	••	•	•	••	
	I	Alves da Silva	•	•	•	••	
	I	São Gabriel	•	•	•	••	
	I	Azeda	•	•	•	••	
	I	Monte Belo	••	•	•	••	
	I	Salgado	•	•	•		
	I	Santa Maria Sul	••	•		•	
	P	Amoreiras	••	•	•	••	
B	P	Az da Varzinha		•			
	P	Troino	••	•		•	
	P	Casal de Figueiras					••
	P	Castelo Velho					••
	P	Liberdade					••
	P	Maltalhados					••
	P	Pinheirinhos					••
	P	Quatro Caminos	•				••
Reformist							
	I	Est dos Ciprestes	•				
	I	Praça do Brasil	•	•	•	••	
	I	Baptista/Tebaida	•				
	I	São Domingos	•				
	P	Camarinha	•			••	
	P	Humberto Delgado	•	•	•		
	P	Vintecinco de Abril	•	•	•		
	P	Viso	•				
	P	Dias					••
	P	Monarquina					••
	P	Terroa de Baixo					••
Self-Help							
	E	Montalvão				•	
	P	Primeiro de Maio					
	P	Reboreda	•			••	
	P	Afonso Costa	•				
	P	Pescadores					

Key: Occupations: •: at least one
                                         ••: many

             Rent Reductions: •: some participants
                                         ••: many participants

             Barrio Type: E: Elite
                                         I: Interclass
                                         P: Popular

the state according to whether experience had indicated they could rely on the cooperation of local government to solve their problems.

Table 4.7

Mass Struggles vs Political Orientation

Struggle	Political Orientation				
	Radical	Reformist	Self-Help	Total[a]	
SAAL	67 %	33 %	0 %	100 %	(9)
Housing occupations	100 %	0 %	0 %	100 %	(5)
Rent reductions	67 %	22 %	11 %	100 %	(9)
None	16 %	50 %	34 %	100 %	(12)
Total	50 %	34 %	16 %	100 %	(32)

[a]The total does not sum properly because three CMs were very active in both the struggles for housing occupations and rent reductions.

In summary, the CMs can be classified into three general political orientations, *radical, reformist,* and *self-help,* according to their attitudes toward mass direct action and the state. Concretely, those CMs which participated in the major urban struggles (SAAL, occupations, rent reductions) found that mass mobilization and confrontation with the state advanced their struggle, and they generally developed a commitment to direct action and independence from public agencies. Those CMs which did not have problems around which the mass struggles developed dealt with their lesser problems through negotiation and cooperation with the local government and did not develop a commitment to independent direct action. Nevertheless, some barrios (e.g., public housing barrios that were institutionally dependent on the *Câmara*) had individual reasons to maintain their autonomy from the state. The political orientation of each CM was essentially the result of its participation in struggles involving (1) mass mobilization around major problems faced by the barrio's inhabitants and likely to result in conflict with the central government, and (2) associated and other sources of conflict with the local government. Both factors, in turn, depended primarily on the national political conjuncture and the material problems of each barrio rather than on the will of any political actor.

Political Orientation and Party Influence

The preceding discussion has accounted for not only the origin but also the political orientation of the CMs without recourse to the role of political parties as their source. This will seem questionable to many (e.g., Bermeo [1986] argues that conflicts between agricultural cooperatives and the state in Portugal were the product of competition between political parties), so we will briefly consider the relationship between the presence of parties in a CM and its political orientation. If the CMs were controlled by political parties then we would expect a strong tendency for the CMs to take on the orientation of those parties. If the CMs were purely spontaneous one might expect a random distribution of political orientations, or perhaps that all would favor spontaneous action. As shown above, neither of these was the case; rather, the evidence strongly supports the hypothesis that the political orientation of urban movements is primarily determined by objective factors that may result in participation in mass struggles rather than by the intervention of political parties.

Thus, one might ask, did the presence of a party generally determine the orientation of the CM, or, as one would now expect based on the preceding analysis, did the orientation of the CMs determine which parties were present? Two broad political lines distinguished the political parties involved in the CMs, with further differences within each group, which are not relevant to our concerns here. The first was the orientation of the revolutionary left parties, based on mass direct democracy as the means for advancing the revolution and transforming the state, and as the model for a participatory socialist society. The second orientation was shared by the Communist Party and part of the Socialist Party, which—after an initial period of ambivalence— saw community organizations as an important vehicle for local involvement and resolution of problems in cooperation with the state. The two political lines are quite similar to those distinguished above as the "radical" and "reformist" orientations of the CMs, and we could expect the relative strength of the parties to be divided correspondingly.

While the data are incomplete, such a correlation does hold. Among the radical CMs, the strongest sympathies were expressed first with the revolutionary left, second with a nonparty-identified conception of popular power, and third with the Communist Party. Among the minority of reformist CMs expressing party sympathies, nearly all supported the Communist Party. And among the self-help CMs the majority expressed support for the broad project of popular power, not tied to any party.

Consideration of only those CMs identified by others as *dominated* by specific parties, two conclusions result: (1) the association between political orientation and party is strongly reiterated, but (2) domination exists in only a minority (20 percent) of the CMs. In this case, the data is probably quite complete and indicates that of the thirty-two CMs active before November 25, only six were clearly dominated by a single political line:

three Communist Party and three from the revolutionary left. The three revolutionary left CMs were all among the radical barrios, including two shantytowns and one Interclass CM; the three dominated by the Communist Party included one radical shantytown and two reformist CMs.

Thus, while a strong correlation exists between the political orientation of the CMs and the presence in them of different political parties, it is a result of the congruence of political positions rather than the product of political organizing. That is, the possibility of a political party gaining strong influence in a democratic CM was largely a product of the party's attitude toward the CM's independently derived participation in mass struggles involving direct action. Still a minority of cases cannot be completely explained in this way, cases in which the actions of specific parties or party members were especially important, and further analysis of the relationships between parties and movements should focus on the specific conditions under which parties had a marginal impact on the structural dynamics.

Conclusion

Careful analysis of extensive data concerning the origins, political orientations, and involvement of political parties in the CMs of Setubal demonstrates conclusively that the popular movement during the Portuguese revolution did not develop in response to the "manipulation" of any outside political forces nor are they "spontaneous" in any simple sense. Rather, the popular movement developed according to a dynamic of its own; this is the objective situation that led to popular organizations being considered spontaneous. But their origin, development, and political orientations were neither homogeneous nor random. Rather, they were determined by objective structural factors: the national political conjuncture, the social base of the movements, and the objective problems to which they sought to respond. The urban problems the neighborhoods faced and the national relation of political forces together resulted in different types of barrios forming CMs at distinct times, as well as their involvement in mass direct action and conflict with the state, and finally in distinct political orientations according to their experience of struggle. There were also many attempts by political parties and other actors to produce, stimulate, and direct these movements. On the whole, however, these attempts failed except when they corresponded to the opportunities and constraints of the objective conditions.

This is not to say that political parties had no role or significance in the popular movements. Parties were certainly important in mediating the role of the movements in national political debates; their militants were involved in the daily affairs of movements, and their actions and interactions had a major impact on the evolution of individual CMs—an impact that was generally inversely proportional to the extent of mass participation at the time. In the vast majority of cases, the origin and political orientations of the CMs was the product of the refraction of the national political relation of forces through the neighborhood class composition together with the material problems of the neighborhoods, resulting in the differential development of CMs, and their participation in mass urban struggles and conflict with the state. With these structural determinants clearly established, organizers can seek an appropriate role in practice, while further research can focus on the important original contribution popular movements provide to political parties, to revolutionary change, and to improving urban living conditions.

FIVE

Transforming City and Society: The Impact of Urban Social Movements

Urban social movements arise in response to political conditions that facilitate and living conditions that necessitate immediate improvement or change. Participation in these movements reflects a belief that by organizing democratically and acting directly, ordinary people will succeed in bringing about change and improving their situation. Can urban social movements affect the populations' material and political situation? What aspects of the relationship between the cities' services and their residents can they change? Are these changes deep and lasting or fleeting and insignificant? What political impacts are possible, and how do they shape the depth of urban effects? These are some of the questions posed when we seek to evaluate the impacts of urban social movements, yet after decades of urban movements there is still no theory of effects of urban movements or even a scale upon which to compare them. Most discussion of movements and their effects is quite limited, saying they did (did not) gain the initial goal; that the movement was stronger (weaker) as a result. Nevertheless, by analyzing movements in terms of their dual role as urban and political change agents, and focusing on a period of dramatic social struggles with potentially great impacts, we can put greater conceptual order in the discussion of the effects of urban movements and begin to develop a theory that ties them into societal change as a whole. This chapter presents an evaluation of the urban and political impacts in Portugal, while at the same time proposing a conceptual framework for analyzing the effects of urban social movements in other contexts. Before considering those effects, however, we should first describe the context of urban problems which participants in the CMs sought to resolve.

Background: Housing Crisis and Urban Problems

For centuries, Setubal's economy and population were dependent primarily on the sea and agriculture. In the first quarter of the twentieth century, the town grew as some of these activities became more industrialized, and it then remained stable for several decades after 1930. When foreign and domestic capital began making large investments in Portugal in the mid-1960s, Setubal became one of the leading poles of national economic development. In a few years the city was radically transformed: it suddenly became a center of heavy industry, population increased rapidly, and the city doubled in area.

Impressions gleaned from the local newspaper and interviews with the local population, supported by the reports of the local planning office and a survey of 10 percent of all households conducted in 1976, present a stark picture of a city suffering a dramatic housing crisis with several components. First, of a total urban population in 1975 of about 20,000 families, nearly 1,400 families lived in shanties, in dire need of decent housing. Second, some 3,500 housing units were found without an interior toilet or in seriously dilapidated condition. Together with the estimated 1,400 units required to provide housing for families forced to double-up, meaning that in 1976, the city needed 6,300 units to provide basic housing for the 40 percent of the city's population living in totally inadequate shelter. Finally, an additional 10 percent of the households, living primarily in housing built since 1970, had to pay more than 20 percent of their income for rent, at a time when the citywide average was 14.4 percent and the national average was even lower (GPS, 1975c and 1977).

In the midst of this housing crisis, approximately 520 units of new housing were finished and empty, some 450 units of old housing lying uninhabited (although not all of it was in good condition), and some 3,500 units of new housing under construction—in all, roughly 4,500 units of vacant housing. If we consider those living in shanties or dilapidated housing and needing new housing, those sharing housing with relatives, and those paying extremely high rents, we see that 50 percent of those living in the city were directly affected by the lack of sufficient housing at an affordable price. These same people could see thousands of units of vacant new housing around them that neither they nor anyone else in the city could afford.[1] Thus, the housing issue lay at the heart of the principle urban social movements that developed during 1974 to 1976.

Next, lack of physical infrastructure was a serious problem for virtually all of the shantytowns and older barrios (both Popular and Interclass), but not for anyone else. This indicates that—excepting the shantytowns—it was largely a problem of the age of barrios. In addition, other problems were found with regard to physical infrastructure, including especially access roads lacking entirely or in bad condition, and individual homes and sections of the city which lacked street lighting and electricity.

Social infrastructure was also quite deficient. While the general level of education and number of school rooms in Setubal was above the national average, 14 percent of the total city population (and 18 percent of heads of households) were illiterate and existing schools were operating at about 50 percent in excess of capacity. The need for more school rooms was chronic throughout the city and acute in the areas of most recent development. There was a severe shortage of spaces in preschool centers. The city as a whole had very little public recreational space, whole sections had none at all, and the only green space—composed essentially of one park and one wide avenue with a promenade down the middle—provided an incredibly low total of 1.8 square meters per inhabitant. Finally, commercial, health and other service facilities were concentrated mainly in the center of town and entire neighborhoods were virtually without them (GPS, 1977).

In addition to the problems of housing and physical and social infrastructure, there were others related to the lack of democratic control over the local government and over the process of urban growth. The Administrative Council of the *Câmara Municipal* was appointed by the central government, and in turn appointed *juntas* (councils) for its six *freguesias* (wards). There was no previous experience of local participation or accountability to the local citizenry; these offices were solely the local representatives of the central administration. The *Câmara*, in turn, had very little control over the process of housing and urban development, and what authority it had had been greatly reduced by two decree-laws (46673-1965 and 289/73-1973) designed to increase the freedom of action of private developers. Beginning in 1969, with the plans for major industrial development around Setubal, urban development came largely under the control of large developers and speculators tied to national finance capital. By 1975, private developers had requested permits to build on virtually all of the open land surrounding the city, enough land to double the city's total surface area. This situation alarmed the new local government particularly because construction was beginning on rich agricultural land, and development was following a hopscotch pattern whose sprawl raised the costs of providing physical infrastructure (GPS, 1975a/b).

In summary, the population faced many major problems. The most severe problems had to do with housing: 7 percent of the population lived in shanties; nearly 20 percent lived in housing that was seriously dilapidated and/or lacking in basic sanitary facilities; nearly 15 percent were sharing housing because they could not afford the rapidly rising housing costs; and an additional 10 percent were paying one-fifth or more of their incomes for high rents; while all around them they could see several thousand units of empty housing. In addition to these housing problems directly felt by 50 percent of the city's residents, many more faced other problems due to lack of urban physical and social infrastructure. These problems affected virtually every neighborhood and every class in the city of Setubal. Under such conditions it would have been difficult for even a responsive local government to deal with the problems of the old and new populations. But, in this case, the government was not under the democratic control of the local citizenry, and the process of urban development was essentially in the hands of medium and large speculators in land and construction.

During 1974 to 1976, these problems became issues for many neighborhood organizations and some became the foci of urban movements. The demands of the CMs correspond quite closely to the problems of the city's barrios indicated by the preceding discussion (see Appendix F). Furthermore, the CMs pointed out problems in public services and maintenance not noted in previous studies, and indicated their relative intensity and importance with clarity, although they did not give much attention to problems of the management of urban development, for example, the control of urban sprawl. Those problems significantly affecting a limited number of barrios were clearly and precisely identified by the CMs. Problems which affected the city as a whole but were not concentrated in any specific neighborhoods were not usually addressed by individual CMs, although some were later explicitly formulated when citywide organization developed. Finally, issues of urban administration and planning were neither more nor less likely to arise through the CMs than through other forms of local political representation. It is interesting—although not terribly surprising—that without any detailed quantitative studies, the CMs were able to accurately specify the problems of their neighborhoods. But, were they able to do anything about them?

Urban Effects

We will consider three basic aspects of the urban effects. First, what was the immediate effect in terms of the demands of the movement (e.g., building or repairing housing, a street paved, a day-care center)? Second, what was the effect on the overall relationship between the population and the city (changing or reproducing the urban structure)? Third, in what ways was the logic of reproduction of the urban structure affected?

Immediate Urban Effects

There were, of course, many specific effects within the general categories of problems referred to above: housing, physical and social infrastructure; the exercise of community control over local government and the use of local resources; in addition, there was tremendous development of cultural, political, and sports activities (see Appendix G). Many of these changes were part of changes in the urban structure, and in the logic of reproduction of the urban structure. They were possible because of the political conditions that existed, especially during 1975, but were brought about specifically by the actions of the popular movement, in conjunction with actions of the local government. Following is a summary of the immediate urban effects.

Housing: All of the housing problems were at least partially addressed. All the shantytowns were integrated into SAAL projects to construct housing for those in need of it, including approximately 1,100 families, or 6 percent of the city's population (see Appendix H). About 2 percent of the city's families moved into better housing through direct action occupations of old and new vacant housing. Rents were lowered for 8 percent of the families living in the most expensive housing in the city, through the struggle against speculative rents. Repairs were carried out in the public housing barrios requiring them, and the barrios with housing in need of major rehabilitation all received some.

Physical infrastructure: Old roads were repaired and new ones built, and basic physical infrastructure was extended or provided in areas where it was previously lacking. Still, only slightly more than one-half of the demands of this type were answered, and these were most often the simpler ones. Virtually all the provision of new infrastructure took place in Popular barrios, while major and minor repairs were done in both Interclass and Popular barrios about equally.

Social infrastructure: Traditional basic social infrastructure was gained about equally by Popular and Interclass barrios, except for the shantytowns, which received much less than they had asked for: school rooms, pharmacies, bus routes, trash pick-up, and other municipal services were provided or improved. Upon closer examination, however, it is evident that most of the barrios that apparently gained traditional basic social infrastructure received services rather than material infrastructure (such as schools). This was especially true in the Popular barrios where half of these accomplishments were accounted for by clean-up of trash or garbage (often gathered by the CM, then carried away by the local government). After "trash clean-up," the most common accomplishment in this category was the installation of a playground, most often in the Popular barrios.

The newer types of social infrastructure were also spread fairly equally throughout the Popular and Interclass barrios. Almost all of them are accounted for by a combination of headquarters for the CMs, social centers, and day-care facilities—often all in the same building. At least one-half of the CM headquarters (and nearly all the social centers) were the result of occupations carried out by the CMs with that end in mind. The role of direct action in resolving demands is most visible in the seven day-care centers the CMs opened for the use of the working population of the city.[2] Finally, two pharmacies were established, one in an Elite and the other in a Popular barrio.[3]

Community control, political, cultural and sports activities: Nearly half of the declared achievements of the CMs came in the areas of community control, political education, and cultural and sports activities. Community control effects were essentially the result of direct action on the part of the CMs, rather than of demands made on some other institution. One-half of them involved occupations of abandoned housing (or the coordination of its occupation, distribution and use) to meet the social needs of the barrio, as a headquarters, social center, or day-care center. In addition, many of the previously mentioned effects, as well as the cultural and social activities carried out by the CMs, had a strong element of community control and direct action. While the various attempts to create or impose new social uses occurred in all types of barrios, they were somewhat more common in the Interclass and Elite barrios than in the Popular ones.

In addition to these effects, there were others from actions taken by the local government in an effort to control and redirect urban development, specifically the actions taken to stop further development in the rich agricultural land in the northern part of the city, and the suspension and review of all building permits.

Many of these changes were brought about by the direct action of the CMs. This is especially true for the improvements in social infrastructure (community and day-care centers, CM headquarters) as well as some of the improvements in housing conditions (occupations) and in physical conditions, which were consistently the result of actions carried out by the CMs, often against the wishes of the local government. Once such actions were carried out, the CMs needed the support of state agencies to maintain them and supply personnel; nevertheless, their existence depended on the initial action of the CMs. Other changes came about as a result of cooperation between the local population and the local government (cleaning up of barrios; building some of the roads), while still others were primarily the result of local government action in response to locally indicated needs (provision or maintenance of physical infrastructure).[4] Finally, while the *Câmara* gave some support, most of the changes in the cultural or social aspects of the quality of the urban environment were the result of the actions of the CMs.

Some of these direct effects were one-time events (e.g., draining a swamp or picking up trash). Once the initial change had taken place, its continuation or permanence depended, with a few exceptions (e.g., the community center or a CM headquarters building), on supportive action by the

government. This might mean a relatively long-lasting action such as investment in physical infrastructure, or the legalization of an occupation, or ongoing actions such as hiring a teacher or assigning resources to support day-care
centers or street repairs. The changes most dependent on the contribution
from the state were thus also most subject to reversal if the control or orientation of the state changed. In turn, those less dependent on ongoing cooperation (e.g., a legalized occupation; completed SAAL projects) were less subject
to changes in state control and were reversible only with much more major
shifts in the political conjuncture.

These effects clearly resolved some problems for some people, and
this, in itself, is important. But did their impact go beyond their immediate
effects? In a given case, were the changes outside the range of normal variation in urban conditions, for example did they improve the situation of those
normally excluded from the benefits (services and facilities) of the city, or
did they simply remedy an anomalous bad situation in ways that would
normally be expected to happen eventually? The question must thus be
raised of what impact these movements had on the overall relationship
between the population and the distribution of the social services and physical structure of the city as a whole or, in other words, what, if any, net alterations did they make in the urban structure?

Effects on the Urban Structure

In considering the effects on the urban structure, we must determine
the extent to which the relationship between the population and the city is
qualitatively changed. The issue is not to make a value judgment regarding
the different effects, but rather to determine what conditions enable movements or governmental agencies to modify some aspect of the city as a
whole. We can use several guidelines to help determine when the urban
structure is altered. First, if the effect involves only the specific group demanding the change, it is unlikely to affect the urban structure. For example, if the
people living in a particular shantytown were able successfully to demand
that they be provided with electricity and sewers, this would be important,
but the change would be limited to them. On the other hand, if all shantytowns were to gain basic physical infrastructure, this would be a change in
the urban structure. Second, is the change relatively permanent, that is, are
the changes secure under prevailing political conditions? For example, the
provision of public transportation to outlying poor areas for a single sports
event or political rally would not be considered a change in the urban structure, whereas the permanent provision of bus lines to these areas would.

The third guideline involves the type of change: whether the change is
an alteration in the historically developed normal relationship (for that soci-

ety) between the class structure and urban services or only the correction of a problem situation that was actually a deviation from the norm, an anomaly created by peculiar circumstances. For example, a new Interclass neighborhood without electricity or paved roads because the developer had gone bankrupt would probably receive a positive response to protest, and the change should be considered the correction of an irregularity rather than a change in the urban structure.

Having established guidelines, we may now look over the immediate effects mentioned above to assess which of them produced or were part of larger changes in the urban structure. SAAL projects were carried out in all the shantytowns of the city. This rehousing of the population living in shantytowns in and of itself changed the relation between the lowest income, worst housed part of the population and the city as a whole. While public housing programs had existed before, this one was different for many reasons, including its higher housing quality, its coverage of all shanties and its vesting people with the right to remain on the site where they had previously lived, as well as the higher level of community participation in the process itself.[5]

Assessment of the housing occupations, rehabilitation, and the rent limitation struggle all lead to the conclusion that they modified the urban structure in some ways, but in other ways they simply reproduced it. Occupations and rehabilitation brought housing back into the housing market, but mostly they did not fundamentally alter its social distribution. But some occupations, especially where they were combined with the struggle to limit rent levels, did serve to lower rents and to allow people with moderate incomes to live in areas that would otherwise have been inaccessible to them, thereby changing the patterns of social segregation within the city.

The preceding evaluations indicate that, first, the urban structure was affected by the provision (or repair) of housing for those who generally had worse conditions. But in these programs the state had to assume a significant role in providing resources and expropriating the necessary land. In turn, this required appropriate political conditions to provide the necessary sectors of the state with the desire and the resources to act. Second, the urban structure was affected by redistributive actions in housing to the extent that they did not simply involve relocation of people, but rather relocation across class and income lines. This required that the normal economic logic and legal stipulations relevant to distribution of goods such as housing be changed. This condition was met through the effective imposition of a maximum rent per room in the city and movement toward a policy to base access to housing on need and rent on ability to pay. Furthermore, while these changes resulted from the actions of grassroots movements and organizations, they would have eventually required validation by the state.

The extension of basic physical infrastructure into areas previously lacking it provided at least some change in the urban structure. It was a change brought about largely through the technical and material efforts of the local government, often with the assistance of the local population (e.g., for laying new roads). While the improvement in Interclass barrios should be considered the correction of an anomaly, improvements in Popular barrios generally represented changes in the urban structure. Similarly the improvements in trash pick-up and bus service to some parts of the city represent slight changes in the urban structure.

Turning now to the social infrastructure of the city, we find another area where significant changes were made in the urban structure. Perhaps the most important change was the creation of the seven new day-care centers, doubling the availability of such services at a low cost. Most of them were a result of the direct action of the radical CMs which occupied facilities and established day-care centers during the summer of 1975. They were dependent initially on volunteer help to fix up the buildings and then on the central government's family assistance agency to subsidize their operation and supply trained personnel. Generally open to the population of the city as a whole, with priority for lower income people, they were a significant change in the relationship between the population and the city. Nevertheless, they were nearly all located in Interclass barrios, consistent with the tendency to locate general service social facilities in such neighborhoods rather than in Popular ones.

The community centers and CM headquarters created in a large share of the barrios was another change in the urban structure and provided the facilities to house neighborhood social, cultural, and political activities. Most of these facilities were the result of direct action on the part of the CMs which sometimes occupied buildings and sometimes constructed new ones. Once built, they did not require any ongoing services or upkeep and thus did not depend on the local government to sustain them.

A few other social services were also expanded. Increased educational services were usually the result of direct action activities of the CMs (e.g., providing a vacant apartment to use as a school room), with the central government then providing the personnel. In virtually all cases these were in areas where more school room space was clearly needed and had already been planned. It is possible that construction was somewhat accelerated, and the interim deficit problem was partially resolved through the actions of the CMs. Nevertheless, we would probably not consider this to be a change in the urban structure because these deficits would probably have been resolved as priority government actions in any case. Two new pharmacies were established (one free one), as well as some first aid posts. But most of these were in Interclass barrios, which would normally be expected to have them. Their existence was not a change in the urban structure, although the provision of broader access to them might be. Once again, they all were created during the spring, summer, and fall of 1975. Thus, while some of the concrete effects produced changes in the urban structure and many did not, both types required political conditions that allowed the CMs to overstep the normal limits on grassroots activity and use of the physical infrastructure of the city.

Finally, several actions of the local government directly affected the urban structure, even though none of the CMs were directly involved. In early 1975, virtually all of the open land surrounding the city was in the hands of private developers, and some construction had already begun on rich agricultural land extending into the city. Applying a new interpretation to existing legislation, the *Câmara* was able to stop further development on that land; and through a new national law proposed by the local Planning Office, it was able to suspend and review all existing development permits, and permanently annul those contrary to its new guidelines for the city's growth.[6]

Many additional aspects come under the rubric of improvements in the general quality of the urban environment and which generally were also changes in the urban structure. A large number of barrios, both Interclass and Popular, inaugurated cultural programs which included film showings and debates, as well as more traditional sports and social activities. Changes in the use of public spaces (whether for demonstrations, meetings, or putting up posters), together with name changes in some barrios, and the visibility of the CMs and their work (through such activities as occupations, projects, and headquarters), produced a major qualitative change in the atmosphere of the city and working people's identification with it.

Thus, many of the specific changes that took place in the city of Setubal also changed the relationship between the population of the city (and the social classes of which it is composed) and the physical and social infrastructure of the city, producing a qualitatively different urban structure. Furthermore, in most cases these changes were the result of CM direct actions, but they required subsequent governmental cooperation if they were to continue. Now let us take the evaluation one step further: would these changes in the urban structure be maintained over time? Would they be extended throughout the city? In other words, was the logic of reproduction of the urban structure changed?

Effects on the Logic of Reproduction of the Urban Structure

Reproduction and extension of changes in the urban structure depend on whether the interests, agents, and rules involved in the reproduction of the elements and relations of the urban structure are changed. The preceding discussion suggests that a new, more egalitarian process of producing and distributing basic urban and social services was developing, based largely on a higher level of basic services entitlement and partially on a new logic of distribution, sustained in part by the pressure of grassroots direct action. Had it continued it would have necessitated a process of urban development which was different from the crisis ridden speculative private production of the early 1970s. The key elements to the developing new logic of construction of the urban fabric were based on public control of land and public initiative in development. While nationalizing urban land was proposed, it never took place; rather, the government was able to take decisive steps to gain control over the spatial process by nullifying private development proposals contrary to public priorities and expanding its role as builder and contractor for housing to the point where it could orient most housing construction. SAAL was one of the first examples, producing housing for those living in shantytowns according to a process which was quite different from both previous private and public housing. The central government also began a program of guaranteed purchases of moderate-income housing to sustain private developers, with the state providing the land and ensuring production of a cheaper product—a system applied quite extensively in Setubal. In addition, the *Câmara* helped in the formation of the first of several production cooperatives composed of unemployed construction workers, and the government dedicated more resources to the social programs demanded by the population. Together these measures can be considered elements of a new logic of urban development that was, however, never fully articulated. This new logic would have required an investment of resources and legal controls only available to state action.

The preceding discussion can be summarized in a coherent framework for analyzing the effects of urban social movements. There are three basic types of urban effects on the differential distribution of public goods and services to the various sectors of the city's inhabitants. First, a group may *win the specific demand* (or gain some other specific change). This improves the situation of the immediate group involved and may be relatively easy to achieve (e.g., when correcting a sudden relative deterioration of their situation) or very difficult (e.g., providing a net historic improvement in housing conditions). But they do not necessarily involve the systematic improvement of the conditions of all those in a similar situation or any significant changes in political power. That is, this level of effect does not ensure any change in the urban structure nor necessarily require change in the relations of political power.

The second level of urban effect is a *change in the urban structure*. The immediate change may be more or less generalized, according to whether it involves many or only a few sectors of the population (providing housing titles to all current residents versus rebuilding all shantytowns), but if it involves all of those in a given situation it signifies a change in the urban structure. In general, changes in physical conditions (e.g., housing and facilities) were more dependent on actions of the local government (often acting in response to the specific demands of the CMs), while changes in social services and cultural and political conditions were much more dependent upon the initiative of the CMs (although often requiring state action to sustain them). Changes in the urban structure require some involvement of the movement (or allied political organizations) in shifting relations of political power, for although changes may be carried out by the direct action of the movement, their continuation often requires government recognition and a commitment of public resources.

All of this may take place without the third degree of effect, a *change in the logic of urban development*. Just as the first level effect may be limited to a certain group in space, so too the shift in the urban structure may be limited to a certain group in time. Those present at a moment of crisis may benefit through the resolution of existing problems, but the underlying processes producing and differentially distributing the city's goods and services—and thus its problems—remains the same (e.g., continuing to result in new shantytowns or high rents in new housing). For the change in urban structure to extend to future city residents the logic of urban development must be altered. This requires national shifts in the structures of political and economic power and institutions. As one element of this, the state must be willing not only to accept specific changes the movement carries out, but also to take the initiative in developing an alternative method of producing and distributing the goods and services of the city.

Thus, only the most limited effect is possible without a shift in the structure of political power—in the political conjuncture and in the state. The second type of effect requires state action, alternately spurred on by, mobilizing, and supporting local direct action. The third and most profound type requires ongoing state initiative, which is only possible with a more complete change in political and economic power. Thus, the degree of mobilization and organization of the urban movements, and their ability to immediately effect the urban structure, depend upon the state of offensive or defensive of the popular classes and change with changes in the conjuncture, while the ability to have lasting impact on the urban structure depends finally on the control of state and economic power.

Political Effects

We now turn to consider the political effects of the urban movements. These may be divided into two broad categories: first, the effects on the general conditions of class struggle and political relations between classes; and second, the effects on the relationship between the population of the city, organized in CMs, and the state, that is, the transformation of the state apparatus and the relation of the population/CMs to it.

Effects on General Political Relations and Class Struggle

In the evaluation of the effects on general political relations and class struggle, the primary issue is the extent to which the urban movements contributed to developing a stronger, larger, and more united popular movement. This can be broken down into three main aspects: first, the effects on those involved in the movement; second, effects on extending organization to other parts of the population and bringing them into the urban movement; and third, the contribution to building a broader popular movement, including especially workers' organizations. A fourth collateral effect with which we will not deal much here is the movements' impact on the unity of those opposed to the popular forces. Unfortunately, sufficient information does not exist to draw broader conclusions regarding the importance of this issue.

First of all, who took part in the CMs? Were they socially representative of their barrios? The study indicated that only a small proportion were "not employed," thus we can infer that the CMs were largely composed of employed workers. Regarding the types of occupations, the composition of the CMs varied with that of each barrio—that is, manual workers were most strongly represented in the Popular barrios, and barrios with greater proportions of white collar residents had more such people on their CMs—but even in the Interclass and Elite barrios the CMs were primarily composed of manual workers, many of whom were CT members or union delegates. Not only were the CMs mainly organizations dominated by manual workers, but among manual workers those from modern and heavy industries (principally shipbuilding, automobile assembly, and other heavy metal work) were represented by nearly three-times their share of the employed population.[7] Because the modern and heavy industries were also those in the leadership of much of the workers' movement, this was one of the mechanisms linking the two movements and intertwining their fates.

With regard to women's participation in the CMs, there were far fewer than a proportional share of women on the CMs in spite of the fact that women seemed to be more than proportionately active in the work of the CMs.[8] This latter fact is a strong argument against concluding that neighborhood movements were simply an arm of the (predominantly male) workers' movement, although it also indicates the existence of obstacles to the full participation of women in all aspects of the movements.

Thus, in their membership, the CMs were organs of a working-class offensive that maintained links to the other sectors of the population by organizing around problems shared in neighborhoods. While they mobilized and involved many people not integrated into workplace organizations, their members were drawn heavily from the most politically active industries, rather than people who lacked an avenue of political expression and involvement at the workplace. Nonetheless, even if they had involved only people who were politically active at their places of work, the movements and struggles would still have developed according to a logic reflecting their urban rather than employment situations.

Were the specific struggles of the CMs an effective way of expanding the urban movement to produce unity and common organization with other neighborhoods and classes, broadening both the geographic and social class base? We have seen many specific impacts related to the expansion and development of the urban movement as a whole, and each of the principle movements made a specific contribution.

The SAAL program came to include all of the shantytowns of the city, involved high levels of political mobilization in those barrios and led to contact and conflict with both the central and local governments. Most of the CMs involved in the SAAL struggle developed a radical political orientation committed to mass mobilization and direct action. Nationally, it was the most organized and significant urban movement, although in Setubal it was relatively less important, reflecting the lower proportion of the population living in shantytowns and the greater importance of other problems and their corresponding movements.

Three waves of housing occupations accompanied the shifts in the political conjuncture. They moved from new public housing, to old public and private housing, and then to new private housing, showing a progression, radicalization and generalization of consciousness and organization among occupiers and in terms of their targets. The most advanced step was based both on the development of a new situation of dual power with coordinating bodies having a broad enough base and organization to consider such actions and the development of the struggle for 500 escudos per room which began placing a limit on the rents people expected to pay. Extensive participation in occupations generally produced a radical direct action political orientation among those CMs involved, much as the SAAL struggle did for the shantytowns. In addition, the conflictive relationship between local government and CMs was strongly shaped and reinforced by this process.

The originators of the struggle to limit rents to a maximum of 500 escudos per room intended it to be a grassroots direct action activity to improve immediate housing conditions, pressure the central government for more profound changes in housing policy, and radicalize or "unmask" existing reformist CMs and local governments. It was also intended to integrate heretofore uninvolved people into the revolutionary political process in a way that would radicalize them and demonstrate the viability and effectiveness of direct action and direct democracy. It developed in all barrios where housing rented for more than 500 escudos per room and came to include some four-fifths of the people paying such rents. It, too, was a critical element in the development of the political orientation of many of the more radical CMs. The great success of the struggle was to develop the revolutionary alliance by successfully spreading it to middle-class sectors, involving people who were economically better off than those in the SAAL program and not previously politically active. But the demand was considered reformist because its benefits were limited to these same people.[9] Even those in modern expensive barrios who strongly supported the struggle were apologetic, while those in shantytowns were often much more critical and suspicious of their new allies. Over time, with the development of the struggles and continued mutual support and coordination between CMs, these tensions lessened. Together with SAAL and occupations, it underlay the political orientation of the CMs favoring a more radical direct action approach.

The urban movements certainly expanded the numbers in the popular movement, but did they contribute specific urban issues to the consciousness and program of the broader popular movement? They brought up and redefined many issues and concerns that would not have arisen in the popular movement had there not been an urban movement. These issues were particularly those discussed earlier that involved development of grassroots direct representation and more democratic distribution of basic urban services and housing. Support for housing those living in shantytowns, limiting rents, and providing day-care as a right spread throughout the population and was discussed and adopted by CTs (see Appendix I). In turn, problems of the workplace and the economy were discussed in the neighborhoods. In the process, they also contributed to defining a relationship of conflict and cooperation with the local state apparatus, leading to a proposed alternative of "popular power."

As a result of the conflicts in which they were involved, the urban movements tended to contribute a focus on (1) conflicts with the social service bureaucracies generally, and housing ministry in particular, especially regarding budgetary and program issues; (2) administrative and bureaucratic delays, producing a strongly antibureaucratic ideology; (3) centralization of decisionmaking in the capital, leading to demands for decentralization—sometimes to local government and sometimes to the popular organizations; and (4) the repressive and judicial apparatuses, leading to demands for institutional reform and revolutionary laws as well as experiments in popular justice through direct action. In all cases the movements found allies as well as opponents within the state.

Through their interaction, the two main components of the popular movement were able to deal with two general realms of political problems. On one hand, the workers' movement, which provided the basic strength underlying the popular movement, faced issues of workers' control, democracy in the workplace, socialization of production beyond the point of simple nationalization, unemployment, international boycotts, etc. It dealt with the state in terms of basic guarantees for employment and industrial conversion, as well as broader planning and democratic control of the economy and work process. Thus, it encountered the state primarily as either the central economic administration or an organ of repression. On the other hand, the urban movements dealt with many more conditions of daily life and its reproduction, facing the state as an agent of reproduction of labor and of the organization and provision of the material and social conditions of urban daily life. Thus, the urban movements dealt with the state primarily as provider of services and restrictive administrative bureaucracy, and secondarily as a source of repression.

These different structural situations were expressed in the demands and ideologies of the two movements. The workers' movement focused on questions of control and transformation of the economy, the economic aspects of transition to socialism, democracy in the workplace, and the need to have representatives of the working-class parties in government ministries, so that the bureaucracies would provide the necessary support for the control of the economy and working conditions by the organized workers; this movement was premised on the belief that work-place democracy was the key to a democratic socialist transformation of the whole society.

While the urban movements were in many ways analogous, they did not develop an ideology based on "neighborhood democracy." Rather, their ideology of "popular power" was based on the idea of direct democratic control of local and national government policies, leading to a democratic distribution of services, housing, and other government resources. They were concerned with transforming and controlling the local administrative apparatus, and by extension the relevant parts of the central apparatus, rather than with developing neighborhood autonomy. While among CMs there were different specific ideas of popular power, it was still primarily the CMs that provided the basis and impetus for the discussion of the transformation of the local state apparatus, for a 'popular power' whose focus was on those parts of the state apparatus responsible for governing and administering the conditions of daily life of the population. The two parts of the popular movement made distinct and critical contributions to the ideology, focus, and concerns of the movement as a whole.

Finally, the development of the urban movements also affected those who were opposed to this process. In the same way that it contributed to the definition of concerns and strengthening of a radical popular movement, it also may have contributed to a definition of concerns and unity among those who were attacked. Did this process push some who might otherwise have sided with or accepted the popular movement onto the side of its opposition? It was the fear of this happening that caused the Portuguese Communist Party to urge a more moderate approach, while the center and right tried to mobilize support by using housing occupations and demonstrations as examples of the chaos that needed to be stopped.

Effects on Relations Between the Population and the State

The other main type of political effect involves the reform of the state apparatus, particularly at the local level, and the change in the population's relationship to it. At the time of the overthrow of fascism in 1974, the *Câmaras* were essentially local administrative organs of the central government and were tightly restricted in both their powers and resources. They were not established to respond to the needs of the local populations, and had no democratic legitimacy. Throughout the following two years, there was much discussion about the need to reform and decentralize the central government, but relatively little was done except for some de facto changes resulting from the breakdown of coherent direction from the center. In contrast, there was a significant increase in the role of the local government in providing services and infrastructure, due largely to the pressures the CMs exerted as well as to the resources they offered. The CMs called—often belligerently—for the attention of the local government to the principal problems the population was facing, helped it to focus its resources and allowed it to act in ways that would have visible effect. With the free labor provided through the CMs, both the *Câmara* and IFAS undertook many new activities and expanded existing ones without any great increase in their own resources.

The daily relationship between the *Câmara* and the CMs was, of course, strongly affected by the attitude of the individuals involved, but the limits on that relationship were largely determined by the demands made by the CMs (a result of the problems their barrios faced) and the legal powers of the *Câmara*. The *Câmara's* concrete role and possibilities for action were changed by various national laws. Because the SAAL program required the SAAL brigades to work through the local governments, their projects and expropriations required the *Câmara's* approval. Other laws concerning the registration and letting of unoccupied houses were to be implemented through the *Câmara*, which was given authority to sign leases in the name of land-

103

lords who unreasonably refused to rent. These were limited—although important—changes in the role of local government, and their impact was often determined by the willingness of the *Câmara* to cooperate with the local population in their application.

From the very beginning of its time in office, the Administrative Commission of the Setubal *Câmara* tried to link itself to organizations of the local population, seeking their participation as "democratic advisors" to summarize and focus demands and to help in the resolution of problems, preferably through acting at the level of the *junta de freguesia*. The attempt to establish advisory councils was not particularly successful, but the *Câmara* continued to try to respond to the needs of the local population. For example, it sponsored public hearings and discussions on housing and other problems of the city; it supported the SAAL projects, and also carried out housing rehabilitation using central government funds earmarked to expand the housing stock of the city; it organized lists of vacant old housing in the city and of those in need of housing, and allocated some housing to people, signing contracts in the name of the owners; and it provided small amounts of material aid for improvements to roads and community facilities.

Nevertheless, the effective powers and abilities of the *Câmara* were quite limited; it served at the pleasure of the central government and would be removed if it overstepped its bounds. It could be open and accessible to the population, it could partially respond to their demands for repairs and urban services, it could support their actions where it was the legally defined intermediary with the central state, and it could "enlighten" them concerning the problems, general conditions or specific situations existing in the city. It could also make clear that it was mainly political factors (e.g., the need to broaden and consolidate the revolutionary alliance, or the danger of jeapordizing it) that prevented it from implementing obvious solutions. But it could not provide the solutions itself and was often opposed to CM direct action solutions.

Given these factors, what was the relationship between the CMs and the *Câmara*? Quatro Caminhos expressed perhaps the most common and realistic attitude, saying, "We had the normal conflicts with the *Câmara*—all Administrative Commissions have conflicts with the population." While most CMs probably had some conflicts with and received help from the *Câmara*, the CMs from those barrios which were directly dependent on it expressed a much more negative view. The public housing barrio Afonso Costa reported that they had expected that things would be quite easy, because they only had to deal with one landlord—the *Câmara* itself—but that, in fact, the *Câmara* "only made things harder" by continually involving them in bureaucratic runarounds. Similarly, Primeiro de Maio, a barrio composed primarily of owner-occupied, single-family housing built on land leased from the city, commented that, "The *Câmara* just makes things more difficult. They make a revolution, but don't change the laws inherited from fascism."

As indicated in the previous chapter, the relationship with the *Câmara* was an important aspect in defining the political orientations of the CMs. Whether the *Câmara* was composed of sympathetic people was not of particular concern to the population; what they were interested in was the *Câmara's* effectiveness in solving the basic problems of the barrio. Inevitably, the *Câmara* had much more difficulty succeeding in this in barrios with more serious problems precisely because it lacked the necessary authority and resources. As a result, in the words of Nuno Portas, Secretary of State for Housing from July 1974 to March 1975, the relationship between the CMs and the *Câmara* was one of "conflictual cooperation," in which cooperation was clearly dominant in practical work while conflict characterized many of the individual encounters and the tone of political discussion. This high level of cooperation—and the practical limitations on the possible achievements resulting from it—is important for understanding one of the principle political effects of the urban movements: demands for and views of a system of "popular power" based on the grassroots organizations as an alternative to the "bourgeois state".

Popular Power: Toward an Alternative Model of the State

As the CMs and the political situation evolved, an ideology developed supporting an ill-defined system in which the population, organized at the grassroots, would have a significant role in the politics and administration of the society. Dubbed "popular power," its results—had it reached the endpoint—would have been to link closely the *Câmara* to the CMs. All the CMs in Setubal and the *Câmara* shared a belief in one form or another of "popular power." As the CA of the *Câmara* declared in a public document on September 6, 1975:

> The guarantee of our ability to get beyond the existing insufficiencies of the state apparatus is the creation of a real popular power which in the short or medium term will be able to replace the moribund administrative organization we know so well, and to do this through real intervention of the organized population in local political administration. The quantitative and qualitative modification of the mode of resolution of the local problems people face is in sight.

> It is the opinion of this CA that a real linking of the grassroots organizations to the presently existing structures whose function is to resolve their problems must involve an evaluation of the Câmara's real possibilities to satisfy the necessities of the whole population of the county, based on the list of needs chan-

neled by the CMs. This evaluation should be considered an immediate task of the CA.

The ultimate goal of this CA is—with the help of the CMs—to modify the con-cepts and methods of administration in order to achieve a maximum efficiency. It is a basic principle of this CA that this goal can only be achieved through a real commitment of the decisive weight of the population directly intervening in the resolution of their problems.

In two words, this is "Popular Power."

While all CMs supported something called *popular power*, they were actually striving for two very different models. The CMs all believed they represented the interests of the local population, but the first model of popu-lar power viewed the CMs as autonomous and powerful organizations, able and entitled to act directly to resolve local problems. This model was espoused primarily by the radical CMs, which were resolving through direct action major problems beyond the *Câmara's* competence. This view called for a greater transformation of the state apparatus, and saw that apparatus as something that currently got in the way of the CMs but which could and should be a resource to be used at their direct command. The other model was supported by those CMs whose problems were amenable to solution through cooperation with the *Câmara*. With generally lower levels of mass mobilization and participation, this group of reformist CMs sought to work with the *Câmara* for a better neighborhood and city and saw their function as identifying problems to the *Câmara* and helping in their resolution.

There were two main aspects that differentiated the attitudes of the CMs. The first was their orientation toward the state: whether the CMs should act through and support the state apparatus (reforming it when necessary), or the state should legitimate and support the actions of the CMs; that is, which should be dominant and which supportive. The second was their ori-entation toward direct action: whether it was based on local individual self-help or mass mobilization and action. Those supporting mass direct action under the guidance of the CMs had what could be characterized as a radical or revolutionary orientation, focusing on the need for change in the central government; those favoring local self-help directed by the CMs had an inde-pendent attitude, although they tended to ally with the revolutionary posi-tion regarding national policy reform; and those favoring local self-help in cooperation with the local government had a reformist orientation. There were no CMs supporting mass direct action in cooperation with the state. The absence of this case is a direct result of the dynamics producing the political orientations of the CMs, according to which the orientation toward mass direct action resulted from conflict with the state. While the image of popular power is most often associated with what is here called the revolutionary approach, all three positions had direct roots in the political developments of the period, and the first and third produced alternative national models of state-society relations.

The further development of these models of popular power and of a more democratic and decentralized state were truncated by the shift in the government and the demobilization of the popular movement that followed the right-wing coup of November 25, although many of their issues remained on the public agenda. The 1976 Constitution (drafted in 1975) guarantees the right of the grassroots organizations to a voice in urban affairs, especially those relating to housing, social services, etc. It also calls for the decentralization of the state apparatus and establishes local assemblies to oversee the actions of the *Câmara* and the *junta de freguesia*. When elections were held for these bodies in 1977, their form was partially determined by the urban movements of 1975, but their content was no longer the same due to the lack of the earlier extensive mobilization and participation. While this did institutionalize a representative democracy that was an advance over the situation under fascism—or in many other Western countries—it represented a long step backward from the discussion of popular power in 1975.

SIX

Theory and Practice of Urban Social Movements: Implications of the Portuguese Revolution

The grassroots organizations and urban social movements that developed in Setubal during the two years of social conflict and change following the overthrow of Portuguese fascism significantly improved the conditions of people and changed the city physically, socially, and politically. The development of urban and other social movements to an extent far beyond what most other countries have seen provides an extreme but typical case upon which to base consideration of the fundamental dynamics and possibilities for such movements generally. In Chapter One, a number of questions were posed that provide a framework for understanding those dynamics. The questions focused on the origin and effects of urban social movements; on their relationship to other movements and to the state; and on their significance for debates on alternative models for a participatory democratic society. The preceding chapters have addressed these questions in the context of the specific events in Portugal. This chapter summarizes the basic theoretical approach and conclusions developed in this study, and then poses the relevance of the present study for other contexts by specific discussion of the empirical and theoretical arguments others have made regarding the origin of urban social movements, their political orientations, the development of coordination among movement organizations, their relationship to the state, and the significance of "popular power" as an alternative model for society.

On the Political Conjuncture and Urban Social Movements

In brief, the development of urban social movements is part of a change in the general balance of class forces and is an expression of the attempt by members of those same classes to translate that new balance into corresponding adjustments in access to public resources. At any point in time, the development of a given society has produced a specific class structure and a specific distribution of goods and services to the members of its different classes. The *urban structure* is one part of this, the relationship between the various resources of the city and the members of the classes inhabiting it. The urban structure does not spontaneously transform itself to resolve problems as relations of power change, nor is its transformation the linear result of the actions of any agent—popular or state—which sets out to resolve the problem. Rather, as a relation between class structure and material conditions, it can only be changed as the result of translating shifts in class relations into the material world of the distribution of society's benefits and problems. To the extent that the distribution of problems corresponds to the distribution of power among classes, they will simply be problems and not issues for social movements. When, as the result of shifting relations of alliance, domination, and mobilization, the general balance of power among classes changes, struggles will occur throughout the society as members of classes seek to translate the shift of power into increased access to the various resources of the society, including urban social movements seeking to change the urban structure.

A change in the political conjuncture at the national level—an advance or offensive of the working class and popular classes, or a shift in control over a significant part of the state—will result in local social movements to improve living conditions. Struggling around specific problems is part of the struggle to shift power, and at the same time, struggles by those most affected by a problem are a necessary ingredient for specific change even with a sympathetic government and supportive class relations. The success of these movements depends on the presence of local class forces interested in the outcome (and/or sufficient presence of the central government), for the national change in relations is not automatically transposed throughout the society; it must be reproduced, reinforced, or countered locally. In turn, a change in the political conjuncture is necessary for a systematic improvement in the living conditions of the popular classes. A corollary is that if living conditions worsen drastically with a stable conjuncture (e.g., due to natural disaster), then a protest movement is likely to arise and likely to be relatively successful at reestablishing the old conditions.

The urban effects of neighborhood-based struggles can include improvements in the immediate conditions of the population, alterations in the urban structure, and transformation of its logic of reproduction. These effects are dependent upon the actions of both the local population and community organizations as well as the local government. Only the most limited type of effect is possible without a shift in the structure of political power—in the political conjuncture and in the state. Furthermore, while alterations in the urban structure require state cooperation, spurred perhaps by local direct action, the most profound effect, developing a new logic of reproduction of

109

the urban structure, requires ongoing state initiative which is only possible with a more complete change in the relations of political and economic power. Thus, a greater effect is only possible if a significant shift in relations of political power has already occurred, or if the particular struggle is the final element necessary to bring about that shift.

The political relation of forces is more than just a "context" for the development or understanding of urban movements. It reflects the state of mobilization of different classes in society and the control exercised over different state apparatuses by the organizations of those classes. Shifts in the national relation of forces among classes affect the likelihood of local class alliances and, therefore, movements. Changes in the national political conjuncture favoring the popular classes will bring greater participation, help develop a mass movement, create the possibility of different kinds of actions and effects, and qualitatively change the nature of the movements and their possible significance. They change the main issues of concern to movements, the tactics people and movements are willing to employ, their likelihood of success, and the possibility of affecting both their immediate conditions and the urban structure. In short, the political conjuncture determines the limits on the essential qualities of the urban movements, both in their own internal dynamics and their urban and political effects. Keeping in mind that the urban movements also help define the political conjuncture, the essential limits on urban movements (and specifically on their urban and political effects) cannot be changed by any simple action of a movement or organization, but only with a change in the conjuncture.

The clear focus on the independent role of the relation of class forces also sharpens understanding of the importance of the two variables most commonly referred to in discussions of urban social movements: social base and urban issues. They are not simply descriptive categories nor the arbitrary creation of organizers; the content of each is significantly defined by the state of and changes in the political conjuncture. The popular movement as a whole is defined in terms of its social class composition, but it actually comprises many smaller movements, defined partially in terms of their class composition, but principally in terms of the problems on which they are focused. The conjuncture and class base define the opposing sides, but leave a majority unmobilized and simply observing the contest, only joining in when they see how it relates to their own interests. Thus, one of the ways in which the conjuncture can be changed, that is, how the concrete composition of the popular movement—the bloc of classes on the offensive—can be altered, is through the addition of class fractions mobilized around some issue of concern to it.

Due to the confluence of the effects of social segregation in space with the concrete problems of the city on one hand and the political conjuncture on the other, the social base of a movement is not simply a demographic category to be filled and from which we can then expect consistent behavior at all times. The social base of a movement is composed of members of the different classes whose power relations at the national level are described by the conjuncture; and those who are most active tend to be from the classes whose mobilization characterizes the conjuncture. As the conjuncture shifts, it will differentially affect members of the various classes, mobilizing or demobilizing them, and giving them more or less access to the government. As a class gains (or loses) power there will be a strong tendency for its members to be more (or less) active in social movements. Thus, movements with the same general class composition are likely to be dominated by different class fractions in different conjunctures, and furthermore these movements are also likely to act differently. Finally, these limits are not rigidly determined; differences in social base may serve to either divide or broaden a movement, and movements may develop with class compositions different from that of the relations in the national conjuncture, thus contributing to the change of the latter.

The answer to the query "what problems become issues for the neighborhood organizations" is simply "the most basic problems of the neighborhood," conditioned by the state of the political conjuncture. The definition of issues is not a simple restatement of problems, rather it is mediated by those groups and individuals mobilized in the neighborhood. Thus, the issues are generally those problems most important to the mobilized sectors of the population. While these sectors may be mobilized partially because of the particular problems of the neighborhood, the basic source of mobilization is the local impact of shifts in the national conjuncture resulting from broader class offensives. This is the filter that transforms problems into contradictions.

Several other hypotheses derive from the preceding analysis, in addition to the effect the conjuncture has on the nature, development, and implications of movements discussed above. First, a certain amount of resistance and conflict always exists around any problem. The development of mass movements depends partially on the nature of the problem involved, but essentially on changes in the national balance of power among classes. As the conjuncture shifts in favor of the dominated classes, movements will develop, based especially (but not only) in these classes, and developing around some of the more serious material problems suffered by these classes.

Second, the movements that arise are not simply caused by a shifting conjuncture, but are real struggles over the division of social resources, expressed in a certain way in a given conjuncture. Furthermore, each specific issue will mobilize others for whom it is also important, producing movements whose social base is broader and less well-defined than that of the general political conjuncture. The political importance and probable impact of different movements thus does not come from the demands themselves, but rather through their drawing less mobilized portions of the population into the broader popular offensive and increasing the weight and impact of the class forces mobilized around the demands.

Third, the involvement or mobilization of new groups will bring up new issues of struggle at the local level. As new problems become issues they will bring further social groups into the struggles around them. These groups may, however, be divided by the relative priority they give to different problems as well as by being on conflicting sides in the principal class offensive defining the conjuncture.[1]

Fourth, while movements based on different social bases in isolation may have characteristic problems, resources, modes of activity, and so on, when struggles become more intense, or the conjuncture involves an offensive on the part of a particular class or class fraction, then members of that class tend to be pulled into movements and conflicts on the basis of their social composition and identification, without regard to sharing the same initial problem. Thus, a narrowly based movement may be broadened or an initially broad-based movement may be split by realignment of class forces at the national level. Similarly, the class lines drawn by the national conjuncture may tend to develop relatively less important aspects as problems, or even cause major problems to go undiscussed.

The analysis presented here is based on urban social movements and organizations that developed during a period of increasing class conflict. Attention to the role of the conjuncture reminds us that the qualities of community organizations in a period of dual power are no more their "true" characteristics than are those of a demobilized period. The range of characteristics of movements in each period is determined by the nature of the period. The revolutionary upsurge in Portugal was followed by relative defeat and demobilization which affected the grassroots organizations correspondingly. Had it instead been followed by a degree of victory, consolidation and advance on the part of the popular forces, the nature of community organizations would have changed in ways that cannot be determined a priori, but which certainly would have been different from what developed.

Nevertheless, because specific movements are responses to real problems, most of their goals and activities remain essentially the same regardless of the conjuncture. Changes in the conjuncture may involve more people in movements and organizations, and may make them more effective, but those who are involved still continue to do what they were doing previously. New political issues may develop, as may new tasks of coordination, control, and perhaps new forms of action as well. But most of the original activities will continue as long as the original problems do, even in a dual power conjuncture. Grassroots activity in a revolutionary period is not intrinsically different from that in other periods, but it is qualitatively transformed by the change in the political conjuncture.

In summary, because class domination and struggle are the main dynamics of social life, development, and change, the development of local urban movements closely reflects the general shifts in class relations in the society as a whole, and potentially affects them as well. Given the existence of a conjuncture favorable to the popular classes, such movements will develop widely and large numbers of ordinary people will have a role in changing the city and society. Without such a conjuncture, they will not. Major shifts in the political conjuncture—whether initiated by a significant reduction in the use of repression or increased receptivity of the state on the one hand, or an offensive of the popular classes on the other—are likely to produce urban social movements. From that point on, the degree of popular participation they exhibit, their evolution, relations with other organizations, possible actions and effects, and eventual end, all depend largely on changes in the political relations of forces between classes in the society as a whole, and not on any specific feature of the movements themselves, except insofar as their concrete development contributes to changing those relations. This conclusion provides a basis for replacing a voluntarist romanticism with a realistic optimism about the possibilities of large numbers of people becoming active in social movements and transforming their society.

On the Origin and Development of Urban Social Movements

Authors discussing the process of development of specific neighborhood associations often argue that three basic preconditions must be met for mobilization to occur: first, agreement as to a significant threat to or problem of the neighborhood; second, a sufficient possibility of collective action in response to the problem; and third, a reasonable belief in the possibility of achieving positive government response. Nonetheless, the experience of Portugal suggests that changes in the balance of power among classes have a far greater impact than any immediate activity on fulfilling these three oft-cited preconditions for the development of neighborhood organization and movements. For example, while actors in a movement often focused much attention on convincing others that a problem existed, for many people this awareness always existed, and it developed for the majority as movements arose around the issues with which they were concerned. Furthermore, people were sensitive to conditions opening the possibility of redress, and whether a collective problem was viewed as subject to redress depended largely on whether the possibility of collective redress existed. Analysis of urban movements frequently considers factors that are likely to increase or decrease the chances of these preconditions pertaining and thus of a move-ment developing, focusing especially on specific characteristics of the neigh-borhood, and of organizers' strategies. The development of the urban social movement in Setubal provides material for commentary on this analysis.[2]

Neighborhood Characteristics

Neighborhood characteristics supposedly related to mobilization can be separated into demographic factors and material problems. Considering first the demographic factors, it is often assumed that urban movements are largely a political phenomenon of poor neighborhoods.[3] Within this group, those neighborhoods argued to be most likely to organize are those with a higher mean income or greater resources generally, a higher mean educa-tional level, and greater neighborhood stability (Henig, 1982:156-63). In Setubal, however, community organizations developed in neighborhoods of all social compositions, although most commonly in shantytowns and other neighborhoods with a predominantly working-class population. Mean neigh-borhood levels of education and income were not important in CM forma-tion, and neighborhoods which had a percentage of recent migrants such as that of the city as a whole were more likely to form CMs than neighborhoods with either high immigrant or high native populations, while neighborhoods with the lowest percentage of migrants (which were also the older ones with lower proportions of income going to rent) were least likely to form CMs. Thus none of the demographic factors often connected with the formation of urban movements were actually applicable in the context of Portugal.

Which demographic factors are considered as increasing the likelihood of organization are actually only correlates of the neighborhoods mobilized at any given time, a cumulative result of the different specific processes that lead to organization. Had one conducted a survey in the spring of 1975, conclusions would have been quite different from those of this study, for at that time the vast majority of CMs were in working-class neighborhoods (one-half of which were shantytowns) and two were in elite neighborhoods. One would have concluded that, excepting the two elite neighborhoods, CMs develop only in working-class areas of town, and that among nonelite neigh-borhoods, those with *less* education and income were *more* likely to organ-ize in order to collectively counteract their individual disadvantages. Six months before that it would have seemed obvious that CMs were an activity *only* of the shantytowns, presumably the poorest and least educated part of the population. What passed during the two years was not simply time, but

distinct periods of class mobilization, struggle and political conjuncture during which neighborhoods with varying social compositions and specific problems formed CMs as grassroots initiatives.

Some authors have argued that certain local problems make mobilization more or less likely. All authors tend to agree that a localized disaster
(e.g., flooding, urban renewal) is an important stimulus to organization. But
for more generalized organization there are few strong hypotheses. Shantytown dwellers are argued by some to be among the most likely to organize
and by others to be very difficult to organize. Insecure landtitles and incomplete neighborhood infrastructure are argued to be important causes of mobilization, especially for homeowners, but less so for renters. Peripheral
neighborhoods are seen to be more often organized than central city ones.
Finally, neighborhoods begun by an organized activity such as a land inva-
sion often give rise to an association at the same time (Nelson, 1979:254-61;
Handelman, 1975:52-56; Henig, 1982:59-63).

In Setubal, it was the shantytowns that first organized, but in the ensuing months they were followed by all other types of neighborhoods. Insecu-
rity of tenure or incompleteness of neighborhoods were important factors in
many neighborhoods, regardless of whether renters or homeowners predom-
inated. Central city neighborhoods were the least organized, but all others
were about equal. The two main problem categories spurring the development of CMs were housing and incomplete neighborhood infrastructure (e.g.,
streets, schools). The housing issue was extremely important, involving issues
of both quality and cost. As a result, there was a very strong correlation
between rates of CM formation and the share of income going to rent: barrios with higher proportions of income going to pay rent were more likely to
form CMs; those paying an average percentage had a lower rate of CM formation; and those paying less than average had the lowest rate of formation.

Once again, these empirical conclusions are a product of analyzing the
situation at the end of 1975 and are largely explained by the organizing among
areas with high rent/income ratios in the summer of 1975 (and the lack of an
equivalently motivated spread of CMs in the older parts of the city—the areas
with low rent/income ratios). The situation one year earlier shows the same
broad categories of problems, but the high rent issue had not yet arisen and
several of the CMs were not yet formed. Thus, neighborhood commissions
were formed around major neighborhood problems, but *which* problems
were important depended on the cumulative effect of changing conjunctures.

Organizing Strategies

It is often argued that organizers should principally focus on trying to
"raise the consciousness" of those around them. In much of the literature,

two basic approaches are found to the question of the development of con-sciousness in urban (and other) movements, emphasizing either that politi-cal consciousness is a prerequisite to the development of a movement; or that consciousness develops slowly over an extended period of time, as a result of much organizing and involvement in progressively more radical activities. In Portugal, however, where both consciousness and action were widespread and reached much higher levels than in most other countries, consciousness developed and changed suddenly with shifts in the conjunc-ture, showing that the consciousness of people does not necessarily develop slowly over time. Nor is it necessary or possible to first change all of con-sciousness, then make social changes. Rather the consciousness of large masses of individuals can only change—and does change—with shifts in the conjuncture. What once seemed—and was—utopian dreaming among a few overnight becomes the accepted position of many, and the old organizers may be left behind.

Consciousness and practice change not because people want them to, and not because people meet and discuss the need for them to be different. Their change depends on having the right conjuncture and other concrete questions. In general terms, broad changes in attitude come about with changes in the conjuncture; more specific changes come about through par-ticipation in or identification with specific struggles. Consciousness devel-ops very unevenly, in concrete and specific ways—corresponding quite closely to the objective possibilities of a given situation—and changes because con-crete circumstances change.

Because consciousness changes in concrete ways, one may find appar-ently contradictory ideas and actions in the same people. For example, hous-ing occupiers may continue to expect to pay rent; men who welcome the participation of women in debates in the workplace may still object to women going to meetings at night; and militants who support democracy in the workplace may resent the inconvenience caused by bakery workers decid-ing to start their day a few hours later. Different aspects of consciousness will only be changed when the possibility of their change develops *and* when specific struggles develop bringing the old aspects of consciousness (and material relations) in question and suggesting new possibilities. This suggests that it is through concrete involvement with some aspect of a movement that attitudes and committments are most likely to change. Furthermore, it suggests that to the extent that movements are localized in space, in time, and by social class, then their effects will be similarly restricted. This could lead to growing differences in attitudes between those affected by move-ments and those not—a difference which may begin to appear structural rather than experiential.

Considering the role of organizing strategies in initiating neighborhood organizations, there are few conclusions to draw that do not fall into detailed case analysis. Still, others have argued four general conclusions that are also supported in the case of Portugal. The most general conclusion is that, while much effort has been dedicated to finding "most effective" organizing strategies (e.g., Fainstein and Fainstein, 1972; Ash 1972), on the whole different organizing formulae have little impact in initiating broad urban movements (Henig, 1982:67 69 and Chapter VIII; Piven and Cloward, 1977:Chapter I). When the conditions are right, they will develop with or without organizers; when not, they will not. These conditions are not created by organizers, but organizers will be more effective if they understand them. For example, while organizing efforts had little impact overall in creating CMs, the development of the rent reduction movement resulted from the conscious strategy of one political group. It is not likely (although not impossible) that such a movement would have developed at about that time without that group's intervention, although it is unlikely it could have developed much earlier even with their organizing.

The second general conclusion is that neighborhood associations and urban movements only develop around important local problems. While they may also take up national political issues, they cannot be successfully begun by appealing to the general "needs of the national political situation," nor by simply trying to copy the actions of other neighborhoods without attention to an area's own problems and priorities.

The third conclusion is that while good organizing strategies cannot produce urban movements, bad or sectarian strategy can be quite divisive and inhibit the development of the movement. These destructive tendencies can be counteracted by zealously guarding principles fundamental to grassroots organizations—that they should be nonpartisan, open to all, and independent of both political parties and government.

Finally, contrary to the arguments of many who observed the development of urban struggles in Chile (e.g., Castells, 1977b:272-73), outside political organizations need not intervene to provide the analysis and links necessary for the development of an urban social movement. If organizing strategy is seen as focusing on providing leadership and articulating demands, the Portuguese experience shows that this is much less of a problem than often supposed, for the people in any given neighborhood were conscious of their problems, able to understand them in a broader context, and able to generate competent leadership. Preexisting groups, organizing drives, agitation, propaganda, and the like may, of course, be important in the specific history of a given movement, but their importance is not due to their giving rise to movements in the first place.

117

In summary, with a given national balance of power among classes, the determinant factors for formation of community organizations are the class composition of the neighborhood and the problems faced by the people living there—and these two factors often overlap considerably. To the extent that serious problems affect a large part of the population of the neighborhood, and to the extent that it seems these problems can be dealt with by pressure or actions of a neighborhood organization, then one develops based on the problems people immediately face. The likelihood of people being able to obtain outside assistance to resolve their problems, or of solving them directly themselves, depends on political conditions which include the control over the state and the degree of mobilization of the population.

On Castells' Structural Models of Urban Movements

The implications of the approach developed here are highlighted by comparison with Manuel Castells' five models of urban movements based on his 1977 to 1979 study of the Madrid Citizens' Movement (Castells, 1983). His models show how, he argues, under specified necessary conditions, correct political party strategy produces urban social movements. While many criticisms of Castells' work have been made (see Lowe, 1986 and Pickvance, 1985 for summaries), it nonetheless remains the principal attempt to provide systematic models of the structural factors underlying urban movements, and is a useful point of departure. The approach outlined above considers many of the same factors as Castells, but has significant differences in weighting and interpretation, reflecting in part the specific circumstances covered in each study. The framework developed here therefore provides a basis for reexamining Castells' study, and leads to significantly different conclusions for both theory and political strategy.

Starting from the position that urban social movements have, each factor is indicated by its presence (+) or absence (−). Table 6.1 outlines these factors.

Before turning to his specific models of urban mobilization, the differences between the apparently similar concepts in Castells' Madrid study and this analysis of Portugal should be highlighted. First, Castells does not distinguish among the various possible urban demands. The study of Setubal demonstrates the importance of distinguishing between (1) demands for the resolution of problems that lead the local neighborhood to participate in broader mass movements and confrontation with the state to change government policy, and (2) demands to resolve problems that do not lead to such participation. This is not a question of the inherently more radical nature of some demands, but rather of their correspondence to neighbor-

Table 6.1

Components of Castells' Models of Urban Movements

Cy · City		Active mobilization around urban demands.
Pw · Power		Participation in political mobilization.
Cm · Community		Development of community social network by movement activities.
M · Movement		Explicit consciousness of being part of a broader social movement, identified as citizen, and distinct from other movements.
Cp · Class Position		Predominantly working class composition.
Cc · Class Consciousness		Self-definition as part of working-class movement.
Sm · Solidarity		Active and conscious involvement by neighborhood in struggles of other social movements.
Md · Media		Coverage of movement by mass media.
Pf · Professionals		Support and advice from established and legitimate professionals.
Pt1 · Party-1		Presence of a political nucleus in movement.
Pt2 · Party-2		Autonomy of movement in relation to party.

The different degrees of effect are indicated by:

U1	Fulfilling immediate demands.
U2	Fulfillment of demand modifies existing logic of urban development.
P1	Increased electoral support for opposition parties whose programs reflect popular class interests.
P2	Expanding and broadening democratic institutions, reinforcing decentralization, participaiton, and grassroots control.
C1	Improving community life and local social networks.
C2	Transforming the urban culture; making the city a meaningful social setting.

hood problems and national movements. It is a question of the possibility of individual versus collective resolution of the problem, and of doing so with community resources or only with governmental ones.

Second, for Castells, the important aspect of the issue of power (Pw) is the neighborhood movement's adoption of the national issues on the agenda of political parties, in particular antifranquist democratic demands, such as human rights and open elections. This is involvement in national politics and not based on the urban problems of the neighborhood. In Portugal, virtually all community organizations took positions on national political issues. This did not serve to distinguish among them or their effects. Rather, it reflects the pervasiveness of debate on those issues throughout society. The analysis of Portugal shows that the important aspect of power was whether or not the neighborhood movement came into conflict with the state as a result of the movement's action around its urban demands. Thus, the model from

Madrid maintains that the posing of the question of power is a result of action based on ideological commitment, while the analysis from Portugal argues that the issue of power is posed as a result of action to resolve urban demands.

Third, Castells' consideration of U1 urban effects is the same as the treatment of "immediate urban effects" above. His U2, however, differs from the above discussion of structural effects in two regards. He attempts to classify the intrinsic nature of the demand as fitting within or breaking the existing relation between classes and urban conditions, which is referred to in this text as the urban structure. His distinction may be useful for some analyses, but the real impact of the movement's effects is more important than the supposed logical implications of the specific demand. It is important to distinguish the extent to which the improvement is shared by all in similar circumstances (changing the urban structure) and whether the change will be reproduced in the future (a change in the logic of development of the urban structure). Castells does not distinguish between these levels of effect, categorizing all indiscriminately in U2. Furthermore, Castells links all effects to each neighborhood and its movement. That is appropriate for the immediate changes and fulfillment of demand, but not for larger structural changes, which are dependent upon broader movements, political relations, and policies.

Fourth, several factors which Castells considers necessary for urban social movements may be, according to analysis of Portugal, corollaries of movements but not causal factors. For example, urban demands (Cy) exist by definition if one is discussing urban movements. If they are not present, then one is dealing with an organization—or even a movement—that happens to be in a neighborhood, but ought not to be considered an urban movement. This is confirmed by both the Portuguese and Spanish cases. The focus on development of community social networks (Cm) is a necessary concomitant of neighborhood activities that are both grassroots based and mass movements. Thus, this may help distinghish urban social movements from other types of urban activities, but it does not cause the difference. Rather than being a causal variable for urban social movements, the support of recognized professionals (Pf) is virtually a given, not only for urban social movements, but also for many other levels of demand activity. With broad movements, professionals are drawn in out of both political and professional commitments. Some even specialize in working with community groups, and if programs are established in response to the demand, this, too, will bring in professional involvement. Similarly media coverage of movement activity (Md) is not a causal variable for urban social movements in either Spain or Portugal. The media, when not absolutedly censored, attempts to cover important local events, thereby seeking movements as they arise.

Thus, these factors may certainly be important, but are not problematic, as confirmed in both Spain and Portugal.

Fifth, Castells' discussion of the role of political parties provides both one of the strongest differences and one of the clearest agreements between our two approaches. For Castells, the presence of an organized political party nucleus (Pt1) in the local movement is absolutely essential, for it is the necessary link to outside political practices and to his conception of contesting power.[4] The Portuguese experience indicates that this is far less important, for in the context of neighborhood-based mass movements party militants become involved in the organizations in their own neighborhood and as grassroots activists seek to frame their activities within a broader perspective. The importance of the autonomy of the neighborhood movement with regard to political parties (Pt2) is supported by both the Spanish and Portuguese cases. The analysis of Portugal suggests that this autonomy is based on two principle conditions. First, that the neighborhood organization maintains its responsiveness to its own grassroots, a condition most likely to obtain if there is an active grassroots movement underlying and pressuring the organization. And second, that party militants do not continually seek to divide or control the grassroots movement and its organizations.

Finally, in his analysis of the movements, Castells concludes that the presence or absence of a working-class majority (Cp), class consciousness (Cc), and active solidarity with other movements (Sm) are not important explanatory variables for the development of movements. While the research in Setubal largely concurs with this conclusion, it shows that class composition is very important for the development of each specific movement and its impact on the political conjuncture. This is clear when the changes in the composition of the movement over time are examined, but is lost when the movement is considered as a whole, at a relatively late period in its development.

While the variables Castells considers are important for describing and understanding movements, this study clarifies the relative significance of each variable and leads to strategic conclusions different than his. The Portugal study demonstrates that, first, the existence of urban social movements is a reflection of broader relations of political forces involving a popular offensive; and, second, in a mass movement based on urban problems, the essential characteristics of the movement are contingent upon whether the nature of the principal urban problems leads to participation in national movements and to conflict with the state to provide necessary conditions for collective solutions. The rest is secondary. Reviewing each of his models shows that this approach is compatible with Castells' data, but produces a different understanding than the one he suggests.

Castells defines five types of urban movements and presents a structural model for each. *Urban social movements* are defined as ones that have "effects of high level, multi-dimensional change," that is, with both immediate and structural urban, political, and cultural effects (U1+, U2+, P1+, P2+, C1+, C2+) (1983:393). *Urban reform movements* are ones with a "low level of multi-dimensional change," producing immediate urban, political, and cultural effects without deeper structural impact (U1+, U2−, P1+, P2−, C1+, C2−) (1983:393). They are the products of mobilization around urban and political demands by an organization under the control of a political party. Castells argues that this illustrates that "when the basic dimensions to foster social change were present but were orchestrated by a political party, the level of change was lowered and reform substituted for social movement" (1983:281). *Urban utopias* are movements that produce urban and cultural but not political change (U1+, U2+, P1−, P2−, C1+, C2+). Castells considers these to be the products of apolitical movements, involving no political parties and not challenging the political system, arguing they "cannot be projected on to the entire city because of their political alientation, but in their local area accomplish substantial changes that suggest an alternative city and culture" (1983:281). *Urban corporatism* (urban trade unionism) has only urban effects (U1+, U2+, P1−, P2−, C1−, C2−), and results when "a political party becomes an urban trade union to defend residents' interests without connecting its practice to other realms of society" (1983:281). Finally, *urban shadows* are those situations in which neighborhood mobilization produces no effects (U1−, U2−, P1−, P2−, C1−, C2−) and are characterized by a political party's use of the neighborhood as a pretext for political agitation. Thus, according to Castells, " . . . parties may try to invent a domesticated neighborhood movement, but they will end by projecting urban shadows, instead of fostering urban change" (1983:284).

If his formulae are modified by deleting those variables which are not, as argued above, causally related to urban movements, the structural formulae underlying the five models are as follows:

Table 6.2

Formulae Underlying Castells' Models of Urban Movements

	Cy	Pw	M	Pt1	Pt2
Urban social movements	+	+	+	+	+
Reform movements	+	+	−	+	−
Urban utopias	+	−	+	−	+
Urban corporatism	+	−	−	+	−
Urban shadows	−	+	−	+	−

Castells considers "urban demands" (Cy), the contention of power (Pw), and the presence of a political party (Pt1) whose strategy respects movement autonomy (Pt2) as the necessary independent factors for urban social movements. He argues that the difference between urban social movements and the other types of movements are either bad party strategy (reform, corporatist, shadow) or the complete absence of a party (utopian). While having good party strategy is preferable, the analysis of the Portuguese urban social movement suggests that "better strategy" can never produce an urban social movement. Strategy may determine whether the movement is reform, corporatist, or a shadow, but the basic factor separating all of these from becoming urban social movements is the absence of a grassroots mass movement. Similarly, the basic guarantee of movement autonomy is not the will of the party, but the existence of a mass movement.

These factors are present in the urban utopias, which involved intense local participation, but did not produce involvement with broader movements generated by the same demands and involved in conflict over state policy. Therefore, types of urban demands must be distinguished, for contention of power is the product of *some* urban demands but not of others. Thus, a local mass movement with demands that make it part of a broader movement and bring it into conflict with the state produces urban social movements; if it is not part of a broader movement seeking to change state policy around its demands it produces urban utopia. In both cases, the outcome is a consequence of the movement and its demands, and the productive role for a political party is based upon its respecting the autonomy of the movement. However, if there is no mass movement, then party strategy becomes much more important. In the best of circumstances it may produce an urban reform movement if the strategy is appropriately urban focused and broad (considering other political and cultural issues). It may produce urban corporatism if urban focused and narrow; or nothing but an urban shadow if it is a bad strategy which treats the neighborhood primarily as a forum for partisan activity, with no real urban focus at all. But good strategy can never produce an urban social movement.

On Political Orientation

A particularly clear and important indicator of the possible significance of urban social movements for broader change is their political orientation. Assumptions about this factor strongly influence the organizing and alliance strategies of political groups and the judgments of observers. Analysis of the development of the CMs in Setubal enables us to more fully understand the orientation, the sources of differences, and the possible significance of urban movements for political development.

The most basic question here is: Do community organizations, when part of an urban social movement, have an inherently radical (leftist) political orientation? Secondarily, what is their relation to political parties and the state? Five different answers have traditionally been given to the first question: (1) a simple yes or no, migrants (the poor, workers) are (are not) radical; (2) some are, on a scale directly related to poverty and being manual workers; (3) the poor may be radical, but it is an ultraleftist rather than leftist radicalism, based in the petty bourgeoisie and lumpen proletariat; (4) they may appear radical, but cannot get beyond an "economistic" reformism unless an outside organization intervenes to provide links to nonurban issues; and (5) it depends essentially on what party organizes them. These five answers are considered below, as well as an alternative sixth answer, which based on the neighborhoods' participation in the major urban struggles and the resulting interaction with the state.

Perhaps still the most common assumption is that of the essentially radical nature of the urban poor, whether migrant or worker. This position has been argued by both those who feared and those who eagerly awaited their entrance on the stage of urban and national politics. In a comprehensive review of this literature, Nelson (1979:Chapter 3) argues that the poor have shown themselves to be much better integrated into the political system than many imagined, with political behavior not differing greatly from that of other parts of the population. Radical political developments are rare, she says, and when they arise are based more often in the organized working class and middle class. Nonetheless, Handelman (1975:63-65) argues that while they may indeed be rare, radical developments do occur and provide the best indication of intrinsic political orientations. Pointing to Chile and other cases where these groups were a significant basis for parties and politics of social transformation, he argues that they are radical but realistic, choosing to support the most radical alternative within the viable. Thus, we should not expect to always see radicalism in these neighborhoods, but can only judge its potential when it is politically viable—and in these situations the poor should enter the stage of history on the left. This conclusion does generally correspond to the Portuguese experience.

The argument made by many, especially those in the revolutionary left of the 1960s and 1970s who became involved in neighborhood organizing and struggles, is that while the poor are naturally a radical (even revolutionary) force when organized, as one goes up the scale of class and stability of work, people are more integrated into the existing society and there is a rightward shift, with well-paid, stably employed workers being reformist and office employees more conservative. This continuum does often correspond to the apparent appeal of different political parties (see Castells, et al. 1973b for this observation in the Chilean context). The problem is that this analysis is based primarily on experiences of only minor popular offensives, when most movements were protests by the poor.[5] As the conjuncture shifts and other sectors join the offensive their political position also becomes more radical, as happened in Setubal where the more revolutionary CMs came from neighborhoods of all social bases.

The traditional left parties often reacted to the situation of protest by the poor by arguing that what may appear radical in their behavior is actually an unreliable ultraleftism based in the desire for immediate improvements by nonworking-class elements (lumpen proletariat and petty bourgeois). This analysis suffers from the same flaw as the previous revolutionary left view of failing to consider developments in a conjuncture of greater popular offensive, when a revolutionary orientation may arise. In addition, even accepting a narrow definition of the concept of working class, the social base of much participation in radical urban movements comes from the working-class population (Cherki, 1974).

The fourth argument follows a well-established debate regarding the trade union movement, insisting that the radicalism which may develop from urban issues is limited to economistic reformism unless an outside organization intervenes to bring nonurban issues into the movement. For example, Castells argues that:

> In order to have a social movement, it is absolutely necessary that there be a deep and profound union of a series of contradictions, which may only be formed by an organization imported from other *practices*. The most that a solely "urban" organization can be is an instrument of *reform*. In all other cases, the organization, while intervening in the system of urban agents, has an external origin. (1973a:340; emphasis in original)

Once again, this view is contradicted by developments in periods of great popular offensive when a revolutionary orientation and grassroots links to nonurban organizations may arise; and it is specifically rebutted by events in Setubal. The "simple linking of spontaneity" may very well have the reformist limits indicated, but getting beyond this does not necessarily require "an organization imported from other practices."

The fifth view is that there is a general progressive orientation inherent in neighborhood organizations of the popular classes, but the exact orientation depends on what political party organizes the neighborhood.[6] Furthermore, according to proponents of this view, a certain predisposition of different types of neighborhoods is found for different parties. This argument is illustrated in the conclusion of Colectif Chili:

[t]he type and strength of participation of the campamentos in the political struggle depend directly on the characteristics of the political organization dominant in the campamentos. . . . [W]hile the presence of a party is not sufficient in itself for the political development of the campamento, its presence is absolutely necessary, and the orientation of the campamento to the struggle bears its mark. (1972:50-51)

What then is the source of the political orientation of urban movements and the relationship of parties to them? Specifically, did the presence of a party generally determine the orientation, or, as we would now expect based on the preceding analysis, did the orientation determine which parties were present? I argued that the political orientation of urban movements is primarily determined by objective factors that may result in participation in mass struggles and potential conflict with the state rather than by the intervention of political parties, and in Chapter Four we saw a close association between the political orientations of the CMs and the partisan orientations they expressed. This was, however, not related to the social base of the neighborhood, nor was it the product of party-based organizing activity. Rather, the political orientation of each CM was essentially a result of its participation (or lack thereof) in struggles involving mass mobilization around basic problems, likely to result in conflict with the central government, and associated conflicts with local government.

Involvement in the mass struggles around shantytowns, rent levels, or occupations was the principal base upon which a radical direct action political orientation developed and in which a revolutionary left analysis gained support. Nonparticipation in mass urban struggles resulted in an institutional reformist orientation when cooperation with the government successfully improved a barrio, or an independent position when there was much conflict between local government and the CM. Overall, it was this process that produced CM political orientations and that, in turn, provided more or less fertile ground for the political line of particular organizations (Communist Party or revolutionary left).

Does that mean that to radicalize a neighborhood organization one need only get it involved in mass struggle against the state? In a sense, but this experience of struggle is not something produced by the political will of an opposition party or group (although it could be influenced by the attitudes of the local government). It is the product of the principal demand of the local population leading it to participate in one or another of the national mass urban struggles that developed. The possibility of a party becoming dominant in a democratic community organization is largely a product of that organization's relation to mass struggles with direct action, and the party's attitude toward such action.

In conclusion, during a conjuncture characterized by generalized popular offensive, neighborhood organizations as a whole will have a progressive orientation. But their specific orientation—whether more revolutionary or more reformist—depends not on the presence or absence of any particular party with its political line, nor of a particular social base. Rather, it depends primarily on the nature of the principal demands of the neighborhood and whether these demands lead it to participate in national mass struggles which come into conflict with the state.

On Coordination Within and Between Movements

Urban social movements never exist in isolation from other movements, because the change in the political balance of class forces that produces the former also produces others. The struggle for a broad positive program begins with the development of joint activities at a greater than neighborhood scale. Until then, it is an issue of more or less abstract discussion. But with such coordination, the potentials for struggle and program qualitatively change. Those involved in individual struggles often look upon such coordination in support of their demands as the key to victory. Both observers and participants sometimes view it as the key to advancing to higher stages of social revolution, modern day equivalents of soviets: the organ of dual power and the institutional form of a new popular power, at each step able to link together more issues and propose and carry out a more complete program of change (Nelson, 1979:287-92; Vieira and Oliveira, 1976; Pastrana and Threlfall, 1974). To the extent that the urban and popular movements produce an alternative to the existing state, it is embodied organizationally in those coordinating bodies. Most authors insist that such bodies are quite rare. Under what conditions do such bodies arise, and can they be effectively created as organizers' strategy?

Three distinct types of movement coordinating bodies are: (1) those linking all of the neighborhood associations sharing a particular problem; (2) those linking all the neighborhood associations of a particular city or geographic area, regardless of specific problems; and (3) those linking neighborhood associations to other working-class organizations. These three types of coordination represent a scale of qualitative advancement in the potential range of problems dealt with and the comprehensiveness of the solutions proposed. The first seeks to strengthen the movement of those with one demand (e.g., replacing shantytowns, lowering rents), and is basically a defensive structure, to give mutual support, share information, and plan tactics, according to the simple logic that in unity and numbers there is strength.

The second broadens the perspective to potentially include all the interests of the population as users of the city (e.g., supporting individual housing struggles *plus* proposing that all vacant housing be distributed according to need with rents set according to ability to pay) and represents all the citizens of the city as consumers. The third broadens this perspective to include interests of the inhabitants as both producers and consumers of the city, as well as providing the possibility of directly solving certain problems (e.g., directing idle construction firms to begin construction of public housing; organizing direct distribution of locally produced products). In a conjuncture of broader popular offensive and deepening crisis of the state, many of its actions are related to the political struggles of the moment, but because this third type of coordination involves representatives of the workers' organizations it has both the legitimacy and access to resources necessary to consider broader issues of the production and distribution of the city, permitting qualitative advances toward the solution of problems bridging consumption and production.

While in Portugal coordinating bodies developed in the above order, this was not a natural progression from one to the next, but rather a product of changes in the general political conjuncture, to which corresponded different kinds of organizations. Each type of organization had a characteristic breadth of composition, range of issues with which it was concerned, types of actions it took and types of internal tensions. They all were oriented toward direct action, but their ability to successfully carry out such actions depended largely on the political conjuncture in which they existed, while their goals or programs depended largely on the breadth of organizations coordinated, that is, on the type of coordinating body.

In other words, while the first type of coordinating body sometimes had a program calling for a wide range of changes, the ones it was able to try to directly implement (as opposed to simply support) were those directly related to that organization and its base. Its ability to allocate resources from one area of activity to another depended on the holders of those resources being among those in the organization. Organizations of the second type were able to develop a broader political base, and could act to carry out some internal redistribution of resources (whereas the first group could only try to gain resources from others outside the group), or propose general political reorganizations outside of its direct control (i.e., seeking to change access to urban resources that were subject to political control). Nevertheless, they were not able to directly affect the economic logic or decision-making for the production and reproduction of the urban structure. Organizations of the third type were potentially able to directly exert control over such decisions and allocate production as well as distribution.

The experience we have examined allows us to put forward a number of further hypotheses. First, coordinating bodies are far more likely to be successful if formed in response to particular concrete problems requiring coordination, as opposed to only being part of a general project of coordination. With the exceptions of COPS and the popular assemblies initiated following the MFA's Guidelines Document, all of the coordinating bodies discussed here had both aspects. Furthermore, while all three types of bodies may exist simultaneously in a conjuncture of broad popular offensive, without such an offensive, the coordinating bodies will be thrown into crisis, and the more advanced ones will atrophy although the simpler ones may continue. If there are no concrete functions to focus on, they will quickly either become the front of some organization or end altogether.

Second, while there is no need to limit their vision to the initial specific problems, coordinating bodies become weaker if they begin to ignore their concrete focus. Even with a higher level of coordination established, the lower levels must continue to function rather than being dissolved into the new one. Similarly, the coordinating body must maintain its focus on the needs and conditions of the grassroots. Even with people aware of its importance, maintaining this focus without some direct contact with and accountability to the grassroots organizations can be extremely difficult, and requires the creation of appropriate intermediate structures, which may be the lower-level coordinating bodies.

Once beyond the simplest form of coordination, these bodies are subject to certain structural tensions, although some tensions can be reduced through appropriate organizational forms. For the broader organization to work well, some problems must be dealt with in smaller more homogeneous groups—both because those groups directly involved can often best deal with their own problems and because they tend to take up excessive amounts of time of the general group in which concern over a given problem is not universal.

The Portuguese case shows the importance of linking community organizations with others dealing with other contradictions in order to form a broader base and have increased possibilities of effects, with a resulting greater structural impact. It also shows that those links can be developed between grassroots organizations dealing with other issues, without the need that the links be imported by political parties. Parties existed and took part in debates and organizations, but the links were not essentially provided by them. This study also indicates that the basic argument that revolutionary change requires a linking of contradictions and social bases rather than being the product of any single base—is equally applicable to the inherent limitation of organizations restricted to the workplace. The ideology and program of popular power arise not from any one sector alone, but from the combination of popular movements.

On Relations With the State

The struggles of urban social movements are rarely, if ever, completely outside or against the state. The relationship between the grassroots organizations and the state is a critical aspect not only for determining the political orientation of the organizations, but also for carrying through changes in the urban structure and logic. The deeper changes we have seen must become imbedded in state action if they are to last. For example, neither a nationwide housing program nor nationalization of industry can be carried out by a movement; local housing efforts (on a national scale) and local exercising of workers' control are dependent upon national conditions, created by the broad political conjuncture and embodied in formal institutions. Only the state can nationalize a firm; nationalization without socialization may not be sufficient, but socialization without nationalization is only temporary.

Strong urban social movements not only constrain the state, but also create possibilities for action by those within the state, particularly for actions that can transform the city. Movements provide a forum for discussion of the major issues facing the city, and of the preferences of the residents for both general and specific solutions adjusted to local conditions. Furthermore, they may provide considerable volunteer labor to cooperate in the solution of their problems. Through direct action, movements may overcome certain hurdles in the provision of social or physical infrastructure, and the state may then provide needed specific resources. They help provide the political context and support for the local government to consider and act upon issues previously outside its scope of real authority, and to take basic measures to permit democratic control over the development of the city.

There is much that would argue for cooperation between urban movements and local governments that sincerely wish to solve the problems of the people of the city. Yet the various state apparatuses are sometimes unwilling and often unable to act in ways the movements desire, and conflict may arise. For, this reason, the relationship between the CMs and the local government may be characterized as one of conflictual cooperation. While cooperation is inherent in any program applying government resources, conflict is a necessary concomitant to increased participation; it produces new ideas, programs, and alliances and is necessary to continually push the state into action.

Others have concluded from the dependence of urban movements on the state for structural change that actors in movements must carefully seek as smooth a relationship as possible, arguing that the most vulnerable targets are those most sympathetic to the objectives of the movements, producing the ironic result of making enemies of potential allies (e.g., Fainstein and

Fainstein, 1974). While it is true that more progressive institutions do seem to be among the most vulnerable targets, whether this turns potential allies into enemies is another question. In considering a "sympathetic institution" it is important to distinguish between the people working in it, who may have many sympathies they are unable to act on, and the rules and functions of the institution itself. These "potential allies" may be converted into enemies to the extent they identify and are identified with the institution and support it against criticism; or they can become allies to the extent that struggles outside the institution can be linked to struggles within it, providing mutual support toward a common goal.

The preoccupation with not antagonizing allies ignores the way that popular movements shape the conjuncture, including the conditions under which the bureaucracy functions. It is often only when pushed and supported by outside movements that progressive internal reforms are possible. There is always dissatisfaction which can grow into opposition within any bureaucracy. But it is often individual, isolated, powerless; and it rarely has a clear program for change or reform. Even a relatively solid bureaucracy is likely to show such differences under pressure from outside. Some of these factions will always seek to align with the movements, even if in a somewhat conflictual alliance. It is precisely disruption and opposition from outside, as well as demands for concrete changes, that create the conditions for the development of "allies" inside, and for them to offer an alternative and act. Ironically, these allies are more likely to be effective even in their own terms (and in terms of the goals of the movement) if the movement continues to pressure them. If it appears the protest will be satisfied with the program of one group—because other interests are defended within the bureaucracy as well—then the resulting compromise will necessarily meet fewer of the protestors' demands. To the extent their demands are met, it is not out of some rational discourse, but rather out of necessity, as a way of resolving a crisis under given conditions. Conflict is part of that crisis and those conditions.

State structure and programs are the crystalization of past social conflicts, power relations, and compromises in a given society; sectoral agencies of the state are composed of and function to defend the relevant class interests in relations of alliance and domination in the society. To the extent that grassroots movements and organizations are mass activities, they will represent interests that are at least partially in conflict with those of the central state. These conflicts occur for several reasons. First, local organizations are forced to seek to represent local interests or lose their base of support, and this requires the state to use its resources to solve local problems. This may conflict with the state's priorities, plans, or interests. Second, the central government seeks to maintain a broader coalition of classes, and the interests of local organizations—especially those based in classes suffering more extreme conditions—often call for a greater shift in priorities than the balance of forces between classes allows. A difference between the class interests represented at the local and central levels of the state may also exist. This necessary tension is expressed in the development of a grassroots movement with an ideology and practice of direct democracy, which also produces conflict because different class interests are represented by parliamentary and direct democracy.

While some strategies seek to by-pass the state entirely, a strategy often proposed is that of "occupying the institutions" in order to then peacefully cooperate with external movements. While not denying the importance of directly influencing the institutions, the Portuguese experience illustrates several problems with this approach. First, as already suggested, those institutions represent past social compromises that are bound to be adopted to some extent by anyone in them. Second, those occupying institutions generally desire protest and conflict to end. But experience shows that the occupation of *some* institutions is not sufficient to bring the state under the control of the popular classes. Thus, even for the services of the occupied institutions to continue—let alone be expanded—continual protest and outside pressure are often necessary.

Third, occupation of the top of some institutions may certainly affect the way they act. But experience shows that the institutions must be not only "occupied" but also *transformed*: in their goals, mechanisms of decision-making and accountability, bureaucratic structure and regulations, administration and personnel. Such transformation also comes about through conflict and concrete experience. Conflict and dialogue with the popular movement can indicate areas that need to be transformed and suggest some alternatives.

Fourth, even if the entire state were taken over by the institutions of a popular alliance, and that state were also transformed to reflect the new interests it was to serve, sources of conflict would still exist. The material problems would continue to exist and, to the extent that grassroots organizations represent their base, they would seek a commitment of state resources to solve local problems. Given freedom of democratic expression, this would mean a *conflictual complementarity* rather than a peaceful administrative one. Furthermore, the occasions for both cooperation and conflict are likely to be increased with state apparatuses directly under the control of progressive forces.

None of these conflicts need be fatal to either progressive local government or to the urban movement. We saw that in Setubal such conflicts existed, but no attempt was made to remove the *Câmara*. These conflicts are part of the relationship to be expected between even progressive local governments and strong urban movements, rather than the relation of simple cooperation which many in government and parties seem to prefer.

The urban movement, like the popular movement generally, was at the same time dependent on the state and independent of it, and the movement developed a practice and consciousness of itself as an alternative to the old state—in terms of its organization and the classes it would serve—an alternative embodied in the idea of "popular power." As demonstrated, in a situation of dual power the neighborhood and workers' commissions and their coordinating organizations developed into organs of dual power. Most of the characteristics they had (participation, actions, results) can be traced to this national political conjuncture. When the situation was resolved against them, they lost much of their role and reality. Had the situation been resolved in their favor, what might have happened? In periods of dual power, organizations and movements of the popular classes exercise certain forms of power: economic, administrative, ideological, and repressive. But they do so as expressions of a societywide confrontation of power, rather than because of the extreme development of their own intrinsic characteristics—this is what is meant by saying they are part of the political relation of forces. With victory or defeat the organizations could continue to deal with some of the concrete problems that gave rise to them in the first place, but their operation as organs of dual power would cease. Were the more advanced forms of coordination essentially forms of political struggle during periods of intense class conflict (i.e., organs of dual power), or could they have become organs of mass democracy and class power? In short, if they are organs of dual power, can they be institutional organs of democratic power?

Popular Power: Embryo of a New Society?

A fundamental question for evaluating community organizations and urban social movements—a question often raised when these movements are most intense—is: are these grassroots organizations the embryo of a new society? Specifically, is this the form of political organization appropriate to a truly democratic socialist society, an egalitarian society based on wide sharing of power and the full participation of all in the benefits and decisions important to their lives?

The experience of neighborhood-based movements in the Portuguese revolution provides several indications of what such a new society might be like. First, it shows that masses of people are quite willing and able to participate in politics and development if given the opportunity; direct democracy can work. Second, that experience gives a sign of what a more democratic city and society could be like, with a sense of full participation, a flowering of cultural, educational and social service activities, a different sense of justice giving greater consideration to need, and a less bureaucratic functioning of the state with greater direct contact between citizens and government. Third, it presents a specific organizational structure for local involvement: independent grassroots committees, democratically elected, recallable, responsible to all within their area, and federated together with committees representing all sectors of the community to express the clearest voice of the people's will. All of these lessons do fit within the various conceptions of a democratic socialist organization of the city and society. But these aspects were, in fact, all side effects of urban social movements that developed in a period of class conflict and crisis of the ruling bloc, and provide only a weak basis for speculation on the role of urban movements in a socialist society.

The CMs and urban movements did not simply develop during a period of conjunctural change and dispute over the control and direction of the society; rather, they were part of that process of conflict and change. The April 25 coup had destroyed the unity and hegemony of the dominant bloc of classes, while the basic state structure remained intact but divided and immobilized. Furthermore, one sector of the state, a part of the armed forces, increasingly legitimated the creation and actions of the popular movement rather than repressing them. It is this crisis of the ruling bloc—and thus of the state—that created the general conditions for the popular movement to develop and to realize the necessity of building an alternative to the existing state.

While virtually all the CMs, the Communist Party and the revolutionary left were able to unite behind slogans calling for popular power and an end to the bourgeois state, two different models of popular power developed in the movement, closely parallelling the different political understandings of the main left forces. The first clear view of popular power to emerge was based primarily in the shantytowns and occupiers, and later reinforced by those in the struggle against speculative rents. These groups, which often suffered from bureaucratic delays and reversals, called for power to the grassroots organizations rather than to the state bureaucracy, proposing that the CMs allocate money, expropriate land, decide on the legality of popular actions, etc. The second view was based primarily in the political parties and CMs close to the local government. Beginning shortly after April 25th, the local government sought to gain the organized participation of the local residents in the definition and solution of the problems of the city. Initially simply called *democracy*, this later became a proposal for a popular power in which the CMs would act as the neighborhood branches of local government, supplementing and supporting the state institutions, which would be modified as necessary. Under this view, CMs would be responsibile for minor tasks on the local level, while, nationally, CMs could be involved in reorganizing some of the main regulatory institutions, such as the courts and legislature. The two views often overlapped, but the first view envisioned a greater transformation or elimination of the bureaucracies, whereas the second envisioned replacing some people and policing their actions. The debate over which model would have eventually become the center of a broader alliance was never settled, but the direct focus on developing a new more democratic state was an important contribution of the urban movements.

Conceptions of popular power varied primarily according to the dominance or subservience attributed to grassroots organizations in relation to the state, and secondarily on whether direct action focused on mass or local self-help activities. The combination of these two factors results in the following matrix of models of popular power:

Table 6.3

Models of Popular Power

		Dominant Force	
		Grassroots Organizations	State
Direct Action	Mass	revolutionary	mobilization
	Self-Help	independent	reformist

Once the various social bases mobilize, their political orientation follows their experience of organized struggle: those involved in mass struggles that come in confrontation with the state adopt a revolutionary attitude; those without the specific material problems that lead to such experience adopt a reformist attitude, unless other particular factors enter to bring them in conflict with the state (e.g., public housing neighborhoods for whom the state is the landlord). In Portugal, only the revolutionary and reformist models received clear articulation in grassroots proposals. That experience also suggests that the revolutionary model—the one most often associated with the image of popular power—is viable only as long as mass direct action continues as a necessary support to the existence of mass movements in conflictual complementarity with the state.

All of the above models of popular power were present in Portugal. Are all of them "real" popular power? Are all of these variants appropriate to a socialist society? Only some of them—or none at all? This discussion must be inconclusive because the two countries where urban social movements were most developed and most studied—Portugal and Chile—did not pass beyond the early stages of a possible transition to socialism. Other countries often considered to have systems of popular power have not been studied from this angle. The best-known (although little-studied) contemporary example of a system of popular power is the Cuban, which shares certain formal characteristics with structures envisioned in Portugal and Chile, and has a very different history based in centrally directed administrative reforms rather than grassroots movements (perhaps putting it in the mobilization category).[7] The origins of grassroots organization in Nicaragua have great similarities to Portugal and Chile, while more recent developments have many similarities to the Cuban system (Serra, 1985; Downs, 1985). Massive participation in the revolutionary insurrection organized in Civil Defense Committees has since taken on other functions of representation, participation, mobilization, local improvement, and defense. It is, however, still too early to determine its mature form. More study is necessary to compare these systems with the alternative models identified through the Portuguese experience, and to determine their implications for the possibility of a stable system of popular power.

The urban movements in Portugal arose in a period of generalized popular offensive in a capitalist society. They developed during a period of conflict over state power, resulting in part from the collapse of the dominant alliance that had controlled that power. Movements were able to bring about certain changes through direct action which the state then supported under pressure. When this conflict was resolved in favor of a reorganization of the old dominant classes, the urban movements returned to a much more limited importance. Had the conflicts been resolved in favor of the popular classes, would such movements have continued? Would the state take on the role of social innovator and initiator of adjustments in the urban structure to correspond to the new power relations; or would it always require a certain prodding from the grassroots?

Portugal shows that the grassroots hold an important key to revolutionary change. Grassroots movements have shown that mass participation and direct democracy are possible and can produce qualitative improvements in local material conditions and national political relations. Massive and sometimes disruptive movements are part of the process of regime transition, part of the class struggles without which there will be no transition, with an important role to play in mass participation, representation, and problem resolution on the one hand and government reform on the other. This was neither sought nor even considered by those who brought to an end one-half-century of authoritarian rule. While one cannot predict its timing, similar processes of mass democratic participation in reshaping society can be expected to arise in other countries undergoing major regime changes. The period of transition when they can have this effect may be limited, but if their experience becomes embodied in the reform of state institutions, then the resulting society will be significantly more democratic. What their role will be following that period of transition cannot be predicted, but the transition itself critical, and is the moment when great and lasting changes may happen. Urban social movements play an important role in shaping the new society, although whether they will continue into the posttransition period must remain an open question.

Case Histories of Selected Comissões de Moradores

T his appendix presents case histories of seven individual CMs of Setubal, selected to illustrate the development, similarities and differences of CMs based in the various types of neighborhoods. Each begins with a summary of information about the physical, economic, and social conditions of the barrio and its population, followed by the overall history of the CM: how and when it began, its demands, achievements, basic activities, internal processes, and so on. Their participation in and opinions about the major urban struggles are described next, followed by their relation to other movement organizations generally and their role in the coordinating bodies in particular and a summary of their interaction with or opinion of the different local state organs. Each case history ends by describing the situation of the CM at the time interviewed (generally, the summer of 1976).

In reading these case histories, one may be struck by the similarities with activities of grassroots organizations in other places, and may think "this is all very interesting, but the real revolutionaries must have been elsewhere." Other movements were based in workplaces, barracks, schools, and other parts of society. But the mundane activities described herein, or their equivalent, are precisely the content of revolutionary activity at the grassroots level. Movements and organizations became far more widespread, with greater participation, ability to act, and effects, but their basic activities were similar to those of grassroots organizations anywhere; the difference was the political situation they were in and of which they were part. This conclusion is strongly supported by the detailed case histories.

Liceu (Elite: modern expensive)

Neighborhood Characteristics

This barrio constitutes the main expansion of the city toward the north, which began in the early 1960s and continued into the mid-1970s. It has nearly 2,000 units of housing, virtually all in four- and eight-story apartment buildings, of which some 80 percent are rented and some 20 percent owner occupied. The barrio is composed of three segments: Rio de Figueira, built in the early 1960s; Liceu, built beginning in the mid-1960s, with building still going on in the 1970s; and Amoreiras, built in the early 1970s. In the first part, rents are at about the average level of the city as a whole, and income is slightly lower than the city average. Rents are much higher in the other parts (highest in Amoreiras), and income is significantly higher as well (especially in Liceu). These barrios have a larger-than-average portion of recent arrivals to the city of Setubal, some 41 percent, 42 percent and 75 percent arriving since 1970, respectively. About 45 percent of the employed population work in white-collar jobs, and about 30 percent are manual workers, with the white-collar workers relatively concentrated in Liceu, while the manual workers are represented much more strongly in Rio de Figueira and especially Amoreiras.

History of the CM

The first CM was nominated by "certain individuals" from the barrio in the summer of 1974. It included an officer who had been purged from the Army as well as one of the developers of the barrio (which was still under construction in places). It was led by people from the PPD and CDS (two right-wing parties), but it also included some people from the PS and the MDP/CDE.

The CM held its meetings in the parochial center in the barrio. In December 1974, a "leftist group" (based in the CM of Amoreiras) called a plenary of the barrio and declared the existing CM unrepresentative. An election organizing committee was established to prepare elections and get people involved. A member of the MDP commented at the time: "As it is now, the CM is of no interest—but if those people come it will be a serious problem."

The second CM was elected in early 1975. Elections were held by block with some 60 people elected. In order to avoid the possibility of the CM being left without any members, statutes were approved specifying that all who wished to could be part of the CM. About eighteen of the sixty delegates regularly appeared at the twice weekly meetings. Some 300 people took part in a plenary on September 29, 1975. Meetings were held in the parochial center and in a basement put at the disposition of the CM by the workers' commission of the firm constructing further apartments in the barrio.

A member of the second CM interviewed commented that, "The CM always met a certain resistance from the residents of the barrio because many of them are reactionary, bourgeois people well set in life. But there are already a lot of working people here as well." The main demand of the first

139

CM was for a parking lot; "They also talked about a day-care center, but never did anything," according to a member of the second CM. This CM decided to focus on more basic social services, specifically demanding a creche and a pharmacy for the barrio which had neither. Both of these goals were achieved through actions undertaken at the initiative of the CM, but with some conficts.

> Many things were done behind the backs of the residents, and even without the knowledge of some of the members of the CM; partisan propaganda and attacks on parties were carried out there even though the Statutes clearly stipulated that one should not attack parties and the CM should be nonpartisan [*apartidária*]. At one point I got so fed up with it that I didn't show up for a couple of months.[1]

By mid-summer 1975, most of those originally elected to the CM were no longer coming to meetings. Then, on September 13, the CM occupied the municipal tennis courts and clubhouse in the barrio to use as a day-care center and playground. This caused considerable debate because, initially, the *Câmara* opposed the action as did many of the residents of the barrio, some arguing that they used the courts and others that some members of the CM had acted without consulting the rest. After many heated meetings it was decided to use only the clubhouse facilities for a day-care center and leave the courts for tennis.

A year later, the member of the CM we interviewed (who had initially opposed the occupation because he and others were not consulted) said this day-care center was the most important achievement of the barrio, and something of which they should be proud. The center formally opened on January 30, 1976, with a subsidy from IFAS, although it had already been operating with volunteer labor. IFAS gave a subsidy of 1,500 escudos per month per child, and families paid a percentage of their income (some paying as little as 300 escudos per month). There were twenty-two children in the center in April and thirty by June; more would have used it had adequate space been available.

In January 1976, the CM opened a people's pharmacy with free medicines for those not covered by insurance or able to afford them. The pharmacy was established in a basement given by the CT of the company constructing the barrio, with medicines procured by requesting samples from the city's doctors ("even some fascists gave medications"). But the CM insisted that this was not a case of charity and called for the "nationalization of medicine and medical supplies" (*A Nova Vida*, March 15, 1976):

> The CM is against charity; this is not a matter of charity, but rather of people's rights. In addition to giving medications we try to make people conscious of

their rights. We want to put the pharmacy at the service of the unprotected population. Thus we have been going around to the shantytowns to tell them of the opening of the pharmacy. We also want to help and collaborate with the asylums and cooperatives . . . .

In the following months the CM also sent cases of medicine to the MPLA in Angola.

In addition to these two major achievements, the CM carried out a number of other specific activities. When the city trash haulers went on strike in the summer of 1975 for a five-day week, the CM called on the population to support the "just demands of the workers for a weekly rest" by keeping trash inside and helping to clean up. The barrio was cleaned up.

The CM established a library in its headquarters, organized showings of films followed by discussion, and instituted a public hygiene campaign. In April 1976, it was planning to undertake various sports activities, create a theater group, establish a committee to monitor prices in the barrio's stores, carry out a literacy campaign, and obtain some open space from the *Câmara* for a park area for local children. The CM also helped carry out several housing occupations and participated in most attempts at coordinating activities of the popular organizations of the city; and some of its members were active in the "struggle to reduce speculative rents."

Occupations

There were many housing occupations in this barrio, some with the help of the CM and others without. Several entire buildings were occupied: in one case, five families living in shanties came together and occupied a building with an apartment for each family; in another case the Frente Socialista Popular (Popular Socialist Front or FSP) brought together families needing better housing and occupied a building. Both of these buildings were still occupied a year later, in the summer of 1976.

But not all the occupations in this barrio went so well:

There was a couple with three small children living in a shanty behind the mansion of a doctor. The CM discovered the house was uninhabited, but the son of the owner didn't want to cede it, saying he was waiting for some relatives to return from Angola. The CM didn't believe him, and one day broke down the door, got some furniture and put the family inside. But the children continued without any care: the father was an alcoholic and the mother a prostitute. Finally they abandoned the house and kids. The oldest one (6 years old) went to an orphanage [Casa do Gaivoto] and the other two stayed with two couples without kids.

The CM heard about another apartment that had been uninhabited for two years. It had been bought for the wife of the owner to live in during the summer vacation, but since [the owners] also had a trailer they always stayed in the campground. We gave the apartment to a family we saw in need: a couple with two kids, the husband was blind and received benefits of 400 escudos per month, the wife received 300 escudos per month, and the oldest son had just returned from the military and was unemployed. The owner heard about it and went to scare them away, but we found out and drove him off. Then he came back with a uniformed army officer with pistol in hand to force the people to leave; the occupiers were so scared they preferred to go back to the room they lived in before. Then we gave it to a family of six or seven *retornados* [refugees from Angola] who guaranteed they would not abandon the house. The next time the owner tried anything we scared him so badly he never came back. But a little while later a young man came to my house wanting to rent that apartment; the people who lived there had gone north. The retornados that lived there betrayed the cause; they told the landlord they were leaving and he took advantage of the situation to sell the house.

The Struggle Against Speculative Rents

This barrio was one of the main centers for the "struggle against speculative rents": the struggle to limit rents to a maximum of 500 escudos per room. This struggle helped change the composition of the barrio, as the member of the CM interviewed explained saying: "Now there are many workers here, but in the beginning there weren't because the rents were beyond their reach."

It was not this CM that began the struggle for 500 escudos but it was a Commission of Struggle for 500 escudos per room, which still exists and includes some members of the CM. This discussion took up a lot of time, to the point of nothing else getting done sometimes. There was some debate because I did not agree with the struggle, and later because they brought this discussion into the CM. I had a reputation as a conciliator because I didn't agree with these things. There were many opportunists with good salaries who entered into the struggle, but I have no doubt that it was a measure that helped many poor people, though today these people are having problems because this all evolved. At that time there was COPCON, and they even said that Otelo Saraiva de Carvalho told them to carry the struggle forward, "keep up the struggle; it is a revolutionary struggle . . ." etc, etc. They continue with the struggle, but things have gone in the opposite direction, and today people that took part in the struggle are taken to court by the landlords, and the Court has already given some eviction orders. That is the problem.

The "Commission of the struggle for 500 escudos per room" spoke with the Minister of Housing, but [the outcome] didn't depend on them; they couldn't do anything, etc., and people have been dropping out, until today the ones left are the ones who don't have any money to pay. They are in danger of being put in the street—that's the problem. I never supported this measure, and never considered it revolutionary, but if I hear of an eviction order in this barrio, and if my presence could help impede it, then they should call me and I'll go there.

Other Topics

The CM was actively involved in all of the major attempts to form coordinating bodies for the base organizations, and it took part in the city-country link of direct sales of agricultural products from cooperatives. Finally, the person interviewed said the CM had "good relations" with the *Câmara*.

By the time of the June 1976 interview, the CM was in a state of demobilization, "caused by sectarian [*partidária*] discussion." Of the variety of subcommissions initially formed, only two were still active: day-care and pharmacy.

Many present and past members of the CM were then involved in discussion concerning the reorganization of the CM, having decided that "letting everyone be part of the CM doesn't work; you have to have a permanent nucleus." Modified statutes were adopted in October 1976, including the following points:

- The CM is a unitary and nonpartisan [*apartidária*] base organization, representing the interests of the residents of its respective area. (Article 1)
- The CM's objectives are:

  1. to develop and reinforce the expansion and organization of the popular masses, seeking to integrate them in the ongoing democratic process within a perspective of a socialist society;
  2. to promote the active intervention of the inhabitants in the resolution of their own problems through collectively taken decisions;
  3. to participate actively in the exercise of local power; and
  4. to carry out other tasks specified in law or which may be delegated to it by the organs of the *freguesia* [ward]. (Article 3)

- The spirit of the CM is defined by the following rules:

  1. the CM is unitary—this rule guarantees the rights of all residents to be elected to all organs of the CM and to participate in Assemblies of Moradores without any partisan political, social, religious or other discrimination, while maintaining the full submission of all to democratic processes.
  2. the CM is political—this rule guarantees the intervention of the people of the area in the defense of their legitimate interests; and
  3. the CM is nonpartisan [*apartidária*]—this rule confers legitimacy on the taking of decisions that defend the interests of the population of the area in general, and not that of any particular political group. (Article 4)

Alves da Silva (Interclass, modern expensive)

Neighborhood Characteristics

This barrio, just west of the nineteenth-century city limits, is composed primarily of some 350 units of new apartment housing built in an area that was formerly covered by canneries and some housing. A section of the barrio is still composed of older run-down housing. The older part has houses without indoor plumbing or other modern amenities, while the new apartments are in very good condition although they lack many finishings (e.g., paved streets, stairways). This barrio, 65 percent of whose housing is rented, has some of the highest rents in the city (averaging over 500 escudos per room). While income is somewhat higher than the city average, it is not as high as in the Elite barrios, and some 60 percent of renters pay at least 20 percent of their income toward rent. While more than one-half the population is from Setubal, nearly one-third has arrived since 1970. People are employed about equally as manual (40.4 percent) and white-collar workers (42.6 percent).

History of the CM

The first CM was democratically elected, by building, in August 1975. It began with twelve members, many of whom left and were replaced by others. One of its first actions was to occupy an uninhabited apartment to use as headquarters. Some people criticized this action, saying that apartments should be used for housing people in need. In mid-September, the CM held a plenary to discuss the occupation and the need for housing, as well as its need for a headquarters and a day-care center in the barrio. This plenary ended with a decision to occupy an abandoned canning factory for the work of the CM (headquarters) as well as a day-care center, meeting room, bar, and cultural center for the barrio. This was done and the previously occupied house was given to a family in need of better housing. In November, the warehouse of the factory was also occupied to provide more space for the daycare center.

From the very beginning, the CM was created with a political perspective. As CM members expressed it in a social gathering in September 1975, "the CTs and CMs have to get off the ground in order to oversee [*tomar conta*] the government, among other things." But while it was a political organization, "there were no sectarian divisions within the CM—it is *apartidária*" and "quite heterogeneous, including members from the PCP, PS, UDP, and FEC."

In a weekly meeting of moradores on October 29, 1975, a motion of support to the "just struggle of the camrade workers of the paper *O Setu-*

balense"[2] was unanimously passed, closing with the slogan: "Revolutionary Information at the service of the working class; *República*, Renascença *Setubalense*—the same struggle." The CM also supported the shantytowns' struggle for housing.

The demands of the CM focused on finishing the barrio (e.g., paving streets, finishings on buildings), and providing basic community facilities (e.g., day-care center, sports pavilion, and headquarters for the CM and social center for the barrio). Through the occupation of the canning factory, it provided facilities for many of these, and was able, first with volunteer help and later with an educator paid by IFAS, to provide some day-care, a headquarters, and a social center. An area was paved for the sports pavilion, and the CM sponsored a variety of recreational and cultural activities (e.g., films). It forced the closing of a nightclub in the area, which was converted into a small restaurant/coffee shop.

Urban Struggles and Coordinating Bodies

It was this CM that initially organized the city-country link (mostly with PCP cooperatives at the beginning, although mostly revolutionary left ones at the end), and it was active in the leadership and defense of the Committee of Struggle after the right-wing coup of November 25. It also included a large number of people active in the struggle for the 500 escudos per room rent.

Aside from the occupations carried out by the CM, there were no reports of occupations in this barrio. A very large portion of the residents of the barrio did take part in the struggle for 500 escudos per room rent, although this number had been reduced by July 1976. Within this barrio, the people in this struggle were more organized than those in other barrios. Here, they elected one delegate for each building up to five floors and two for taller buildings to coordinate the struggle. Even after being forced to go to court they were still able to impose reductions of one-third in rents.

Other Comments

The person interviewed said the CM never had any problems with RI11 (the local Army barracks) or the *Câmara*; "they did what was possible, neither supporting nor coming out against the CMs."

In the period after November 25, conflicts developed with a new member of the CM (who entered after November 25) "who acted as if he wanted to take over the CM." As a result of ensuing events, nine members left (over a period of two or three months) and later were active in the creation of a GDUP.[3] At the time of the interview (July 1976), eleven to thirteen CM members were divided into work groups on the city-country link, infancy, and housing. But the only one functioning at the time was infancy, which had outside support (IFAS). The CM was quite demobilized, and the nine who left earlier had proposed a joint meeting to reactivate it.

Monte Belo (Interclass: modern expensive)

Neighborhood Characteristics

This apartment development is on the extreme eastern edge of the city, composed solely of eight-story apartment buildings all built since 1970. All of the roughly 250 apartments have the normal furnishing, although not all of the barrio was complete in terms of finished streets, working elevators, and basic commercial facilities. Seventy percent of the apartments are rented, and rents are quite high—more than 80 percent are over 500 escudos per room. As would be expected, a high percentage (65 percent) of the family heads arrived in Setubal after 1970. Families are quite young, and a large percentage of the manual workers are employed in modern or heavy industry (35 percent out of the 48 percent of the active population involved in manual labor). An additional 30 percent of the active population are employed in white-collar jobs. The average family income level is slightly lower than that of the city as a whole; given the rent levels, this means that the share of income going to rent is one of the highest in the city (with more than 75 percent paying more than 20 percent of their income in rent), and twice as high as in the city as a whole.

History of the CM

A pre-CM was formed in May 1975. They had hoped to form a CM together with Camarinha, but the latter went ahead and formed its own. In early June, the pre-CM (Monte Belo) occupied an abandoned prefabricated building which the builder of the barrio had constructed to use as a sales office. It then called a plenary of the barrio to discuss the use of the building and the formation of a CM. The first CM was elected with eleven members on June 10, 1975 in that General Assembly, which also decided to use the building as a headquarters and a child-care center. From then on the CM normally had assemblies of up to 300 people once each month (with its own meetings every week) and focused its attention on the problems of the barrio:

- it secured a teacher from IFAS for the child-care center which had twenty children by the winter of 1975-76;

- it sought a good road to Camarinha (the main access to the barrio) and public transportation. The *Câmara* provided the supplies, and the CM put in the road and blacktopped it;
- the bus line was extended into the barrio in mid-December 1975;
- the CM also sought to have the barrio's internal streets finished off. This was done in August 1975;
- lighting for the public areas of the barrio, and water and electricity for the day-care center were all obtained; and
- elevators that did not yet work in some buildings were finally put in working order.

In addition, the CM maintained a number of other activities:

- together with the CM from Camarinha, it maintained a security watch over the primary school between the barrios;
- the headquarters was used for films and theater pieces which were then followed by discussion;
- an adult literacy course was organized in July 1976, with twenty students, mostly women, taught by a Civic Service teacher; and
- finally, at least one issue of a barrio newspaper was produced.

Urban Struggles and Coordinating Bodies

At least one entire vacant building was occupied, in addition to the prefabricated building. Most of the people occupying were from outside the barrio, but in need of housing. Some of them were living in shanties, others living with their families, and still others who had no housing, for example, some army officers. There were also some people living in shanties on the edge of the barrio who took part in this occupation. These occupations were legalized and contracts signed.

Many people from the barrio took part in the struggle for the 500 escudos per room rent, but according to the person interviewed, this was always an individual decision. While this may be true, the CM was also active in the beginning of the struggle, as indicated by a note in the barrio newspaper in August 1975: "Friends, in relation to the payment of the 500 escudos per room, the CM of our barrio—as long as there is no communication to the contrary—thinks that all moradores should continue in the struggle."

The CM did not take part in the city-country link. It did take part in both the earliest and latest intercommissions, although the person interviewed disavowed any participation in the Committee of Struggle (referring to the period before November 25). It also took part in many meetings with others CMs on specific topics, for example, infancy, legalization of CMs.

Other Comments

Finally, the member with whom we spoke reported that "contacts with the *Câmara* always went well." And the *Câmara* supplied materials to open the road between Monte Belo and Camarinha as well as for other repairs.

This CM was affected by the same demobilization that hit most other CMs after November 25. By the end of August 1976, it decided to "freeze" its activities until the population, which was no longer appearing at assemblies, demonstrated more interest. However, a subcommittee continued to operate the day-care center. In January 1977, this subcommittee was still meeting, and involved six of the eleven people who had initially been elected to the CM (all six were production-line workers).

Santa Maria Sul (Interclass: old historic core)

Neighborhood Characteristics

This barrio together with Centro Histórico, covers the area of the medieval city of Setubal, with a significant number of buildings from the eighteenth century, a majority from the nineteenth and some from the twentieth. There has been more renovation in this part and more new construction in the other. Both areas together are often referred to as the historic center of the city. Their separation is based on their being in two different *freguesias* (a geographic boundary provided by a central square surrounded by some stores), and the fact that there was an attempt to organize a CM (although it was not fully successful) that defined its own area as corresponding to the southern part of the freguesia of Santa Maria, thus excluding the area referred to here as the Centro Histórico. Approximately 800 housing units are in this area, all in three- and four-story multiunit buildings, and virtually all rental housing. More than two-thirds of the housing units in this barrio lack an indoor bath and more than one-third lack an indoor toilet. Rents are generally quite low, although a few rents are in excess of 500 escudos per room. Income is also quite low, so while more than 40 percent of families pay less than 5 percent of their income in rent, nearly 20 percent pay more than 20 percent of theirs. Santa Maria Sul appears not to have the extent of very low and high per capita incomes that Centro Histórico has, although this is not certain because a much larger percentage report "variable" incomes, which generally includes both the lowest and highest incomes. Relatively more manual workers live in this barrio than in Centro Histórico: 40 percent of the active population are manual workers, about 25 percent are office workers, and another 20 percent are personal service or commercial employees. An additional 6.5 percent are commercial owners, and there are a few other owners as well. Finally, 57 percent of the family heads are natives of Setubal, while 11 percent have arrived since 1970.

History of the CM

In August 1974, the MDP called a plenary to form a Democratic Commision at the level of the *freguesia* of Santa Maria to struggle for improvements. "Half a dozen people showed" and nothing more was heard of this commission (*O Setubalense*, August 9, 1974).

The first real attempt to form a CM in this barrio came with the formation of a Dynamizing Group (organizing committee) comprising seventeen people on August 28, 1975. This group organized a plenary in early October 1975, attended by more than 100 people, where a pre-CM was elected, composed of the committee and a few others. But despite several more plenaries held over the next few months, the pre-CM was never able to "pass on to become a CM because not enough people showed up."

> The idea of our forming a commission here followed the example of others that were formed and the process that unleashed. We saw that it was necessary that a CM be formed in our area. This initiative came from various members of the Dynamizing Group, which, with the development of the process, grew to include twenty-three members.

> At the beginning people accepted the idea, gave a lot of support, and cooperated until about half way; then they began to lose interest. There began to be problems and more work to do, etc., and they began to pull away. They thought: "when I have a problem I'll go there and take care of it." Sometimes we didn't even know why people turned away and stopped working with the commission.

> It seems to me that people react according to how the political process is: i.e., if it is more to the left they react more to the left, and if it is more to the right they react more to the right. At that time [a few months before the interview] the means of communication were not completely controlled; rather, there was a certain openness, certain leaks that told the people more than they say now. The process is going more to the right and people are drawing back with a little fear.

In January 1976, the CM called a plenary to discuss proposals of the population and the pre-CM for the passage to CM, as well as discussion of the city-country link. It remained a pre-CM due to lack of sufficient attendance.

Then they decided that one way to show the population the usefulness of a CM was to create a playground.

> We tried to make a playground to show the residents some work and that the commission was good for something. We had some problems with it because

the owners of the land didn't agree. This was after November 25th, and we were not strong enough and didn't have a chance.

By ourselves we couldn't do anything. We needed the support of the *Câmara*, but we didn't get much. It gave us strength before November 25th, but afterwards took a step backward. The *Câmara* gave its support in legal processes, and in the so-called illegal ones it had to support what was called "revolutionary law" because there was a certain pressure from the workers, and the *Câmara* was afraid. After the process went to the right they began to retreat. And that was not only in the case of the playground, but also with rental contracts they had signed for occupied houses, and other things . . . .

Urban Struggles and Coordinating Bodies

Besides the children's park, the other main demand of the CM was for repairs to buildings of the barrio, some of which were carried out by the *Câmara*. At least some of the repairs were done in houses the CM helped occupy. The CM member interviewed reported that the CM was involved in the occupation of eight or nine houses within the barrio. In addition, it occupied at least two in an adjacent barrio:

The CMs took the position that they would act in areas that did not belong to them as long as there was no CM formed in that area. We acted as the nearest CM in one area where we occupied two houses.

We had no big problems with occupations. We asked people to tell us if houses were empty; we wouldn't occupy a place that had things inside because that would cause problems and the people occupying wouldn't be secure. With five of the occupations the people are not paying any rent because they are in buildings where the landlord has had a request in the *Câmara* for six years for demolition to build new apartments. The *Câmara* never authorized it before, and certainly won't now. The *Câmara* was not able to help with repairs, etc, since the demolition request had been made, but it did authorize the requisition for water and light.

There was another case that wasn't really an occupation. The landlord refused to sign a lease with the tenant. He wanted to knock down the walls and make the apartment into a warehouse. When we heard about this we went to the *Câmara* who then sent us to COPCON—when we had COPCON and a certain strength of our own we were able to occupy because we always had COPCON on our side—they stopped the landlord from knocking down the wall. The tenant stayed there and gave us the key, and we then gave it to COPCON until the *Câmara* decided what to do. It was finally resolved and the person is depositing his rent in an escrow account because he didn't want to sign a lease.

There were also other houses occupied in Santa Maria Sul by people who did not say anything to the CM, but:

150

> If problems came up after the occupation they would come to the CM. The CM never turned its back on anyone; the CM is here to take care of things.

> People occupying houses never had to leave. Up to now we have had no problems like that; the only disagreements we've had concerned leases: we've sometimes had to insist that people either sign a lease or deposit their rent in escrow. There were also cases where the landlord wanted to put the occupier into the street, but there has been mass support for the occupations, and they haven't been able to put anyone out. Even people who vote for the PS or PPD here wouldn't accept any evictions. The police could put someone out in the street, but I guarantee you that within a few hours the house would be occupied again and the people would be back in.

Finally, the CM also occupied an apartment for its own headquarters in October 1975.

The person interviewed reports there were three cases of people from the barrio involved in the 500 escudos per room rent struggle. The CM took part in the city-country link (it was one of the last to stop sales in June 1976). It also took part in the intercommissions that existed during its own lifetime. The member interviewed says they were all ridden with sectarian division. The real basis of the CMs strength was their link with the CTs, but there was often political division between them. However, while "parties and sectarian divisions always weakened everything, in moments of crisis there was a certain level of basic unity."

Other Comments

> This is all a very new process. We have very little experience and in fact people become frightened when they see that things aren't going like they were; they become frightened, start to abandon things and leave. What we are living through in this country is all very new [recent], and people react according to how things are. Even if people don't seem very involved now, they have changed and learned, and they do think differently.

> After November 25th all the CMs went under. The support they had from COPCON, the *Câmara*, the J.F.—from everyone—ended. We can no longer count on them, and the CMs demobolized but are holding on. Now it's just a matter of holding on until we see what will happen.

In July 1976, four members of the pre-CM were meeting regularly.

Primeiro de Maio (Popular: public)

Neighborhood Characteristics

This barrio is on the extreme eastern side of the city. It is actually an area of municipally owned land, rented in lots on seventy-year leases, on which people have built 500 single-family homes. This barrio began in the early 1960s as an attempt to give a partial subsidy to moderate income people, while also providing access to home ownership. In fact, three-quarters of the houses are owner-occupied. Rental on the rental units seems somewhat high (and may indicate some measurment error) but not excessively so and the levels recored are certainly possible. Rents average 430 escudos per room, with none more than 500 escudos. The age distribution of this barrio is much like the rest of the city, except that there are few young children, and a large bulge of people in the six to seventeen age range. One-half of the active population are manual workers, including some in modern and heavy industry, but with greater weight in more traditional and lesser skilled occupations, while an additional 30 percent work in white-collar jobs. The income level is a little below the average for the city as a whole. Finally, most of the population is either from Setubal or has been there a long time: 41 percent were born there, while an additional 37 percent arrived before 1960; only 8 percent have arrived since 1970.

History of the CM

The first CM was self-nominated in the summer of 1974, in a meeting called by GAPS. At the time, it included the shantytown Terroa de Baixa. There was some tension between the two parts of the barrio (and their representatives on the CM), and the CM fell apart in May 1975, as the result of a confusing story of sectarian and personal manipulation (instrumentalization) by the PCP. The second CM was elected in a plenary in the early summer of 1975, with the presence of a delegate from the MFA. Eight people were elected to the CM which no longer included Terroa.

The demands of the CM focused on improving basic physical and social conditions in the barrio. Initially one of the main demands was for houses for those living in shanties in Terroa, as well as for sewers and water for those houses lacking them. Otherwise the most important problem, as the CM saw things, was to get a school for the barrio. They also demanded a day-care center, a playground, a public telephone, and a canteen for the school.

By the summer of 1976, the CM had cleaned up an area and arranged a playground. It had built a center for cultural and recreational activities, which was also used as a headquarters and was usable as a day-care center whenever IFAS provided an educator. Streets had been improved (again through the work of the CM, although the *Câmara* loaned the equipment), a public telephone had been installed, the CM had organized dances and film showings,[4] and it had the equipment to establish a kitchen in a school, if a building could be provided. If more was not done, the person interviewed believed, it was because of lack of cooperation from other institutions, partly for partisan political reasons ("If I were from their party, I'd have everything."), and partly because no one really thought their problems were important: "Liceu, Salgado, Monte Belo are the barrios who always had the priority in the resolution of their problems."

Urban Struggles and Coordinating Bodies

There were no occupations, nor did anyone from the barrio take part in the struggle for 500 escudos per room rent. The CM also did not take part in the city-country link.

The CM took part in demonstrations of support for the construction workers' strike, and the women of the barrio took food down to the strikers. It also took part in the occupation of the newspaper *O Setubalense*, and "the whole population took part in the demonstrations in support of Otelo."

The first CM had been partly PCP and partly FSP, but fell apart due to internal sectarian struggles. The second CM was left-oriented but tied neither to any particular reformist or revolutionary left party (although the woman interviewed had been a PCP militant for many years). But, while the CM continued to support popular struggles and tried to participate in intercommissions, its experiences were quite bad, and it blamed much of the difficulties of the period on the political parties:

> We went to all of the meetings where all the barrios would come together in the *Câmara* to make the Conselho de Moradores, or popular power, or whatever. We'd get there and find the parties were already there, fighting amongst themselves. And what did that give: we'd get there at 10 p.m., the soldiers were there, and everybody. We'd get there and that struggle would be going on, and it would get to be 11 p.m. and we would have to leave. I had to get up at 5 in the morning—and we were going to stay until midnight with something that was going nowhere, and then begin the meeting at midnight?! And once we'd left, do you know what they'd do? The tactic is always the same; there's always an opportunist, because opportunism didn't end. They already had the list of all the CM that had been there, a lot of commissions, but when they got to the point of voting on things, the ones they wanted were the only ones there, because everyone who got fed up with it had left. If things went badly here in Setubal ... if the Revolution isn't ... well, it was the parties that destroyed everything and nobody else. This happened many times, and I'll say that to their faces. We couldn't stay mobilized like that forever, and we stopped going.

Other Comments: Relations with State Institutions

The CM member who was interviewed gave a strong impression of distrust and bad experience with the majority of institutions with which they had to deal:

- "the *Câmara* just makes things more difficult;" "they make a revolution, but don't change the laws inherited from fascism" [a reference to the process for the distribution of land by the *Câmara*, giving surface rights for seventy years];
- there were some problems with IFAS, which "lacks receptivity and doesn't give support"; "it does not respect the 'organs of popular power'" (negotiations had been carried out with a person from IFAS who finally promised money for a day-care center, if certain guidelines were followed, but who was then transferred and no money was ever provided); "if they're not going to give money they have no business sticking their noses in here."
- (the State proposed the CMs take full responsability for creches, day-care centers, etc) "they want to turn the CMs into bosses [*entidades patronais*]"; "that is the responsibility of the State—the State should create the agencies of technical and material assistance, and the CMs should have an active voice in the choice of personnel and functioning."
- "the survey carried out [by SAAL] was poorly done, bureaucratic, and did not detect the real needs"; "the distribution of houses is incorrect, based on friendship"; "the program is made for those who have money, and not for the poor"; "the architects from SAAL and the *Câmara* do not work properly. Liberty is respect, and if we have no respect we have no liberty."

The one exception to this overall negative response to the institutions concerned the Setubal Planning Office: "GPS had an important role in the dynamization of [local] organization, and in indicating possible ways to solve problems."

Of the eight members elected to the CM in the summer of 1975, only three were still working at the time of the interview in June 1976. The CM was reorganized in a plenary on October 22, 1976.

Casal de Figueiras (Popular: shantytown)

Neighborhood Characteristics

This barrio on the western expansion of the city is largely the result of individuals building their own homes on the outskirts of town during the 1920s and 1930s. According to a survey carried out by the CM, there are 529 housing units in the barrio, including 344 shanties. Some of the rest are more solid, single-family houses, but most are one- or two-story, two- to four-family buildings. Approximately 75 percent of the units lack some kind of infrastructure: nearly all of these lack an indoor bath, 50 percent lack running water, and one-third are without electricity. Two-thirds of the housing is owner-occupied (the figure is higher for the shanties), and rents in the remaining third are quite low. The age distribution on the population is about the same as that of the city as a whole. Almost 80 percent of the economically active population are manual workers, including 16 percent fishermen, 20 percent cannery workers, 4 percent workers in modern and heavy industry, 15 percent construction workers, and 20 percent "other workers". A few people are involved in service and commerce work, as well as about 8 percent office employees. Both family and per capita income are considerably below the city average. Finally, about 90 percent of family heads are from Setubal, and fewer than 2 percent have arrived since 1970.

History of the Barrio

This barrio was always very poor. I was born here fifty-three years ago, when there were only four or five shacks and the neighbors all knew each other. We didn't have any water or electricity, bakery, or grocery store. When it rained, we were in the mud up to our knees. There wasn't anything here. My grandparents lived on the beach below, but they were forced off the beach and sent here where there was nothing because the beach was needed for buildings for classes in a more comfortable situation. That is, since the most underpriviledged classes, living in the worst conditions, couldn't be there mixed in with higher classes, they were pushed off to these fields; and all around us were the rock quarries to build Setubal. Ten or fifteen years ago, when the city began to develop more and the population grew, life began to change here, and the people who couldn't pay the rents down below went where? They came here.

Everything in this barrio was made by the moradores; neither the *Câmara*, nor the government, nor anyone else ever cared about this place. Five or six years ago the moradores began to insist, and went to the *Câmara*, and the *Câmara* put in sewers, but not in the whole barrio. Up to the middle of the barrio there are sewers, but from there on there aren't. There was water up to the middle of the barrio, but the part further up had none. You could count the street lights, and from there up there were none.

The land here was never sold to the moradores; four landlords own it [one has most of it] and rented it out by the year. Five or six years ago when we went to pay, the landlord told us he couldn't receive the money because there was a court process over the land for an inheritance. Then it was sold. ... The new owner wanted to get us out of here and put up big buildings—skyscrapers—that he could then do business with. He once even told us he expected to make some 3,000 to 4,000 contos [thousands of escudos] here. Turns out he was wrong. Patience!

At one point he sent someone to offer to sell us the land for 200 escudos per square meter (he had paid 8). That's how it was done then, that's how big fortunes were made … The delegate the owner sent was very poorly received by the population, who threw stones at him. …

History of the CM

Even before the 25th of April we formed a commission because of the land problem. When we went to the *Câmara* right after April 25th there were three of us, but two were very afraid, saying "Marcelo Caetano will be back and have us arrested," and quit.

Then, even before the new Administrative Commission was nominated to the *Câmara*, the owner tried to carry out some transactions with the land. In a meeting of interested people we nominated a pre-CM to deal with it. With the help of two members from the *junta de freguesia* we had a plenary in a local cafe in July 1974. Some 300 to 400 people were there, and the pre-CM was confirmed as the democratically elected CM.

We were able to at least temporarily stop the owner from selling the land, or building on it, but we didn't want him to go around saying: "the people of the barrio stole my land from me." We wanted to pay, but a price we were able to pay. We knew he paid 8 escudos per square meter, and it wouldn't have bothered us to buy it at 20. He refused, saying he wouldn't sell for twenty or for any-thing, and we could fight it out in the expropriation process.

The people from the planning office [GPS] also told us that expropriation was the only way the barrio would be better off; if each bought his or her own little piece, we'd just continue living there without minimum housing conditions. The land was expropriated, as was the land around it necessary for building a new social barrio [SAAL].

As a result of the requirements of the SAAL process, the CM became a legal *Associação de Moradores* on July 1, 1975.

Other Comments

In addition to resolving the problems mentioned above (lack of hous-ing, expropriation, sewers, water, electricity, improvement of streets), the CM also tried to get a medical clinic and pharmacy in the barrio, a day-care center, and social center, as well as developing programs for the children of the barrio and local primary school. "There is already less misery than before, and many things have been done. [But] people only notice the big things that get done; they don't notice the little things. But the big things can't be done from one day to the next."

By July 1976, the main area and one other had been expropriated, and two others were in process. Electricity and street lights had been installed in the upper part of the barrio, streets were being fixed up (even if slowly), and a subsidy for the construction of a water pump and tank was assured. Both on its own and working with the teachers at the local school the CM had organized sports groups, films, cultural visits (to museums, factories, and so on) and festivals for both Christmas and the Popular Saints.

> Parallel to all this we have continued our main struggle for housing. Our biggest struggle is for the expropriation of the land so that we can build our barrio. We think that workers generally and people of our barrio in particular have entered an epoch in which we, too, deserve houses like any other person. We don't want luxury, but we want to be able to enter a house without having to hear the father told: "Go outside because your daughter wants to undress, she wants to lie down." In many houses here, if the daughter wants to lie down, she has to go over the bed of her father or the father over the bed of the daughter, because there are six people and only one bedroom.

> We think the time when that was necessary is long since past, and if there really has been a revolution in our country, then the most underprivileged class should benefit now. It will take effort and work; we don't want anything we don't work for. We have gone everywhere, but many things have also been cut off from us since the coup of November 25th. Our barrio should have been begun a long time ago, but everything was frozen then; the money was frozen and never appeared again.

> Still, I have faith. Before now, didn't we go to the Fourth Government, didn't we go to the Fifth Government, didn't we go to the Sixth Governemnt? And now if we need to we'll go to this one, too; there is no problem with that, we've gone to all of them.

The member of the CM interviewed also said that: "The *Câmara* has worked with and helped all the AMs. But something happens: there's money for first one barrio, and then for another one when it has problems, but when our turn comes, there's nothing left." Many repairs and improvements have been made, but "they take time and we are always told to wait and be patient."

The CM cooperated with the *Câmara's* attempt to create a priority list and distribute vacant housing according to need (three of the thirty-three families from the barrio on the list got housing), but it thought the struggle for the 500 escudos per month rent was "not correct." On the other hand, the CM went quite early to the *Câmara* to protest threatened expulsion from the land, right after April 25, and returned there when necessary as well to take part in national demonstrations about problems with SAAL or other housing issues. The person interviewed said: "We support all popular struggles at the level of CMs and workers' commissions, including the intercommissions, even though they don't always work too well. Perhaps this is due to lack of experience—this is all a very recent process."

At the time of the interview, in July 1976, the CM continued with regular weekly meetings of its three work groups: construction/repairs ("works"), reception ("to receive the people of the barrio who have something to propose, or some problems"), and culture and sports. They met on Monday, Wednesday, and Friday; on Saturday, the CM held general meetings open to the population of the barrio. The last such meeting had between sixty and eighty people present.

The CM includes several people close to the PCP, or with other political positions. While the members do not support direct action type activities, they do support militant pressuring, which they have found both necessary and successful in the past. As the woman interviewed stated, "We weren't born revolutionaries; it was beaten into us."

Liberdade (ex-Cova do Canastro) (Popular: shantytown)

Neighborhood Characteristics

This shantytown lies in a hollow on the far eastern side of the city. It is composed of some 300 units of single-family housing, generally built by the owners, one-half of which are in very precarious condition, the other one-half somewhat better. More than 80 percent of the units lack some basic infrastructure, including 51 percent without electricity. The barrio as a whole lacks public lighting, and the street entering the barrio is made of dirt and is subject to flooding and gullying in the rain. Three-fourths of the units are owner-occupied, while rents on the remaining one-fourth are quite low by absolute standards (two-thirds are below 500 escudos per month). They may still be significant compared to the income of the families involved, although the mean share of income going to rent is about 10 percent. In addition, 82 percent of the land is rented. The population of the barrio is younger and the rate of participation in the labor force is higher than the city as a whole. Nearly three-quarters of the economically active population are manual workers, with the largest share accounted for by construction workers (31 percent), followed by "other workers" (26 percent) and cannery workers (7 percent). In addition, 12 percent of the population are engaged in personal services, 9 percent are involved in commerce (both street salespeople, as well as regular employees and one store owner), and 3 percent have office jobs. Average family income is about two-thirds the level of the city, although the average worker earns only the minimum wage. Finally, approximately 60 percent of the family heads are from Setubal, while about 10 percent have arrived since 1970.

History of the CM

The barrio's main problem is housing. Like Casal de Figueiras, Liberdade was threatened with expulsion before April 25. In the months preceding the overthrow of fascism, the city had a proposal to renovate this area and put in a park, followed by new development. There was some organizing within the barrio in opposition to this plan. The first CM was formed following the occupation of some housing in the adjacent social housing barrio Humberto Delgado (then Marcelo Caetano), in May 1974, to try to get housing for everyone. It was one of the first barrios to become actively involved in the SAAL process, and following SAAL requirements, it became a legalized AM on February 15, 1975. The other AM legalized at the same time was in Castelo Velho, and both of them took an active role in organizing an intercommission of the shantytown CMs to help them start the SAAL process and obtain housing for all.

The following excerpts from the statutes of the AM Liberdade indicate its goals:

The *Associação de Moradores do Barrio da Liberdade* has the following goals:

A. Improve the housing conditions of the associates:
   1. obtain the land;
   2. promote the construction of houses; and
   3. promote the construction of social and collective equipment (creches, first aid posts, community centers, etc.).
B. Defend the interests of the members before public and private entities:
   1. administer and maintain the patrimony of the Association;
   2. resolve all the problems of the Barrio, or have them resolved by the Public Administration (State, Municipal *Câmara* of Setubal, etc.);
   3. obtain those material benefits for the members that the Board of Directors deems possible and within the limits of the funds of the Association;
   4. organize and carry out cultural and sporting activities that will result in the development of associative spirit; and
   5. make known to other populations with the same living conditions the advantages of the associative life and cooperation. (Article 2)

The Association is at the service of the Moradores of the Barrio da Liberdade and will develop its activities within a solidary and

159

nonlucrative spirit, guaranteeing that in political matters the Association will remain always strictly nonpartisan and absolutely neutral religiously. (Article 3)

Work soon began on constructing the new barrio, and the land was already being prepared in March 1975. But the first of two major problems that were to hit this SAAL project soon arose: the land on which it was being built was not solid. Work stopped after a couple of months, with many of the basic structures already in place. The situation was exploited by the right to show the unsoundness of SAAL, while there were mutual recriminations as to how bad the situation really was, and whose fault it was (the technicians from the SAAL brigade, or the local AM).

A new directive council for the AM was elected in June 1975, comprising six members. This new directive council took a more activist outlook, and their relations with the local SAAL brigade were not as smooth as had been those of the first. In September 1975, a polemic developed as the SAAL brigade accused the CM of not having the power to mobilize the barrio. The CM responded that, contrary to the opinion of the SAAL team, the future day-care center was not yet in proper condition to be used. (In mid-November 1975, there was a note in the local paper asking for kitchen equipment for the future day-care center, in order to get it ready for use.)

The second big problem this SAAL project faced was in part a result of beginning work prematurely, without first having the land expropriated. Legal proceedings had begun because the landlord refused to sell the land, but it was still in court during this period. After work had stopped because of the geological problems, the court imposed an injunction against further construction until the problem of expropriation should be settled. With the coup of November 25, this became even more complicated because, while the laws for expropriating remained in effect, the probable cost increased greatly, and procedural rules were changed to make it more difficult. Nevertheless, the expropriation was finally completed, and by 1978 the housing was ready.

While housing was the issue of principal concern to the AM, it also made many other demands focusing both on basic physical infrastructure and on some social facilities. It demanded sewers, water, lighting, and electricity for those parts of the barrio without them. It also demanded a day-care center, as well as a school and playground. It sought a sports field and improvement of the dirt streets of the barrio. In addition, there were demands for a pharmacy and medical/first-aid post, as well as for facilities for the elderly, and for a consumer cooperative, a general social center for the barrio and a headquarters for the AM.

Although problems existed, work on providing housing began quite early, and progressed reasonably well for a while. Very early on, the SAAL brigade helped provide materials for a wooden building to serve as a social center and CM headquarters. Soon afterward, and as part of the SAAL project, a permanent multipurpose center was built by AC (a major construction company operating under workers' control), which was intended to provide a social center, day-care center, facilities for the elderly, first-aid post and food distribution, etc. Several factories contributed to this by providing either materials or games and toys for children.

Two public baths were constructed, the streets were improved, and electricity and water were extended to buildings that did not have them (although sewers were not put in—it would have been more work, and appeared completely unnecessary given the expectation of moving into the new housing in a matter of months). A cafe was also established and run in association with the AM.

IFAS provided an educator for the day-care center, and a cook and one other aide were paid by the AM. Because a need was ascertained, the AM had decided that instead of using a sliding scale they would simply have one low charge, admit the neediest, and expand when possible. At the beginning of May 1976, thirty children between the ages of two and six were using the center daily; this increased to forty by the end of June. They paid a flat charge of 100 escudos per month per child, which included three meals a day at the center.

Urban Struggles, Coordinating Bodies, and Other Comments

The AM Liberdade was one of the more active ones in the mobilization of the population and militant struggles around SAAL. It took part in almost all of the intercommissions and sold products in the city-country link.

The AM included some people from FEC/ML (later União Democrático Popular—Popular Democratic Union or UDP), and the population generally supported the left. As the person interviewed stated, "The population goes to left demonstrations, but the CM is *apartidária*. There is no support for Eanes in the barrio—almost everyone voted Otelo—they are all communists."

The CM strongly supported the demands and actions of the popular movement, and this support continued long after the popular movement as such was no longer very active. At the time of the interview (July 1976) they were busy taking care of the ongoing concerns of the barrio and were fighting to get construction under way once again. They were still very active a year later, when they commented, "The demonstration of April 25 [1977, commemorating the overthrow of fascism] lost all meaning for poor *moradores* when two slogans were eliminated: 'For the Right to Housing—Housing Yes, Evictions No!' and 'Houses Yes, Shacks No!' "

Guidelines to the Alliance Between the People and the MFA

I. Introduction

The PEOPLE-MFA alliance has been a constant reality of the revolutionary process up to the present moment. The liberating action of April 25, 1974, continued by a whole series of attitudes on the part of the MFA and the progressive political parties and by the measures of a political and economic nature that have been carried out, has made it possible to maintain a sufficient degree of cohesion between the PEOPLE and the MFA. However, the maintenance and consolidation of the PEOPLE-MFA alliance is dependent, in a preliminary analysis, on the satisfaction of the deepest aspirations of the exploited classes. In this regard, the work started on April 25, 1974, must be continued. It is within the scope of a Cultural Revolution, through the application of military and civilian potentialities in the technical, human and material fields, that the People will be decisively mobilized for the Revolution. Experience is beginning to prove the truth of this idea, which is obvious in any case. This *sine qua non* premise of the consolidation of the Revolution is being developed and will create the conditions necessary for the maintenance and consolidation of the Portuguese revolutionary process.

On the other hand, and still with the intention of mobilizing the People for the Revolution, it is necessary that the working masses be assured conditions of active participation, which involves forms of popular organization that are, in practice, democratic, independent, and unitary.

Practical advantage must be taken of this fundamental reality—the PEOPLE-MFA alliance—stimulating and supporting it in order to defend and DYNAMIZE the Revolution that is under way.

Defending and dynamizing the Revolution, in its present phase, involves carrying out the following tasks:

a. Fomenting the revolutionary participation of the masses, in the sense of creating and developing unitary groups, so as to set up real organs of popular power.

b. Defending the Revolution from the attacks of reactionary forces by making people fully aware of the requirements of the process and the need for the creation of defense organisms.

c. Winning the BATTLE OF THE ECONOMY. As long as output is insufficient to meet the overall needs of the country, a great effort must be made by the working masses. It is therefore essential to win the battle of the economy, overcoming the feeble development of the productive forces, extending and developing worker control, enlarging the field of the State sector and seeking to achieve an accumulation that is necessary for our economic independence. To assure the carrying out of the above-mentioned points, care must be taken:

A. *In the Domestic Field*

a. to create and develop a large State sector that is a reflection of the domination of the national economy by a Democratic State, in substitution of a private economy dominated by monopolistic capitalism, which paralyzes the development of production;

b. to replace an agrarian structure with deep feudal roots by another that allows for the expansion of progress, an objective that is clearly defined in the Agrarian Reform, the application of which should be scrupulously controlled by the organized rural working masses;

c. clean-up of the State apparatus as well as its decentralization with a view to the construction of a new State apparatus with a popular basis so that, through effective coordination, the potentialities of the initiatives of the local people's organs can be made dynamic, this being associated with an ample autonomy of decisionmaking and ability to reply in the field of financial power, which will place the product of national labor at the effective service of the working masses;

d. to stimulate and support the forms of control of the means of production by the workers;

e. to define an overall economic policy into which the priority development sectors are fitted; and

f. to define an economic policy for each of those sectors.

B. *In the External Field*

a. to guarantee, up to the ultimate consequences, the carrying out of the process of decolonization in Africa because, in a historical, lucid, and dispassionate perspective, the independent future of Portugal will have to be based on fraternal relations with our former colonies in the domain of political, social and economic relations;

b. to avoid any kind of ideological, political or economic hegemony over the Portuguese revolutionary process; and

c. to guarantee the maintenance of cordial relations with all the peoples of the world; and to consolidate an economic power that will guarantee national independence.

There is no intention of IGNORING THE PARTIES devoted to the construction of socialism or of MILITARIZING THE PEOPLE.

The idea is to seek to create a mass organization which, at the present moment and within a correct perspective of the class struggle, can join together all the workers and take on the concrete tasks of the Defense of the Revolution that have been described above.

It should be explained that the Revolution is defended through the CONSOLIDATION OF EXISTING ACHIEVEMENTS, involving ORGANIZATION, VIGILANCE, WORK, DISCIPLINE and AUTHORITY, and through an EFFECTIVE ADVANCE toward setting up the POWER OF THE WORKING MASSES.

This mass organization, by promoting, through its formation and functioning, the unity of the working masses, will create conditions that will enable the political parties interested in building socialism to find ways of cooperating and achieving mutual understanding that will lead to the unification of their efforts for the correct consolidation of the political vanguard of the revolutionary process.

These objectives involve carrying out the Political Action Program presented by the Council of the Revolution through a unitary practice on the part of the Provisional Government, an information policy at the service of the revolutionary process and the practice by the MFA of exemplary unity, austerity, authority and discipline. This last point includes the revolutionary practice of criticism and self-criticism within the MFA.

In view of the above, the following structure is suggested for the PEOPLE-MFA alliance:

II. Structure of the People-MFA Alliance

A. Organic Explanation

a. The structure of the PEOPLE-MFA alliance will have three basic lines: MFA, Popular, and Governmental.

In this transitional phase, the State apparatus must be cleaned up and progressively replaced. Its administrative and financial powers shall be decentralized, by permitting local initiative under the control, supervision and progressive takeover of power by the popular organisms.

b. The Neighborhood Committees, Workers' Committees, and other basic popular organization will form Local People's Assemblies, for the civil parish or other area to be defined.

c. Municipal Assemblies shall be formed from these Local Assemblies, and so on up to the formation of the National People's Assembly.

d. The physical participation of the MFA will begin in the Municipal and District Assemblies through the Unit Assemblies, in the Regional Assemblies through the Regional Military Assemblies, and in the National Assembly through the Assembly of the MFA. It is to be understood that the Unit Assemblies are assemblies of units of the Army, Navy, and Air Force, and the Security Forces.

e. The Council of the Revolution is the highest organ of national sovereignty.

f. The People's Assemblies are supported by the MFA and organs of the State apparatus and shall exercise control over the public administration of the latter, in which they will participate.

B. Establishing Popular Organizations

a. In the first phase, the Unit Assemblies, through explanatory and informative meetings, will stimulate the formation of Neighborhood and Workers' Committees in places where they do not yet exist. In places where structures of this nature already exist, there will also be explanatory and informative meetings concerning the real objectives of the MFA.

Later, in contact with these basic organizations, information about their practical functioning will be gathered together and the conclusions published in order to improve their proceedings and achieve results.

The organizations will be officially recognized after appreciation by the MFA.

b. In the second phase, over the short term, the formation of Local and Municipal People's Assemblies will be stimulated.

c. In the third phase, over the medium term, the formation of the District People's Assemblies will be stimulated.

d. In the fourth phase, over the long term, the formation of the Regional People's Assemblies will be stimulated.

e. The National People's Assembly, the highest organ of popular participation, will be the last and distant stage in this structure.

III. Statutory Principles

A. Generalities

The proposed popular organization is fundamentally based on the WORKERS' COMMITTEES and NEIGHBORHOOD COMMITTEES. The VIL-

LAGE COUNCILS, COOPERATIVES, LEAGUES OF SMALL- AND MEDIUM-SIZED FARMERS, CLUBS and other basic popular ASSOCIATIONS are also considered to be basic organisms.

Organizations that are being established under various initiatives should link up with the basic organisms defined above—Neighborhood and Workers' Committees—which will enlarge their composition in order to absorb and discipline the intentions to consolidate and guarantee the revolutionary process, as concerns the tasks of the basic organizations mentioned in III.B.b.

In conclusion, the Neighborhood and Workers' Committees and other basic organizations will take upon themselves the tasks involved in the Defense of the Revolution.

The present statutory principles are applicable to those that already exist in the various organizations, which should be amplified in order to include the objectives herein defined.

B. Orienting Principles of the Popular Organization

a. Objective

The fundamental and ultimate objective is the construction of the socialist society defined in the POLITICAL ACTION PLAN of the Council of the Revolution.

As this objective can only be achieved through unity, all the levels of the popular organization should, therefore, be unitary.

This concept of UNITY is defined in the following way:

- independence of any party links;
- democratic representativeness based on populational sectors or units of production;
- association to solve concrete problems.

The best guarantee of the attainment of this objective is the MFA—a supra-party movement—accompanying and encouraging this process by supporting and integrating it and recognizing the organizations which justify it in practice.

b. Tasks of the basic organizations

Besides their specific functions, the Workers' Committees, Neighborhood Committees, etc., should, in accordance with their characteristics, promote the following activities:

- POLITICAL WORK, through information and explanations in the professional or populational sectors;
- SOCIAL ACTION, in the fields of health and assistance, culture and sports, literacy campaigns, housing and town planning, transportation, etc.;

- ECONOMIC ACTION, in the Battle of the Economy, control of the means of production in the nationalized and private sectors, supply and prices, etc.;
- VIGILANCE, in the defense of installations and urban areas through physical permanence in shifts, control of entrances, channelling of information to competent official organs, etc.

In special cases (strategic points of the national economy), on the initiative of the MFA itself and under its control and leadership, this activity may take the form of self-defense tasks; and

- STRENGTHENING OF THE PEOPLE-MFA ALLIANCE, as the constant activity of these organizations.

c. Tasks of the People's Assemblies
The People's Assemblies shall have the following basic missions:

- to transmit the aspirations, opinions and demands of the populations to the appropriate decisionmaking level;
- to intervene in local, regional and national planning through the competent organs, acting as the representatives of the populations;
- to supervise and control the activity of the organs of administration and their ability and the time they take to reply to the needs of the populations; and
- to establish alongside of the local organs of popular power, a people's tribunal to solve noncriminal problems.

C. Process of Formation

a. The leadership of the popular organizations shall be elected at plenary meetings by a show of hands.

b. In the basic organizations, the elected members may be dismissed by the same plenary that elected them.

c. In the People's Assemblies, the elected members may be dismissed by the Assemblies themselves.

D. Composition

a. OF THE BASIC ORGANIZATIONS (Workers' and Neighborhood Committees, etc.)
These shall have their present composition enlarged so as to carry out the tasks defined above.

b. OF THE LOCAL PEOPLE'S ASSEMBLIES

- Delegates of the basic organizations; and

- Delegates of the local governments.

c. OF THE MUNICIPAL PEOPLE'S ASSEMBLIES

- Delegates of the assemblies of the military units;
- Delegates of the Local People's Assemblies; and
- Delegates of the local governments and government bodies.

d. OF THE DISTRICT PEOPLE'S ASSEMBLIES

- Delegates of the assemblies of the military units (including the Commanding Officer of the unit);
- Delegates of the Municipal People's Assemblies;
- Delegates of the local governments and government bodies; and
- Delegates of the trade unions.

e. OF THE REGIONAL PEOPLE'S ASSEMBLIES

- Delegates of the Assembly of the Military Region (including the Commanding Officer of the Military Region);
- Delegates of the District People's Assemblies;
- Delegates of the local government and government bodies; and
- Delegates of the trade unions.

f. OF THE NATIONAL PEOPLE'S ASSEMBLY

- To be defined.

E. Functioning

a. The decisions in all these organizations shall be taken by a show of hands.

b. The representatives of the local governments, government bodies (Regional Planning Bureaus, Agrarian Reform Institute, etc.,) and trade union delegates have the same right to submit proposals, vote and express themselves.

c. The decisions taken by the Assemblies are binding on all the participating organizations.

IV. Final Provisions

A. These principles are not of a rigid nature and their application shall take into account the specific local characteristics and the conditions determined by the dynamics of the process.

B. The present project should be considered a document containing guidelines for the practical action of military units and popular organisms.

The structure corresponding to the present development of the popular organization extends up to the local People's Assemblies.

This phase needs to be duly consolidated. It is through the very dynamics of this process that the feasibility of advancing to higher forms of organization will be verified.

Statutes of the Conselho de Moradores

I. Definition and Objectives of the Conselho de Moradores

1. The Conselho de Moradores shall be the union of all the commissions of Moradores of the city of Setubal, oriented toward organized struggle for the resolution of the problems of the barrios of the city (housing, social infrastructure, health, transportation, etc.).

2. It shall be unitary and nonpartisan.

3. It shall place itself in the vanguard of the people's struggles for the conquest of its rights, and thus must be AUTONOMOUS and INDEPENDENT of any entity before whom it may appear.

4. The activity of this Conselho shall be oriented by the assemblies or plenaries of the respective barrios, and it shall submit itself to the criticism of the popular masses.

5. It shall always act collectively, repudiating all individualist and selfish actions.

6. It shall always try to link the struggle in the barrios with the struggle in the factories.

II. Regulations

A. The Assembly

1. The Conselho de Moradores will hold a regularly scheduled Assembly with three members from each commission present once every two weeks.

a. Special sessions will be held whenever necessary.

2. The members of each commission shall have right to one vote.

a. The members of each neighborhood commission may always vote in the Assembly of the Conselho de Moradores, as long as this is in accord with the spirit of the barrio assemblies.

b. Whenever the commissions find that the questions posed go beyond the spirit of the discussions held in the barrio assemblies, they shall return to consult with the grassroots.

3. The Assemblies of the Conselho de Moradores may be public, but observers shall only have the right to speak (never to vote) when authorized by the Assembly, since it is understood that the matters that would like to see treated should be directly brought up with their neighborhood commissions.

4. Meetings will begin at the time scheduled, with a grace period of 15 minutes, at the end of which the meeting will begin with the members present.

5. A record of attendance will be kept, registered at the entry to the meeting; once the grace period has ended, all entries will be in *red*.

6. A book of minutes will be kept, and the minutes shall be signed by all the members of the Conselho de Moradores. once they have been read and approved by the Assembly.

7. The agenda will be adopted in the preceding Assembly, and can be altered by the Assembly on the day of its meeting.

8. The chair of the assemblies shall always be composed of three members (a president and two secretaries):

a. The two secretaries shall always be nominated by the secretariat, from amongst its members;

b. The president shall be indicated by rotation amongst all of the neighborhood commissions from an alphabetical listing of the names of the barrios;

c. Whenever the members of the commission scheduled to act as president does not wish to chair the assembly, for whatever reason, the presidency shall be exercised by a member of the next commission on the list.

B. *The Members*

1. The Conselho de Moradores shall be composed of 3 members of each comissão de moradores.

2. The following are excluded from membership in the Conselho de Moradores: landlords, owners of construction companies, and any other individuals whose activity is the exploitation of the labor force of another.

C. *The Secretariat*

1. There shall be a Secretariat with 10 members elected in the first meeting of the Conselho de Moradores from amongst those present in the Assembly.

2. Each Neighborhood Commission may have no more than one member in the Secretariat.

3. The members of the Sec. are fixed, are not remunerated, and their position shall last 6 months.

a. Any of its members may be removed whenever the Assembly of the Conselho so determines.

4. The Secretariat has the following functions:

a. Execute the decisions of the Assembly of the Conselho;

b. Convoke special sessions;

c. Register the presences of the members of the Assembly;

d. Prepare the minutes;

e. Take charge of the list of presences and the minutes;

f. Nominate two secretaries, from amongst its members, for the chair of each Assembly;

g. For special tasks, it may request a work group from the Conselho de Moradores.

D. Revision of Principles

The fundamental principals of the Conselho de Moradores can be altered by the decision of its Assembly.

III. Immediate Tasks

A. Support to the struggle of the shantytowns.

B. Support to the struggle to lower rents.

C. Support to the struggle of the peripheral barrios and localities for infrastructure (sanitation, electric energy, water, etc.).

D. Get a HEADQUARTERS for the Conselho de Moradores.

COPS: Proposal for Popular Organization (in the factories, neighborhoods, and barracks)

Only the working classes are competent to decide on their own form of organization. Thus, this proposal does not pretend to be exhaustive or definitive, but is being proposed for discussion in all the workplaces, living places and military units in the area; that is where the conditions necessary to put it into practice will be defined.

I. Background

A. Political and Economic Situation

Fascism as a form of capitalism caused Portugal to be economically and politically dependent on foreign countries. Thus we were obliged to import large quantities of foodstuffs, and our exports were restricted to such sectors as textiles, cork, wine, and electronic materials. All measures designed to increase exports are boycotted by foreign capitalist countries, which, in crisis as well, do not buy our products. At the level of food imports, they demand payment in advance in gold.

Thus we see that all the drastic measures which serve to advance the revolutionary process result in boycott or economic sabotage on the part of national and international capitalism, and cadre identified with capital and with fascism have not been purged, and continue to occupy important positions in the current bourgeois State apparatus. Additional results are the resurgence of a counterrevolutionary campaign at the level of foreign news organs and those domestic news organs at the service of capital, and the distortion of the meaning of the Constituent Assembly elections and later exploitation of that.

B. Lack of Political Definition and the Dilution of Power

After April 25th, two organs of political power arose in Portugal: the MFA and the Provisional Government. Both of them carry within themselves deep-seated contradictions.

a. Analysis of the MFA

Since April 25, the MFA has included "Spinolist and other" members whose political behavior was reflected in the attempt to find a neocolonial solution to the Portuguese colonial problem and in the maintenance of the capitalist and imperialist system in Portugal.

Until March 11, these contradictions were reflected in counterrevolutionary activities, whereas afterwards, this is not what has happened. As Vasco Goncalves observed in his document, which was approved in principle by the MFA Assembly, now these contradictions are reflected in the fact that "It is much easier to characterize an antifascist attitude than a Socialist attitude, mainly because the latter requires that a class option be chosen, and throws open to question the corresponding taboos, namely the class origins of the majority of MFA members. This is the source of the discussions and doubts, and the difficulty in defining ourselves politically."

b. Analysis of the Provisional Government

The existence of a coalition Provisional Government based on class compromise was only possible because of the contradictions within the MFA. That is why there are parties representing capitalist and imperialist interests in Portugal in the government. This is how one can explain the fact that it is almost nonfunctioning.

The workers' response at the political and organizational level is the result of all this, and is determinant.

c. The Creation of Conditions for the Exercise of Power by the Workers

These contradictions can be overcome only through an organized response by the workers, who seek to set up forms capable of seizing and exercising political and economic power as a way reaching Socialism.

For this to occur, there must be a clear ideological definition at the class level, identification of the enemy, and the existence of an organized vanguard.

The organizational forms being proposed will have to respond to all this.

We likewise consider the Institutionalization of Popular Power in the MFA Assembly to be an important advance in the revolutionary process.

II. Preliminary Proposal for Popular Organization

A. In Summary

    a. Workers will have to be organized to take power.
    b. A proposal for workers' organization will have to be drawn up which

looks towards the creation of organizational forms which can take and exercise political and economic power, as the only way of reaching Socialism.

c. Such a proposal for organization would have to include:

- political education of workers;
- purging and replacing personnel;
- workers' control; and
- arming and training workers.

d. Committees of Armed Vigilence will be created as forms of organization which look towards the seizure of power by the working class.

B. *Proposed Statutes*

a. That the Committees of Armed Vigilence be elected in assemblies of firms, neighborhoods, and barracks.

b. That the Committees of Armed Vigilence not be organs of political power, but that they remain within the framework of the political organs of the workers.

C. *Proposal for Organization*

a. The Committees of Armed Vigilence (CVA) in the workplace will be elected in a plenary session of the firm, where at least 2/3 of the workers are present.

- The CVA in the neighborhoods will be elected in a plenary of the neighborhood.
- The CVA in the barracks will be elected in the General Assembly of the Unit.

b. The election of any member may be revoked if the Assembly which elected him/her deems it necessary.

c. The Workers' Commissions, as unitary organs at the base which are essential for the exercise and seizure of power by the working class, must be represented in the SECRETARIAT of the CVA through an election in a meeting of the INTERCOMMISSIONS OF WORKERS.

These meetings should be held soon.

d. The other members of the secretariat will be elected in meetings of:

- the Committees of Armed Vigilence in the Firms;
- the Committees of Armed Vigilence in the Barracks; and
- the Committees of Armed Vigilence in the Neighborhoods.

e. At the Regional level, the process will be similar.

Table D.1

Organigram of the Proposal for Organization by Zone

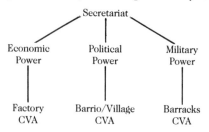

Secretariat: elected in meetings of the INTERCOMMISSION OF WORKERS.

Power: members elected in plenaries of the FACTORY, BAIRRO/VILLAGE, and BARRACKS CVAs, respectively.

CVA: Committees of Armed Vigilance.

This proposal was approved in a preparatory meeting for a Popular Assembly and was to be taken to workplaces, neighborhoods, and barracks in the zone for discussion. It was approved by the majority of Moradores Commissions and Workers' Commissions in the Concelho of Setubal, as well as by representatives of Trade Unions, collectives, and other democratic and popular organizations. At the same meeting it was also decided:

- that the Committee of Unity of the Democratic and Popular Organs would resign;
- that the election of a committee would take place in a representative meeting of all the unitary grassroots organizations (Provisional Coordinating Committee).

This Committee has as its function to dynamize the process in the factories, neighborhoods, and barracks, with the goal being a Municipal Assembly.

APPENDIX E

Occupational Composition of Neighborhoods

Group	Barrio	Occupational Group						
		1	2	3	4	5	6	7
Elite								
A	Liceu	——	0	0	##	##	–	——
	Montalvão	——	——	#	##	0	##	0
B	Ferro de Engomar	——	——	##	#	——	##	——
	Jose Ma da Silva	——	——	##	##	#	——	——
D	Cinco de Outubro	——	##	##	##	——	##	##
Interclass								
A	Alves da Silva	–	——	–	##	##	##	–
	Inf D Henrique	0	0	——	#	##	——	–
	Est de Algeruz	–	0	##	##	##	——	——
	Praça do Brasil	–	——	##	##	#	——	0
	São Gabriel	——	#	##	##	#	——	#
	Monte Belo	0	##	——	0	——	——	0
B	Est dos Ciprestes	——	0	——	##	——	——	##
	Azeda	0	##	0	–	–	#	–
	Baptista/Tebaida	–	##	——	0	——	##	0
C	Na Sa da Conceição	–	——	–	##	——	——	–
D	Salgado	–	##	–	#	——	——	#
	Camilo C Branco	——	##	——	——	##	##	##
	Centro Histórico	–	##	——	——	##	——	#
	Santa Maria Sul	–	##	##	–	——	0	#
	São Domingos	0	##	0	——	##	——	##
	Zona Portuária	0	##	——	0	##	##	——
Popular								
A	Amoreiras	#	——	0	0	——	——	0
	Fonte da Lavra	##	#	——	——	——	##	–
	Areias	#	0	——	0	——	——	0
B	Az da Varzinha	#	–	##	——	##	——	–
	Camarinha	#	0	–	——	##	0	–
	Reboreda	#	##	0	——	——	——	–
C	Afonso Costa	##	–	0	——	——	——	–
	Humberto Delgado	##	——	0	——	——	——	–
	Primeiro de Maio	#	0	0	0	–	——	–
	Vintecinco de Abril	##	0	——	——	0	——	–
	Viso	##	0	#	——	##	——	–
	Pescadores	##	——	——	——	——	——	–

Appendix E

Occupational Composition—Cont'd.

Group	Barrio	Occupational Group						
		1	2	3	4	5	6	7
D	Santos Nicolau	##	--	#	--	–	–	–
	Trindade	#	##	0	--	##	--	##
	Troino	#	#	0	–	--	0	0
E	Casal de Figueiras	##	--	--	--	--	--	–
	Castelo Velho	##	–	#	--	#	--	–
	Dias	##	–	##	--	0	--	0
	Monarquina	##			--		–	
	Liberdade	##	##	0	--	--	--	##
	Maltalhados	##	--	--	--	0	--	–
	Pinheirinhos	##	–	--	--	--	--	##
	Quatro Caminos	#	--	--	0	#	--	##
	Terroa de Baixo	##			--		–	

Key to Appendix E:

1 – manual workers
2 – personal service workers
3 – commerce (owners and employees)
4 – business service workers/white collar professionals
5 – police and military
6 – owners
7 – rural and others

## – very high	(GE)	56.4	11.2	11.9	40.0	3.9	2.0	4.0
# – high	(GE)	49.4	9.2	9.9	35.5	3.2	1.5	3.3
0 – city average		44.4	8.0	8.9	32.5	2.7	1.0	2.8
– – low	(LE)	39.4	6.8	7.7	29.5	2.2	0.5	2.3
-- – very low	(LE)	32.4	4.8	5.5	25.0	1.5	0.0	1.5

APPENDIX F

Complete List of CM Demands

Group	Barrio	Housing	Physical Infrastructure	Social Infrastructure Basic	Elite
Elite					
A	Liceu			oz	1
	Montalvão			ach	12
B	Ferro de Engomar				
	Jose Ma da Silva				
D	Cinco de Outubro				
Interclass					
A	Alves da Silva		hy	mop	
	Inf D Henrique				
	Est de Algeruz				
	Praça do Brasil		hko	op	
	São Gabriel		k	dhgmnps	
	Monte Belo		hoqx	ghiox	
B	Est dos Ciprestes		j	kw	
	Azeda		abcq	dgnq	
	Baptista/Tebaida	2	o	co	
C	Na Sa da Conceição				
D	Salgado			bmnor	
	Camilo C Branco				
	Centro Histórico				
	Santa Maria Sul	2		a	
	São Domingos	2		ao	
	Zona Portuária				
Popular					
A	Amoreiras				
	Fonte da Lavra			acgjkmn	
	Areias				
B	Az da Varzinha		ahion	ado	
	Camarinha		t	ghz	
	Reboreda		l	aghmv	
C	Afonso Costa	3	ht	j	
	Humberto Delgado		hmy	adgmnz	
	Primeiro de Maio		nt	adhoq	
	Vintecinco de Abril	3	m	ajmno	
	Viso		ahluz	afjmn	
	Pescadores		lopt	hjno	
D	Santos Nicolau		op		
	Trindade				
	Troino	12		j	

CM Demands—Cont'd

Group	Barrio	Housing	Physical Infrastructure	Social Infrastructure Basic	Elite
E	Casal de Figueiras	1	bclt	bdnoz	
	Castelo Velho	1	c	m	
	Dias	1			
	Monarquina	1	blno		
	Liberdade	1	abc	abdoprz	
	Maltalhados	1	hpq		
	Pinheirinhos	1	p	cjo	
	Quatro Caminos	1	p	cjo	
	Terroa de Baixo	1		m	

Key to Appendix F, with frequency of demands.

Housing
1. new (includes expropriation of land and rest of process)   (10)
2. major repairs and renovation to existing housing   (5)
3. maintenance   (2)

Physical Infrastructure
1. new provision
   a. sewers   (4)
   b. electricity   (3)
   c. water   (4)
   d. streets   (0)
2. major repairs/works
   h. street pavement, access to interior of barrio   (8)
   i. cut fields surrounding barrio   (1)
   j. drain swamp   (1)
   k. put in sidewalks   (2)
   l. increased water or electrical capacity   (4)
   m. unclog plumbing or sewers   (2)
   n. extend infrastructure to minority lacking them   (2)
   o. street lighting   (6)
   p. sewers, electricity, water for public use areas   (5)
   q. access road   (3)
3. maintenance, repairs, or "finishing" of barrio
   t. street repairs   (5)
   u. fence in dangerous areas   (1)
   x. put elevators in working order   (1)
   y. finish buildings and area (stairway railings)   (2)
   z. access stairway   (1)

Social Infrastructure-Community Facilities
Basic
1. traditional basic infrastructure and integration
   a. playground   (11)
   b. first-aid clinic   (4)
   c. traffic signs and signals   (5)
   d. school   (7)
   f. public bath house   (1)

CM Demands—Cont'd.

g. bus stop/route   (7)
h. telephone booth   (7)
i. mail box   (1)
j. clean up/pick up trash   (8)
k. provide trash cans   (2)
l. exterminate rats   (1)
2. new basic social infrastructure (community facilities)
m. headquarters for CM   (10)
n. community center   (9)
o. day-care center   (17)
p. sports playing field   (4)
q. canteen for school   (2)
r. old-age center   (2)
s. park   (1)
t. library
u. canteen for workers, neighborhood people
3. maintenance of existing equipment
v. sufficient space for buses to turn around   (1)
w. shelters for bus stop   (1)
x. water, electricity, personnel for day-care center   (1)
4. social infrastructure for a wider area
z. pharmacy   (5)

Elite Social Infrastructure
1. traditional—parking lot   (2)
2. new—heating for swimming pool   (1)

Complete List of CM Accomplishments

Group	Barrio	Housing	Physical Infra-structure	Social Infrastructure Basic	Social Infrastructure Elite	Community Control	Cultural Political/ Sports
Elite							
A	Liceu			jotz		f	am
	Montalvão			aj			ak
B	Ferro de Engomar						
	Jose Ma da Silva						
D	Cinco de Outubro						
Interclass							
A	Alves da Silva			mop		fm	12m
	Inf D Henrique						
	Est de Algeruz						
	Praça do Brasil		hko	amo			m
	São Gabriel			djmnu			m
	Monte Belo		hoqx	gowx		fp	ghil
B	Est dos Ciprestes		j	kw			m
	Azeda		cq	dm		f	
	Baptista/Tebaida	2	o	cjo		q	m
C	Na Sa da Conceição						
D	Salgado	2		mout		fm	ilkm
	Camilo C Branco						
	Centro Histórico						
	Santa Maria Sul	2				e	m
	São Domingos	2					m
	Zona Portuária						
Popular							
A	Amoreiras						
	Fonte da Lavra			acgjkm			m
	Areias						
B	Az da Varzinha		i			acefphn	abhij
	Camarinha			jz			
	Reboreda		l	ajm		a	afhlm
C	Afonso Costa	3	ht	o		b	b
	Humberto Delgado		hy	amnp			acdg
	Primeiro de Maio		t	ahmn			ah
	Vintecinco de Abril	3	m	jmnot		f	
	Viso		huz	mn			
	Pescadores		no	j		d	

CM Accomplishments—Cont'd

Group	Barrio	Housing	Physical Infra-structure	Social Infrastructure Basic	Elite	Community Control	Cultural Political/ Sports
D	Santos Nicolau						
	Trindade						
	Troino	2	n	m		f	him
E	Casal de Figueiras	1	blt				bhk
	Castelo Velho	1	c	m			
	Dias	1					
	Monarquina	1		lmn			a
	Liberdade	1	c	fmon			am
	Maltalhados	1	aq				
	Pinheirinhos	1					
	Quatro Caminos						am
	Terroa de Baixo	1		m			

Key to Appendix G, with frequency of accomplishments.

Housing
1. new (includes provision of land and rest of process) (9)
2. major repairs and renovation to existing housing (5)
3. maintenance (2)

Physical Infrastructure
1. new provision
   a. sewers (1)
   b. electricity (1)
   c. water (3)
   d. streets (0)
2. major repairs/works
   h. street pavement, access to interior of barrio (5)
   i. cut fields surrounding barrio (1)
   j. drain swamp (1)
   k. put in sidewalks (1)
   l. increased water or electrical capacity (2)
   m. unclog plumbing or sewers (1)
   n. extend infrastructure to minority lacking them (2)
   o. street lighting (4)
   p. sewers, electricity, water for public use areas (0)
   q. access road (3)
3. maintenance, repairs or "finishing" of barrio
   t. street repairs (4)
   u. fence in dangerous areas (1)
   x. put elevators in working order (1)
   y. finish buildings and area (stairway railings) (1)
   z. access stairway (1)

Social Infrastructure
Basic
1. traditional basic infrastructure and integration
   a. playground (7)
   b. first-aid clinic (2)
   c. traffic signs and signals (2)
   d. school (1)
   f. public bath house (1)

CM Accomplishments—Cont'd.

g. bus stop/route (2)
h. telephone booth (1)
i. mail box (0)
2. new basic social infrastructure
    m. headquarters for CM (16)
    n. community center (7)
    o. day-care center (9)
    p. sports playing field (2)
    q. canteen for school (0)
    r. old-age center (0)
    s. park (0)
    t. library (1)
    u. canteen for workers, neighborhood people (2)
3. maintain existing equipment
    v. sufficient space for buses to turn around (0)
    w. shelters for bus stops (2)
    x. water, electricity, personnel for day-care center (1)
4. social infrastructure for a wider area
    z. pharmacy (2)
Elite Social Infrastructure
1. traditional—parking lot (0)
2. new-heating for swimming pool (0)

Community Control
1. control over local resources
    a. allocation of use of housing (2)
    b. put creche to service of the barrio (1)
    c. coordinate list of abandoned housing and needy (1)
    d. distribution of unoccupied housing (1)
    e. carrying out housing occupations (2)
    f. occupation for CM headquarters or social functions (9)
2. control of consumer prices
    h. food and other retail prices (1)
3. general social control
    m. closed down or converted night clubs (2)
    n. control of noise from vehicles (1)
    p. security force for barrio (2)
    q. internment of mentally ill person (1)

Cultural, Political, and Sports Activities
1. traditional activities
    a. festivals for the popular saints (10)
    b. sports activities (2)
    c. choral group (1)
    d. carpentry shop (1)
2. new types of activities
    f. "dynamizing people" (1)
    g. put out barrio newspaper (2)
    h. show films (8)
    i. literacy classes (4)
    j. sell books and pamphlets (1)
    k. visits by children to factories, cultural centers (3)
    l. theater performance (4)
    m. city-country link (12)

SAAL Projects in Setubal

Barrios	Families	Association Legalized
Casal de Figuieras	310	July 1, 1975
Castelo Velho "Grito do Povo"	67	February 15, 1975
Dias "UnidosVenceremos"	124	Post-November 1975
Liberdade	230	February 15, 1975
Monarquina "Barrio do Paz"	107	Post-November 1975
Quatro Caminhos, Pinheirinhos, Maltalhados "A Luta do Povo"	170	September 12, 1975
Terroa de Baixo	43	Post-November 1975

Communique from the Setenave Housing Group Communique from the Workers

Comrades:

The Setenave Working Group on Housing met on February 5, 1976, to analyze the problem of housing in Setubal, after having made several contacts at the technical and bureaucratic level and having reached the conclusion that no State organ (F.F.H., Gabinete de Planeamento da Habitação de Setúbal, Câmara Municipal, etc.) is willing to take our analysis and proposed solution to the problem to the Central Government. This conforms to point #10 of our report dated December 5, 1975, which states the following:

> The Working Group, in an attempt to find short-term, viable solutions which are compatible with both the needs and the economic capabilities of the workers, suggests that governmental measures be taken to immediately utilize the existing housing in Setubal (calculated at about 3,000 units) by means of expropriation, purchase with indemnization (purchase at 4000 escudos per square meter seems to already include values which would allow indemnization of the owners), or any other method which would make it possible to put these currently uninhabited houses at the disposition of workers for monthly rents they can afford (for example 15 percent of earnings, which is already very high considering that in social democratic countries they defend the principle that rent for housing should never exceed 12 percent of family earnings). It is also suggested that insofar as new construction is concerned, there ought to be a socially oriented land-use policy and a policy of direct aid to construction workers, either through financing which is currently given to contractors, or through official technical aid.

The time has come to demand, once and for all, that those in power set forth on the road to a more just and socialist society.

Our proposal should be put into practice immediately, thus guaranteeing one of the most basic human rights, to live in a house and not in a shack. We will go and discuss this problem with the Minister of Social Welfare and the Environment, and we intend that this same minister will be our spokesperson in the Council of Ministers.

All the workers in the city are part of this struggle, namely, ENI, Secil, Entreposto, Movauto, IMA, etc. They will be willing to move forward with this task no matter what form the struggle will have to take. All news organs in the country will receive a copy of this communique.

THE EMANCIPATION OF WORKERS IS THE TASK OF THE WORKERS THEMSELVES

HOUSES YES, SHACKS NO

THE STRUGGLE CONTINUES, VICTORY IS CERTAIN

Mitrena, February 10, 1976

Abbreviations Used

CA   —Comissão Administrativa
         Administrative Commission (municipal)

ADFA   —Associação dos Deficientes das Forças Armadas
         Association of Disabled Veterans

AM   —Associação de Moradores
         Shantytown Residents' Association (for SAAL)

CAM   —Comissão Administrativa Militar
         Military Administrative Commission (City of Oporto)

CDS   —Centro Democrático Social
         Democratic Social Center

CICAP   —Centro de Instrução em Condução de Auto do Porto
         (military training center, Oporto)

CM   —Comissão de Moradores
         Neighborhood Commission

COPCON —Comando Operacional do Continent
         Continental Operational Command (military)

COPS   —Comité dos Organismos Populares de Setúbal
         Committee of the Popular Organizations of Setubal

CRMP   —Conselho Revolucionário de Moradores do Porto
         Revolutionary Council of Moradores of Oporto

CS   —Comissão de Soldados
         Soldiers' Commission

CT   —Comissão de Trabalhadores
         Workers' Commission

FEC/ML   —Frente Eleitoral Comunista/Marxista Leninista
         Communist Electoral Front/Marxist Leninist

FFH —Fundo de Fomento de Habitação
Housing Development Fund (Ministry of Housing)

FNLA —Frente Nacional para a Libertação de Angola
National Front for the Liberation of Angola

FSP —Frente Socialista Popular
Popular Socialist Front

GAPS —Grupo de Acção Popular Socialista
Socialist Popular Action Group

GDUP —Grupos Dinamizadores de Unidade Popular
Popular Unity Organizing Groups

GPS —Gabinete de Planeamento de Setúbal
Setubal Planning Office

ICBB —Intercomissões dos Bairros de Barracas
Shantytown Coordinating Commission

IFAS —Instituto da Família e Assistência Social
Institute of Family and Social Assistance

JSN —Junta de Salvação Nacional
Junta of National Salvation

LCI —Liga Comunista Internacional
International Communist League

LUAR —Liga de União e Acção Revolucionária
League for Revolutionary Unity and Action

MDP/CDE —Movimento Democrático Português/Comissões Democráticas
Eleitorais
Portuguese Democratic Movement/Democratic Electoral
Commissions

MES —Movimento da Esquerda Socialista
Left Socialist Movement

MESA —Ministério de Equipamento Social e do Ambiente
Ministry of Community Facilities and the Environment

MFA —Movimento das Forças Armadas
Armed Forces Movement

MPLA —Movimento Popular para a Libertação de Angola
Popular Movement for the Liberation of Angola

189

NATO —North Atlantic Treaty Organization

PAP —Plano de Acção Política
Political Action Plan

PCP —Partido Comunista Português
Portuguese Communist Party

PPD —Partido Popular Democrático
Popular Democratic Party

PRP/BR —Partido Revolucionário do Proletariado/Brigadas
Revolucionárias
Revolutionary Party of the Proletariat/Revolutionary Brigades

PS —Partido Socialista
Socialist Party

RASP —Regimento de Artilharia Pesada da Serra do Pilar
(heavy artillery base, Oporto)

RIS —Regimento de Infantaria de Setúbal
Setubal Infantry Regiment (military base)

SAAL —Serviço Ambulatório de Apoio Local
Mobil Local Support Service

SUV —Soldados Unidos Vencerão
Soldiers United Will Win

UDP —União Democrático Popular
Popular Democratic Union

UNITA —União Nacional para a Independência Total de Angola
National Union for the Total Independence of Angola

Factories Mentioned

CUF	Chemicals and diversified heavy industry
Entreposto	Automobile assembly
IMA	Automobile assembly
Lisnave	Ship repairs and construction
Movauto	Automobile assembly
Propam	Yeast and bread products
Sapec	Chemical products
Secil	Construcion materials
Setenave	Ship repairs and construction

Siderurgia	Steel mill
Signetics	Electronics assembly
Socel	Paper products

Monetary Conversion

April 1974:	One US Dollar = 24 Escudos
April 1975:	One US Dollar = 24 Escudos
April 1976:	One US Dollar = 30 Escudos
April 1977:	One US Dollar = 39 Escudos

One Conto = 1,000 Escudos

Notes

CHAPTER ONE

1. This study's emphasis on the role of grassroots organizations in developing the Portuguese revolutionary process may seem strange to some who share the common misconception that it was the Armed Forces Movement (MFA) that brought about the changes that took place in Portugal. While the MFA obviously played the key role in the overthrow of the forty-eight-year-old fascist regime on April 25, 1974, this study shows that the armed forces had little direct role in the development of the community organizations (CMs) and their activities. If they had a role, it was *not repressing* grassroots activity and allowing it to develop, rather than initiating or carrying out the changes that took place. This role is illustrated in an April 1975 letter from the local military base to a newly formed CM in Setubal:

> Acknowledging receipt of your communication requesting our aid in the organization of your CM. At the moment there is nothing that occurs to us to explain to you, given that you have already indicated the principal goals. We only remind you that the initiatives you undertake should come from yourselves. The CM should be united and dynamic. When necessary and convenient for your endeavors, contact the appropriate services of the municipal and other government agencies.

The MFA's role was critical in that it *permitted* ordinary people and their organizations to develop, decide democratically and act in ways that would normally have been repressed. This allowed social experiments and conflicts to develop according to their own logic, permitting the development of democratic mass activity which generated a new model of society and a social agent prepared to struggle for it.

2. See Tilly (1978); Gurr (1970); Ash (1972); Gamson (1975); Useem (1975); Fainstein and Fainstein (1972); Rude (1964); Wolf (1969); and Hobsbawm (1963).

3. Still, this factor may enter in important ways in specific parts of movements; for example, it was in response to the threat of layoffs and plant closings that factory occupations and experiments in workers' self-management developed in Portugal, especially in textiles and construction.

4. See Castells (1973a, 1973b, 1977a, 1977b, 1983); Dunleavy (1980); Fainstein and Fainstein (1972); Gamson (1975); Henig (1982); Lowe (1986); Piven and Cloward (1977); and many articles in the journals *Espaces et Sociétés* and the *International Journal of Urban and Regional Research*.

5. Other frequently cited aspects include: public opinion (Lipsky, 1975), the state of the "movement community" (Useem, 1975 and Schwartz, 1971), openness of

government (Henig, 1982 and Nelson, 1979), repression and other aspects of the antag-onists reactions (Tilly, 1978 and Gamson, 1975), and general economic and social con-ditions (Pickvance, 1985). See Piven and Cloward (1977:32-34) for further examples.

6. Borja (1974) presents a similar argument and breakdown of protest, democratic, and dual power movements on the basis of his research in Chile in 1973. His typol-ogy is discussed in Kusnetzoff (1977) and Walton (1979).

7. Poulantzas (1976) and Skocpol (1979), among others, have made similar argu-ments regarding the development of revolutionary situations.

CHAPTER TWO

1. For a detailed history of the captains' movement before April 25, 1974, see Rodrigues, et al. (1974) and Saraiva de Carvalho (1978).

2. When studies of the strike wave before April 25 were later carried out, the only source for most information proved to be the reports of the various police agencies. See especially, *Análise Social,* 1975: 42-43.

3. While it was now relatively rare, the police or army were still used to end a few strikes. This happened primarily in the communication and transportation sectors (post office, airline), and these were cases where the main demands were not eco-nomic, but rather for purging the old administrators. This also led to the first cases of low ranking officers siding with the strikers and refusing to carry out orders (on June 20), in the postal strike.

4. See Lima dos Santos, et al. (1976 and 1977). By the end of June, such strikes had taken place in textiles, shipbuilding, bread, cork, pharmaceutical products, public transportation, postal service, oil refining, insurance, watch assembly, and others. The real wage for urban workers increased an estimated 25 percent during 1974.

5. Many unions had been demanding a minimum wage of 6000 escudos per month.

6. The Intersindical included all of the major political tendencies in the workers' movement, with the Communist Party holding the strongest influence.

7. The MDP/CDE was considered close to the Communist Party, but involved mem-bers of other parties and unaffiliated individuals as well.

8. Unsuccessful struggles arose against Applied Magnetics in the summer and Signetics in December 1974.

9. That is, Spínola, who sought a federal solution to the colonial wars, wanted as limited purging as possible, and, because he wanted to integrate Portugal economi-cally more into Europe, he sought to maintain its "comparative advantage" of cheap labor; in addition, he had learned as Military Governor of Guine that, in his own words, "democracy is the best way to govern people."

10. Recognized in the draft Program of the MFA, but changed in the final Program at Spinola's insistence. See Saraiva de Carvalho, 1978.

11. Nuno Portas, Secretary of State for Housing and Urbanism, interviewed in *República,* August 30, 1974.

12. Decree-law 445/74. Early demolition was one response of landlords to control over their right to rent their housing as they wished.

13. Decree-law 660/74, November 24, 1974.

14. See "Um Contributo para a Analise do Proceso de Ocupacoes em Lisboa e Arredores," Instituto Superior de Serviço Social, mimeo, 1975.

15. In January, the Alvor Agreement established a transitional government for Angola composed of the three Angolan liberation movement, MPLA, FNLA, UNITA and Portugal, with independence to come on November 11, 1975.

16. They had been told the base was under the influence of Tupamaros and other foreign terrorists.

17. In addition to finance, the sectors nationalized included electricity, air and sea transport, petroleum refining and distribution, cement, tobacco, plastics, rail and road transport, and glass products.

18. This discussion does not include the reactions of those who had opposed these changes but were forced to adapt to them.

19. A slogan of the occupiers' movement.

20. COPCON was the military force created in July 1974, to "intervene directly to maintain and establish order, in support of and at the request of the civilian authorities," rather than having to depend on the unreliable and disliked police and national guard inherited from fascism. Over time it began giving more support to the popular movement, and in April 1975, its commander said: "The Comissões of Moradores are small cells intensely living the revolution; thus, I give them my full support in as much as they can be the real advisors for the resolution of the housing problem."

21. In a Service Order of May 31, 1975 the Comissão Administrativa Militar (Military Administrative Commission or CAM) declared it "recognizes the CMs of the barrios camararios [city-owned public housing barrios, built since the late 1950s, and famous for their Draconian internal regulations] and other CMs as organs of effective collaboration and participation in the decisions within the power of the President of the *Câmara* and of the Camara Municipal of Oporto . . . Within thirty days, these commissions should present a proposal for their organization, procedures and functions."

On June 17, 1975 the CAM announced that "as of today the Administrative Commission will meet weekly . . . with the true representatives of the workers of this city." Until a final structure could be created, a temporary consultative commission was set up composed of six representatives of the CMs (three from the barrios camararios and three from the other CMs), three from the *juntas de freguesia*, and three from the municipal workers. The last meeting of the Municipal Council on September 5, 1975, already included representatives from the trade union confederation and the volunteer firemen, and it was announced that representatives of the soldiers and police would soon join.

The Municipal Council formally ended with the early September resignation of the CAM, in response to both military and civilian objections to its activities, and with the change of conjuncture leading up to the Sixth Provisional Government. A short struggle to defend the CAM and the Municipal Council followed, but they were soon lost in other events.

The Municipal Council did not exist long enough to demonstrate how it would function as a permanent institution, nor what interests would eventually have become dominant as the number of groups and representatives increased. But two things are clear. In this period, bureaucratic decisions that had been stalled for months in the *Câmara* were finally dispatched, and major practical advances were made. On the other hand, it was a time of political demobilization, partly as a result of the sudden ease in getting things done. See Botelho and Pinheiro (1976) for a history of the Municipal Council.

22. Such as the announcement by one Lisbon CM that as of October 1, 1975, it would take the place of the landlord in the renting of housing in its area, or the early October decision by workers at the main chemical factory (CUF) to lower fertilizer prices and provide direct delivery to agricultural cooperatives. See Chapter Three for more examples.

23. The most advanced such center was the Setubal Committee of Struggle discussed in Chapter Three.

24. The negative judgment of at least one sector of the international community was shown by the ITT decision, announced September 10, 1975, to cease further investments and disavow responsibility for debts incurred by its Portuguese subsidiaries.

25. The right's action was planned in advance to take on the appearance of a defensive countercoup, and its offensive nature has generally not been admitted. However, because it was a planned, purposive action, and not merely defensive, I will refer to the events at the end of November 1975 as a right-wing coup.

CHAPTER THREE

1. A few months earlier the landlord had sent a representative to offer to sell the tenants the land at a high price. According to the head of the CM interviewed two years later, "he was very poorly received by the population, who threw stones at him."

2. Not all the members of the delegation went down to city hall, because some were afraid fascism would soon return.

3. Other examples include employees of the local newspaper *O Setubalense*, and of a large modern shipyard, Setenave.

4. For example, Socel was occupied since only the pay increases not the administrative purges demanded on May 1, 1974, were granted; Propam was also occupied.

5. Interview with Francisco Lobo, *Câmara* President from July 1975 to December 1976, quoted in Downs, et al. (1978). Lobo, who was vice president from May 1974 to July 1975, had a much respected personal history that included involvement in an attempted military coup against the fascist regime in 1962, leading to a term in prison followed by blacklisting from his previous job. After release from prison, he left the Lisbon area, moving to Setubal where he worked in an auto assembly plant and was involved in clandestine union activity.

6. The Concelho of Setubal (the geographic area governed by the *Câmara*) contains six *freguesias*, four of them corresponding closely to the urban area (the "city") of Setubal, and two that are rural.

7. These attempts continued as late as November 1974.

8. A Setubal-based organization, soon to form part of the left-wing of the Socialist Party, and then the left breakoff to form the Frente Popular Socialista (Socialist Popular Front or FSP).

9. Formed by part of the elite which had previously supported Marcelo Caetano.

10. Castelo Velho and Liberdade with sixty-seven and 230 families respectively, legal-ized on February 18, 1975.

11. The most active barrios in the early phases of the ICBB were Castelo Velho, Liberdade, Pinheirinhos, and Quatro Caminhos, although it also included the rest of the shantytowns of the city, as well as Primeiro de Maio which then represented Terroa de Baixo.

12. The SAAL struggle had less importance in Setubal, where about 5 percent of the urban population lived in shantytowns, than it did in Lisbon or Oporto where the figure was estimated as high as 25 percent. Nonetheless, the shantytowns provided about 20 percent of the CMs and their own leadership for urban struggles.

13. Beginning February 18, 1975, with the expiration of Decree-law 445/74, the law obliging landlords to rent vacant housing, discussed in Chapter Two.

14. While many people had the impression that several hundreds of occupations took place (one person estimated 1500), all indications are that the number was much lower. Nearly all these occupations were in run-down housing in older parts of the city. Because a February housing survey by the *Câmara* had found about 450 vacant old housing units, of which fewer than one half were considered to be in habitable condition, and because fewer than 100 occupations were legalized by May, I estimate the total number of occupations between 200 and 250, that is, including virtually all the habitable vacant housing not rented out in the meantime plus a certain share of the housing in worse conditions.

15. The meeting was called by Pinheirinhos, Quatro Caminhos, and Maltalhados, and was attended by Vintecinco de Abril, Dias Monarquina, Primeiro de Maio, Humberto Delgado, Castelo Velho, and Liberdade.

16. The main CM participants were Amoreiras, Azeda, and Sao Gabriel.

17. The data from Setubal indicate this presumption may be false, or at least that it depends strongly upon the percentage level chosen as the limit. The barrios with the highest rents were also the ones paying the highest percentage of income toward rent. A rent level of 20 percent of income would have affected basically the same barrios—and many of the same people—as did the struggle for 500 escudos per room rent.

18. According to the 1976 Social Economic Survey, rents in the newer barrios aver-aged over 700 escudos per room, while in the rest of the city the average was under 200 escudos per room. Some 1,750 units cost more than 500 escudos, according to estimates from that survey.

19. Data is not very good, but the coordinators of the struggle estimated 1,500 fami-lies were involved in November 1975, with a minimum of 1,200 in January 1976.

20. In practice most of the "reformist" CMs were not directly affected by this struggle, while it was instrumental in creating new radical CMs, as discussed in Chapter Four.

21. From the Minutes of the Conselho meeting on June 7, 1975.

22. Ibid.

23. FSP, LCI, LUAR, MDP, MES, PCP, PRP/BR.

24. F. Brinca, participant and local journalist, interviewed July 13, 1976.

25. The slogans were: contra o fascismo, contra o capital, ofensiva popular; contra o fascismo, abaixo a social democracia, independencia nacional; operarios, camponeses, pescadores, soldados e marinheiros, unidos venceremos; trabalhadores, soldados, moradores, asembleias populares; casas sim, barracas nao; avancar e armar poder

popular; soldados e marinheiros sempre sempre ao lado do povo; operarios, camponeses, pescadores a mesma luta; militares revolucionarios unidos com o povo
trabalhador; morte ao ELP, morte ao fascismo e a quem o apoiar; aplicação imediata
do documento do COPCON; fora os Nove e tambem quem os promove; contra o
desemprego, contra o capital, poder popular; abaixo a social democracia.

26. See its *Minutes* #75-34 and 75-38.

27. A few days later, there were two cases of different people simultaneously occupying the same vacant apartments. They were eventually resolved by the respective
CMs supported in their authority by COPCON.

28. These goals were expressed in the slogans of the demonstration:

- Reactionaries out of the barracks, Now!
- Soldiers always, always on the side of the people!
- For the dictatorship of the proletariat!
- Against the purging of the left!
- Against the Sixth Government, popular offensive!
- Out with the trash, power to those who work!

(*O Setubalense*, October 17, 1975)

29. The absence of some of the CTs was clearly related to a tactic of the PCP, which
was trying to create an "Industrial Belt of Setubal," as it already had done in Lisbon,
composed of CTs and unions in which it had a dominant influence. Whether this
would have succeeded, and whether it would have destroyed, strengthened, or left
untouched the Committee of Struggle (as a mixed organization) is impossible to know.

30. In an attempt to undercut the activities of the CMs, the Socialist Minister of
Education prohibited their use of schools for meetings as of December 15.

31. In at least one building in Alves da Silva, all the tenants negotiated together with the
landlord, and they finally agreed upon the following rents: three rooms at 1700 escudos
and four at 2200 escudos, rather than 2800 escudos and 3300 escudos, respectively.

32. The CMs that actually attended, in addition to the CTs of the project, were
Primeiro de Maio, Humberto Delgado, Padeiras (Vale de Ana Gomes—a peripheral
area of the city), Santa Maria Sul, Pescadores, Liberdade, AM Luta do Povo (Quatro
Caminhos, Maltalhado, and Pinheirinhos), and AM Casal das Figueiras.

33. All seven projects did eventually go ahead, in spite of many delays with expropriations, financing, and construction, and the roughly 1,050 families initially involved
were rehoused between late 1977 and 1979. Overall the completion rate was much
higher in Setubal than in other parts of the country.

CHAPTER FOUR

1. Table 4.3 indicates the formation of the first CM in each barrio. Once a CM was
formed it would continue to go through other processes of renovation, disintegration,
and so on; some of these will be considered later, but here we are focusing only on the
initial CMs. There were cases where a single CM initially covered two barrios and later
divided, and one case where CMs from two contiguous modern expensive barrios
(Popular and Elite) merged into a single CM. Each barrio is considered separately in
both situations. Housing conditions are classified as A—modern expensive, B—modern
inexpensive, C—public housing, D—old traditional housing, and E—shantytowns.

2. Two actually ended while four others decided that with the lack of active support it was better to suspend activities although not to dissolve the CM. Some of them reappeared soon afterward in citywide meetings.

3. This group includes the CMs with the reputation of being the most hostile and "violent" toward the *Câmara*—although no physical violence ever occurred.

4. Of the two that were not shantytowns, one was composed primarily of deteriorated housing and the other had serious infrastructural problems (sewers) that it tried unsuccessfully to resolve through the *Câmara*.

5. The three shantytowns in this group shared several characteristics. Two of them had physical and economic conditions that were among the most precarious in the city and consciously eschewed militant action (Monarquina spoke proudly of its "nonviolent" reputation with the *Câmara* and SAAL), while all three had earlier been joined with other barrios in CMs that split in highly divisive factional fighting. These were the three shantytowns whose SAAL projects were *least* advanced by summer 1976, while the ones with the most "violent" or militant reputations had the most advanced projects.

6. Three were public housing barrios that dealt with the *Câmara* as landlord; the other two had more idiosyncratic reasons for maintaining their distance from the *Câmara*.

7. These three were still somewhat special cases, because two were public housing barrios and the third had the occupation forced upon it by a labor struggle in a preschool in the barrio.

CHAPTER FIVE

1. Topalov (1976) argues that before 1974, Portuguese housing was being built primarily for a luxury market, far beyond the economic capabilities of all but a very small percentage of the population. This is substantiated by comparing the median asking price for the approximately 600 housing units on the market (but not selling) in Setubal in 1975, with the price for government-guaranteed construction for moderate income families two years (and 40 percent inflation) later: one bedroom apartments went for 341 contos (US$14,210) in 1975 and 325 contos (US$8,330) in 1977, two bedroom for 490 and 373 contos, three bedroom for 589 and 498 contos, and four bedroom for 655 and 544 contos, respectively.

2. Four were the result of occupations of abandoned buildings (carried out by the CMs and later staffed with the assistance of IFAS), one was established in the multipurpose center built as part of a SAAL project, and two were private day-care centers put "at the service of the people of the barrio" by their CTs and CMs.

3. The one in the Popular barrio was a regular commercial pharmacy established in a vacant storefront. The other was a "free popular pharmacy," reasonably well-equipped with drugs and first-aid supplies donated by doctors, factories, and others, and established through an occupation by an Elite barrio's CM.

4. Significantly, while all CMs produced improvements in their neighborhoods, on the whole, the radical CMs had the greatest impact, followed by the self-help CMs, with the reformist CMs having the least effect.

5. It is worth noting that the SAAL projects advanced most rapidly where the CMs were more radical.

6. Decree-law 511/75, adopted September 20, 1975.

7. This is more than *six* times their share of the total adult population; other manual workers accounted for three times their share of the adult population.

8. There is no evidence that greater women's participation was the source of demands often associated with neighborhood family issues (e.g., childcare, and parks), rather these demands arose in neighborhoods with a large percentage of dependent younger population. At the same time, there is not enough information to tell if these demands brought a larger number of women into the work of the CMs.

9. A movement based in eliminating the highest rent/income ratios more than 21 percent) would have been based mainly in the same barrios as the struggle for 500 escudos. It is also probable that it would have involved primarily the same people.

CHAPTER SIX

1. As national politics—the national conjuncture—becomes more clearly defined in terms of open and explicit class conflict (e.g., Portugal 1975), then the class determination of local action becomes much stronger. When the national politics are less clearly defined that way, they may also be less clear at the local level and alternative (e.g., ethnic, regional) determinants may have a greater role.

2. These variables were often found through studies of isolated organizations, and may be important in such cases even though not necessarily important in a case like Portugal which experienced dramatic shifts in conjuncture and movement development.

3. The rich may be less likely to organize because they either do not face problems requiring such actions, or because they have other means of influence.

4. This important point of continuity with his earlier work is ignored in some recent discussions that over emphasize "ruptures" among different periods in Castells' work (e.g., Lowe 1986).

5. In terms of countries that did have major popular offensives, it is important to note a major difference between the campamentos in Chile and the CMs in Portugal. In Chile the campamentos came primarily out of land seizures organized by specific political organizations, who selected participants partly on the basis of political agreement, and who kept the neighborhood organized after the occupation. As a result, the political identification of campamentos was relatively homogeneous, easy to identify, and stable over time, and with an importance overshadowing other possible factors. In Portugal, only the occupants' committees could be expected to be subject to these dynamics. In the case of CMs and most urban struggles, the participants were already living in the area and selected themselves rather than being selected according to political or other criteria. While parties might try to compete within them, they rarely were able to organize as complete control over a given area as had the parties in the campamentos of Chile.

6. Some have also argued that the poor have no inherent political orientation, but are easily radicalizable, and will follow and reflect the orientation of whatever party "captures" them. See Kornhauser (1959).

7. See Harnecker (1980) for a presentation of the structure and functioning of the Cuban system of Popular Power.

APPENDIX A

1. The person interviewed later added:

   I think that if you were to speak with other members of the Comissão de Moradores they would probably say exactly the opposite to everything I've said, and you wouldn't know whether I was telling the truth or lying. I opposed many measures they thought were revolutionary because I didn't think they were since democracy was not consolidated.

2. *A Nova Vida* the city newspaper, March 15, 1976.

3. The paper was taken over by the editorial and production staff in mid-October in response to an attempt by the owner to fire some writers and censor the news.

4. The GDUPs (Grupos Dinamizadores de Unidade Popular—Popular Unity Organizing Groups) were the organizations formed to unite CMs, CTs, and other base organizations around the candidacy of Otelo Saraiva de Carvalho for president (the candidate of the revolutionary left/popular movement). According to the person interviewed, 90 percent of the population of the barrio supported Otelo, "although they wouldn't admit it—it is camouflaged support."

5. From *O Setubalense*, August 9, 1974.

6. These events were organized through the legally constituted Cultural and Sports Association, nominated by the people of the barrio. According to the person interviewed, the PCP boycotted this association and tried to create a parallel one at the time of the formation of the GDUPs, because of the strong support the CM and the population gave to Otelo.

Bibliography

Alvarado, Luis, Rosemond Cheetham, Adriana Garat, and Gaston Rojas. *Chile: Movilización Social en Torno al Problema de la Vivienda.* Santiago: CIDU. December 1972.

Ash, Roberta. *Social Movements in America.* Chicago: Markham, 1972.

Bermeo, Nancy. *The Revolution Within the Revolution: Workers' Control in Rural Portugal.* Princeton: Princeton University Press, 1986.

Borja, Jordi, "Elementos Teóricos para el análisis de los movimientos reivin-dicativos urbanos", *Cadernos de Arquitectura y Urbanismo*, Santiago de Chile: CIDU, Enero-Febrero, 1973.

_____. "Movimientos Urbanos y Estructura Urbana," *Documents D'Analisi Urbana*, Barcelona: Universidad Autonoma, No. 1, January, 1974.

Botelho, A, and M. Pinheiro. *O Conselho Municipal do Porto.* Porto: COPSA, 1976.

Boyte, Harry. *The Backyard Revolution.* Philadelphia: Temple University Press, 1980.

Carvalho, Otelo Saraiva de. *Alvarada em Abril.* Lisbon: Bertrand, 1977.

Castells, Manuel. "Commentary on G.C. Pickvance's 'The rise and fall of urban movements . . . .'" *Society and Space*, Vol. 3, 1985.

_____. *City and the Grassroots.* Berkeley: University of California Press, 1983.

_____. "Urban Social Movements and the Struggle for Democracy: the Citi-zens' Movement in Madrid." *International Journal of Urban and Regional Research*, Vol. 2 No. 2, 1978.

_____. *Ciudad, Democracia y Socialismo.* Madrid: Siglo Veintiuno, 1977a.

_____. *The Urban Question.* Cambridge: MIT Press, 1977b.

Bibliography

_____. *Luttes Urbaines et Pouvoir Politique.* Paris: Francois Maspero, 1973.

_____. *La Question Urbaine.* Paris: Maspero, 1973a.

_____, M. Terecha Chadwick, Rosemond Cheetham, Antonieta Hirane, Santiago Quevado, Teresa Rodríguez, Gaston Rojas, Jaime Rojas and Franz Venderschueren. "Campamentos de Santiago: Movilización Urbana," in Manuel Castells (ed.), *Imperialismo y Urbanización en America Latina.* Barcelona: Gustavo Gili, 1973b.

_____, Eddy Cherki, Francis Godard, Dominique Mehl. *Crise du Logement et Mouvements Sociaux Urbains: Enquête sur la Region Parisienne.* Paris: Mouton, 1978.

Cherki, Eddy. "Populisme et ideologie révolutionnaire dans le mouvement des squatters." Manuscript, 1974.

_____. "Le mouvement d'occupation de maisons vides en France." *Espaces et Sociétés,* No. 9, 1973.

Colectif Chili. "Revendication urbaine, stratégie politique et mouvement social des 'pobladores' au chili." *Espaces et Sociétés,* No. 6-7, 1972.

Cowley, John (ed.). *Community or Class Struggle?* London: Stage 1, 1977.

Dunleavy, P. *Urban Political Analysis.* London: Macmillan, 1980.

_____. "Some political implications of sectoral cleavages and the growth of state employment." *Political Studies,* No. 27, 1979.

Downs, Charles. "Local and Regional Government." In Thomas Walker (ed.), *Nicaragua: The First Five Years.* New York: Praeger, 1985.

_____. "Comissões de Moradores and Urban Movements in Revolutionary Portugal." *International Journal of Urban and Regional Research,* Vol. 6 No. 2, 1980a.

_____. *Community Organization, Political Change and Urban Policy: Portugal 1974-1976.* Unpublished doctoral dissertation, Berkeley: University of California, 1980b.

Downs, Chip, Helena Goncalves, Fernando Nunes da Silva, and Isabel Seabra. *Os Moradores a Conquista da Cidade,* Lisbon: Armazen das Letras, 1978.

Fainstein, Norman I, and Susan S. Fainstein. *Urban Political Movements:*

the Search for Power by Minority Groups in American Cities. Englewood Cliffs, N.J.: Prentice-Hall, 1974.

Ferreira, Vitor Matias. *Movimentos Sociais Urbanos e Intervenção Política.* Porto: Afrontamento, 1975.

Freeman, Jo. "The Origins of the Women's Liberation Movement." *American Journal of Sociology,* Vol. 78, January 1973.

Gabinete de Planeamento de Setubal. *Plano de Estructura do Concelho de Setúbal.* Setubal, 7 vols., 1977.

———. "Relatório de Março." Setubal, 1975a.

———. "Relatório Preliminar do Plano de Estructura do Concelho." Setubal, 1975b.

———. "Relatório Preliminar sobre a Situação Habitacional." Setubal, 1975c.

Gamson, William A. *The Strategy of Social Protest.* Homewood, Ill.: Dorsey, 1975.

Grofman, Bernard N. and Edward N. Muller, "The Strange Case of Relative Gratification and Potential for Political Violence: The V-curve Hypothesis." *American Political Science Review,* Vol. 67, June 1973.

Gurr, Ted. *Why Men Rebel.* Princeton, N.J.: Princeton University Press, 1970.

———. "A Causal Model of Civil Strife: A Comparative Analysis Using New Indices." *American Political Science Review,* Vol. 62, December 1968.

Gusfield, Joseph R., ed. *Protest, Reform, and Revolt: A Reader in Social Movements.* New York: Wiley, 1970.

Hammond, John L. *Building Popular Power.* New York: Monthly Review Press, 1988.

———. "Portugal: Two Steps Forward, One Step Back," paper presented to the Conference on Radical and Reformist Military Regimes, Fredonia, New York, April 1978.

Handelman, Howard. "The Political Mobilization of Urban Squatter Settlements." *Latin American Research Review,* Vol. 10, Summer 1975.

Harnecker, Marta. *Cuba: Dictatorship or Democracy?* Westport: Lawrence Hill, 1980.

Henig, Jeffrey. *Neighborhood Mobilization: Redevelopment and Response.* Newark, N.J.: Rutgers University Press, 1982.

Henriques, Augusta, Cristina Pereira, Francisco Branco, and Rosario Baptista. *Untitled.* Lisbon: Instituto Superior de Serviço Social, 1976.

Henry, Etienne. "Les 'campamentos' et la création d'un pouvoir populaire au Chili." *Espaces et Sociétés*, No. 9, 1973.

Hibbs, Douglas A., Jr. *Industrial Conflict in Advanced Industrial Societies.* Cambridge: Center for International Studies, MIT, 1974.

_____. *Mass Political Violence: A Cross-National Causal Analysis.* New York: Wiley, 1973.

Hobsbawm, Eric. *Primitive Rebels.* New York: Praeger, 1963.

Huntington, Samuel P., *Political Order in Changing Societies.* New Haven, Conn.: Yale University Press, 1969.

IFAS. *Programa do Trabalho*, Fevreiro 1975.

_____. *Annual Reports.* 1976-1978.

ISSS. *Textos de Base sobre Habitação: Ocupações.* Lisbon: Institutio Superior de Serviço Social, 1975.

Intervenção Social, publication of the Association of Students of the Instituto Superior de Serviço Social, Lisbon, 1976 and 1977.

Johnson, Chalmers. *Revolutionary Change.* Boston: Little, Brown, 1966.

Katznelson, Ira. *City Trenches: Urban Politics and the Patterning of Class in the United States.* Chicago: University of Chicago Press, 1981.

Kornhauser, William. *The Politics of Mass Society.* New York: Free Press, 1959.

Kramer, Jane. "Letter from Lisbon." *The New Yorker*, September 23, 1974.

Kusnetzoff, Fernando. "Spatial Planning and Development in Latin America: The Critical Approach." *Journal of Interamerican Studies and World Affairs*, Vol. 19 No. 3, August 1977.

Laclau, Ernesto. *Politics and Ideology in Marxist Theory.* London: New Left Books, 1977.

Lefebvre, Henry. *Everyday Life in the Modern World*. London: Penguin, 1971.

_____. *La Révolution Urbaine*. Paris: Gallimard, 1970.

Lipsky, Michael. "In the Winter of our Discontent." Unpublished, 1975.

_____. "Protest as a Political Resource." *American Political Science Review*, Vol. 62, December 1968.

Lodhi, Abdul Qaiyum and Charles Tilly. "Urbanization, Crime, and Collective Violence in 19th-Century France." *American Journal of Sociology*, Vol. 79, September 1973.

Lopes, Sergio. "Etat et 'Moradores'." Unpublished master's thesis, Paris: L'Ecole des Hautes Etudes en Sciences Sociaux, 1977.

Lowe, Stuart. *Urban Social Movements: The City after Castells*. London: Macmillan, 1986.

Luxemburg, Rosa. "The Mass Strike." In Mary-Alice Waters (ed.), *Rosa Luxemburg Speaks*. New York: Pathfinder, 1970.

Marconi, Francesco and Paulo de Oliveira. *L'Architectura come practica politica: Portogallo: il Saal*. Milan: Feltrinelli, 1977.

Marx, Gary T. *Protest and Prejudice: A Study of Belief in the Black Community*. New York: Harper & Row, 1969.

McPhail, Clark. "Civil Disorder Participation: a Critical Examination of Recent Research." *American Sociological Review*, Vol. 36, December 1971.

Milkman, Margaret E. *L'Articulation entre la Politique Internationale et la Politique Interne au Portugal après le 25 Avril 1974*. Unpublished master's thesis, Universite Catholique de Louvain: Institut des Sciences Politiques et Sociales, 1979.

Moore, Barrington, Jr. *The Social Origins of Dictatorship and Democracy: Lord and Peasant in the Making of the Modern World*. Boston: Beacon, 1966.

Nelson, Joan M. *Access to Power: Politics and the Urban Poor in Developing Nations*. Princeton, N.J.: Princeton University Press, 1979.

_____. *Migrants, Urban Poverty, and Instability in Developing Nations*. Cambridge: Center for International Affairs, Harvard University, 1969.

Bibliography

Neves, Orlando (ed.). *A Revolução em Ruptura: Textos Históricos da Revolução, Vol. II.* Lisbon: Diabril, 1975.

Oberschall, Anthony. *Social Conflict and Social Movements.* Englewood Cliffs, N.J.: Prentice-Hall, 1973.

Orbell, John M. "Protest Participation Among Southern Negro College Students." *American Political Science Review,* VOl 61, June 1967.

Parsons, Talcott. *The Social System.* New York: Free Press, 1951.

Passos, Maria Jose Ferreira and Luisa Maria Gouveia Alves. *O Movimento de Ocupações.* Lisbon: Instituto Superior de Serviço Social, 1976.

Pastrana, E. and M. Threlfall. *Pan, Techo y Poder: El Movimiento de Pobladores en Chile (1970-1973).* Buenos Aires: SIAP, 1974.

Perlman, Janice. *The Myth of Marginality.* Berkeley: Universty of California Press, 1974.

Pickvance, Chris. "Concepts, contexts and comparison in the study of urban movements: a reply to M. Castells." *Society and Space,* Vol. 4, 1986.

_____. "The rise and fall of urban movements and the role of comparative analysis." *Society and Space,* Vol. 3, 1985.

_____. "From 'Social Base' to 'Social Force'." In Michael Harloe (ed.). *Captive Cities.* London: John Wiley, 1976.

_____. "On the Study of Urban Social Movements." *The Sociological Review,* Vol. 23 No. 1, February 1975.

Pinard, Maurice. *The Rise of a Third Party: A Study of Crisis Politics.* Englewood Cliffs, N.J.: Prentice-Hall, 1971.

_____. "Mass Society and Political Movements: a New Formulation." *American Journal of Sociology,* Vol. 73, May 1968.

Piven, Francis F. and Richard A. Cloward. *Poor People's Movements.* New York: Vintage, 1977.

Porfirio, Laurinda Maria, Maria Luisa Cristovão de Sousa, and Rosa Maria Ramos Costa. *Breve Análise da Situação Política, Económica e Social desde 1926 a 1974.* Lisbon: Instituto Superior de Serviço Social, 1976.

Portas, Nuno and Margarida Coelho. "Os Movimentos Sociais Urbanos em

Portugal." Lisbon: unpublished, 1977.

Poulantzas, Nicos. *The Crisis of the Dictatorships*. London: New Left Books, 1976.

Rodrigues, A, C. Borga, and M. Cardoso. *Portugal Depois de Abril*. Lisbon: Intervoz, 1976.

_____. *O Movimento dos Capitães*. Lisbon: Moraes Editores, 1974.

Rogin, Michael Paul. *The Intellectuals and McCarthy: The Radical Specter*. Cambridge: MIT Press, 1967.

Rude, George F. *The Crowd in History*. New York: Wiley, 1964.

Santos, Maria de Lourdes Lima dos, Marinus Pires de Lima, and Vitor Matias Ferreira. *O 25 de Abril e as Lutas Socias nas Empresas*. Three vols, Porto: Afrontamento, 1976.

Schwartz, Michael. *The Southern Farmers' Aliance: the Organizational Forms of Radical Protest*. Unpublished doctoral dissertation, Department of Sociology, Harvard University, 1971.

Serra, Luis Hector. "The Grass-Roots Organizations." In Thomas Walker (ed.). *Nicaragua: The First Five Years*. New York: Praeger, 1985.

Simões, Elvira, Filipa Fontes, Manuela Pereira, and Carmo Sobreira. *Lutas Urbanas—Um Contributo para a Análise do Processo das Ocupações em Lisboa e Arredores*. Lisbon: Instituto Superior de Serviço Social, 1976.

Skocpol, Theda. *States and Social Revolutions*. Cambridge: Cambridge Universty Press, 1979.

Smelser, Neil. *Theory of Collective Behavior*. New York: Free Press, 1962.

Snyder, David and Charles Tilly. "Hardship and Collective Violence in France, 1830 to 1960." *American Sociological Review*, Vol. 37, October 1972.

Spilerman, Seymour. "The Causes of Racial Disturbances: a Comparison of Alternative Explanations." *American Sociological Review*, Vol. 35, August 1970.

Tilly, Charles. *From Mobilization to Revolution*. Menlo Park, Ca.: Addison-Wesley, 1978.

————. "Does Modernization Breed Revolution?" *Comparative Politics*, Vol. 5 No. 3, April 1973.

————. "Reflections on the Revolution of Paris: a Review of Recent Histori-cal Writing." *Social Problems*, Vol. 12, Summer 1964.

Topalov, Christian. "La Politique du logement dans le processus révolution-naire portugais." *Espaces et Sociétés*, No. 17-18, 1976.

United States National Advisory Commission on Civil Disorders. *Report.* Washington, D.C.: Government Printing Office, 1968.

Useem, Michael. *Protest Movements in America.* Indianapolis: Bobbs-Merrill, 1975.

Vanderschuren, Franz. "Mobilisation politique et lutte pour le logement au Chili." *Espaces et Sociétés*, No. 5, 1972.

Viera, M. and D. Oliveira. *O Poder Popular em Portugal.* Coimbra: Centelho, 1976.

Viva a Luta dos Bairros. Lisbon: Escola Superior das Belas Artes, four issues, 1975.

VonEschen, Donald, Jerome Kirk, and Maurice Pinard. "The Organizational Substructure of Disorderly Politics." *Social Forces*, Vol. 49, June 1971.

Walker, Kenneth. "A Comparison of University Reform Movements in Argen-tina and Colombia." *Comparative Education Review*, Vol. 10, June 1966.

Walton, John. "Urban political movements and revolutionary change in the Third World." *Urban Affairs Quarterly*, Vol. 15 No. 1, September 1979.

Wolf, Eric R. *Peasant Wars of the Twentieth Century.* New York: Harper and Row, 1969.

Zald, Mayer and Roberta Ash. "Social Movement Organizations: Growth, Decay and Change." *Social Forces*, No. 44, March 1966.

Subject Index

ADFA (Associação dos Deficientes das Forças Armadas): 31

Achievements:
—(see comissão de moradores, achievements; and effects)

Agrarian reform:
—Law, 30

Allende, Salvador: 21

Armed Forces Movement:
—(see MFA)

Armed forces:
—(see military; MFA)

COPCON:
—creation, 19, 194
—Document, 56
—housing proposal, 26, 56
—and popular movement, 30, 32, 142, 150, 151

COPS:
—(see coordination bodies)

CRMP (Conselho Revolucionário de Moradores do Porto): 27, 194-95

Caetano, Marcelo: 15, 34

Castells, Manuel:
—critique of, 8-9, 118-123
—theories of urban movements, 8, 118-119, 122

City-country link: 58, 59, 62, 145, 147, 149, 151, 153

Colonial war:
—decolonization, 20, 25, 27, 50, 53, 141, 194
—government divisions and, 19

—MFA and, 15

Comissão de moradores (neighborhood commission):
—achievements, 3, 4-5, 67, 140, 145, 147, 150, 152, 156, 182-84
—case histories, 138-161
—class composition, 99 (see also social base)
—conflicts among, 48
—coordination and (see coordination bodies)
—defined, 3
—demands, 26-27, 145, 148, 152, 154-55, 179-81
—demise of, 62, 74-76, 198
—factors predisposing to formation, 77
—housing conditions and issues, 47, 69-70 (see also housing)
—an local government, 4, 47, 101, 103-105, 143, 148, 150, 153-54, 157, 196, 198
—neighborhoods without, 76
—organizational principles, 4, 143, 159
—origins of, 35, 37, 38, 39, 72-77, 197
—political orientation, 77-86, 161
—political parties and, 35, 73-74, 83-86, 144, 161
—relation to state, 76, 78, 143, 145, 151, 161
—role, 3, 46
—social base and priorities, 48, 51, 139
—social base and origin of, 67-77, 144, 146, 148, 152

Committee of Struggle

—(see coordination bodies)
Communist Party:
—(see PCP)
Conselho de Moradores:
—(see coordination bodies)
Coordination bodies:
—Committee of Struggle, 58-63, 147, 197
—Conselho de Moradores, 47, 48-53, 55-56, 58, 170-72, 196
—COPS, 54-56, 57, 173-76
—ICBB, 39, 49, 53, 64, 196
—models for, 54, 127-129, 157, 162-69, 186-87
—political parties and, 53-54
Coups:
—April 25, 1974, 15
—March 11, 1975, 25
—November 25, 1975, 32, 195
—September 28, 1974, 20-21
—threats of, 33, 41

Demands:
—housing, 18, 23, 27, 34, 56, 179-81
—saneamento, 17, 34
—social services, 26, 179-81
—unemployment, 20
—urban, 119, 160-61, 179-81
—wages and working conditions, 17
—workers' control, 28
—(see also comissão de moradores, case studies; issues)
Democracy:
—direct (see direct action)
—economic, 21-22
—(see also models of society; popular power)
Demonstrations, 20-21, 24, 27, 29, 30, 31, 32-33, 36, 37-38, 41, 46, 52, 57, 58, 60, 61, 64, 157, 161, 196-197
Direct action:
—advance of revolution and, 26
—against rightwing opposition, 21, 37-38

—direct democracy, 28, 57, 84
—effectiveness of, 92, 198
—general, 13
—labor and, 50
—limitations of, 53
—and political orientation, 78, 126
—popular power and, 106-107, 133-137
—and reform of urban structure, 95, 96
—self-management, 18
—(see also occupations)

Eanes, Ramalho: 33, 65
Economic reforms:
—antimonopoly, 22, 25, 27, 32, 38
—Melo Antunes Plan, 22
—(see also nationalizations)
Effects, political:
—changing general political relations, 99-103
—reform of state apparatus, 103-105
Effects, urban:
—dependence on political conjuncture, 109-110
—immediate, 90-93, 96, 119, 120
—local government, relation to, 92-93
—on logic of reproduction of urban structure, 96-97, 98
—on urban structure, 93-96, 97
Elections:
—Constituent Assembly, 26, 46, 77
—Legislative, 33, 64, 77
—Presidential, 33, 65, 77
Escudo-dollar equivalency: 191

Foreign involvement:
—electronics assembly firms, 18, 36, 38, 193
—ITT, 195
—reaction to minimum wage, 18
—U.S., 15

GAPS (Grupo de Acção Popular Socialista):

—origin of CMs, 37
Gomes, Costa: 15, 21
Gonçalves, Vasco: 19, 21
Government:
—provisional:
—First, 19, 36
—Second, 19
—Third, 21
—Fourth, 29, 42
—Fifth, 30, 32, 56
—Sixth, 30, 32, 57
—(see also state)
Guidelines Document:
—CM formation and, 70
—coordination bodies (COPS) and,
53-54, 129
—model for new society, 28-29
—text, 162-69
Gurr:
—critique of, 6-7
—theory of relative deprivation, 6

Housing:
—CMs and, 47
—Committee of Struggle, 61
—COPCON proposal, 26, 56
—demands, 18, 23, 27, 34, 41, 56, 160
—impact on popular movement, 100-
101
—laws, 20, 24, 26, 27, 31, 193
—legal proceedings, 52, 63
—local government and, 40, 42-44, 45,
47, 51, 52
—military and, 44
—occupations, 8, 18, 24, 26, 30, 31,
34, 40, 41, 42-44, 45, 53, 64, 141,
144, 145, 147, 150, 151, 153, 195,
196
—rent reductions, 41, 47-48, 51, 52,
53, 56, 63-64, 142, 145, 147
—SAAL, 19, 157, 160-61, 185, 197
—shantytowns, 18
—workers commissions and, 186-87

ICBB:
—(see coordination bodies)
Issues:
—economy, 25
—historical background, 87-90
—and origin of CMs, 114-115, 144
—and political orientation, 78
—political conjuncture and, 110, 111-
112
—and social class, 12
—of urban movements, 9, 101

Labor:
—action, 38
—demands, 36-37
—and direct action, 50
—factories mentioned, 190
—housing and, 186-87
—unemployment, 20
—unions, 17
Laws:
—agrarian reform, 30
—constitution, 33
—criticism of, 20
—demonstrations, 52
—Guidelines Document, 162-169
—housing, 20, 24, 26, 27, 63, 103, 193
—local government, 36
—media, 30, 31
—strikes, 20
Local government:
—attempts to organize CMs, 37, 39
—CM and, 4, 47, 57, 101, 103-105,
143, 148, 150, 153-54, 196, 198
—CM political orientation and, 80, 145
—coordination bodies and, 58
—and housing, 40, 42-44, 45, 47, 51,
52
—limitations on, 35
—1974 reorganization, 35-36
—political parties and, 39
—and popular power, 57, 105-106
—role in changing urban structure,
94-95, 96
—(see also state)

MDP/CDE:
—local government and, 17, 35
—and origin of CMs, 37
MFA (Movimento das Forças Armadas):
—COPS, 54
—and decolonization, 19, 20
—decomposition of, 60
—and economic reforms, 22
—and government, 16
—opposition and, 21
—Political Action Program, 27-28
—relation to CMs, 145, 192
—roots, 15
—rural areas and, 23
—soldiers demands, 18-19
Mass movements:
—(see social movements; popular
  movements)
Media:
—Jornal do Comércio, 21
—laws, 30, 31
—occupations, 27, 60
—Rádio Renascença, 27, 30, 32, 60,
  144-45
—República, 27, 29, 30, 32, 60, 144-45
—Setubalense, 60, 62, 144-45
Military:
—Committee of Struggle and, 58-62
—demonstrations and, 24, 58
—relation to CMs, 145, 192
—resistance to purging of left, 59-60
—soldiers demands, 18-19, 31
—(see also MFA)
Milkman, Margaret: 27, 30
Models of society:
—COPS, 173-76
—Guidelines Document, 28-29, 162-69
—Political Action Program, 27-28
—role of state in economy, 25
Movement:
—poor peoples, 11
—popular, 4, 11
—revolutionary, 11
—working class, 4

Movimento das Forças Armadas:
—(see MFA)
Movimento Democrático Português:
—(see MDP/CDE; political parties)

Nationalization:
—antimonopoly alliance and, 27
—following March 11, 1975, 24, 42,
  194
—laws, 30
—Lisbon water company, 17

Occupations:
—bridge over Tagus, 31
—factories, 34, 36, 192, 195
—housing, 8, 18, 24, 26, 30, 31, 34,
  40, 41, 42-44, 45, 53, 64, 140, 141,
  144, 145, 147, 150, 151, 153, 195,
  196
—impact on urban structure, 94
—local government and, 42-44
—media, 27, 60
—military and, 44
—and political orientation, 81-83
—rural, 24, 26, 31, 61
—social services, 51, 55, 140, 144
—(see also direct action)
Organizing strategies:
—origin of CMs, 115-118
Otelo Saraiva de Carvalho: 19, 33, 65,
  142

PCP (Partido Comunista Português):
—conflicts with other parties, 23, 31
—model of economy and society, 25
—relation to CMs, 84
PPD (Partido Popular Democrático):
—demonstration against, 41
—model of economy and society, 25
—Setubal demonstration against, 24
PS (Partido Socialista):
—conflicts with other parties, 23, 31
—local government and, 17
—model of economy and society, 25

—opposition to Fifth Provisional Government, 29
—opposition to Guidelines Document, 29
—relation to CMs, 84
PSD:
—(see PPD)
Participation:
—gender, 99, 199
—occupation, 99, 199
—political orientation and, 100
Partido Socialista:
—(see PS; political parties)
Pato, Octavio: 65
Piven and Cloward:
—critique of, 7
—theory of poor peoples movements, 7
Political conjuncture:
—changes of, 11-12
—definition, 2
—role of, 2, 9, 108-113, 134-135
—social classes and, 11-12
Political orientation:
—CMs and, 77-86
—direct action and, 126, 198
—neighborhood issues, 78
—relation to local government, 80
—role of political parties, 83-85, 126
—theories of, 123-127, 126
Political parties:
—conflicts among, 23, 26, 27, 28, 29, 31, 39, 84, 153
—cooperation among, 50
—coordination bodies, 53-54
—general, 17, 22, 121
—models of economy and society, 25
—opposition to revolution, 37
—political orientation of CMs and, 83-86
—social movements and, 66
—socialism and, 23
—(see also specific parties)
Popular movements:

—expansion of, 73-74
—factors producing, 85-86, 192-93
—political parties and, 85
—theories of, 7, 193
—urban social movement as part of, 12
—(see also social movements)
Popular power:
—COPS proposal, 173-76
—government and, 61, 103-105, 133-137
—Guidelines Document, 28-30, 162-69
—models of, 67, 102, 105-107, 133-137, 162-69, 170-72, 173-76
—political conjuncture and, 134-135
—support for, 57
Portas, Nuno: 105
Portuguese Revolution:
—antimonopoly reforms and, 22, 26
—April 25, factors underlying, 3, 15, 16
—economic issues and, 21
—issues, 16
—models for change, 27-29
—opposition to, 20-21, 25, 29, 30, 32
—periods, 16
—role of military, 25, 28

Rent reduction, 41, 47-48, 51, 52, 53, 56, 63-64, 81-83, 142, 145, 147, 151, 153, 196, 197
Rural organizing:
—MFA and, 23
—occupations, 26, 31
—workers, 24
—(see also agrarian reform)

SAAL:
—coordination (see coordination bodies, ICBB)
—creation, 19, 27
—local government and, 103-104
—origin of CMs, 37
—political orientation of CMs, 81-83

—shantytown struggles, 64, 185, 197, 199
SUV (Soldados Unidos Vencerão): 31, 58
Shantytown struggles:
—(see SAAL)
Social base (of neighborhoods):
—of CMs, 139, 144, 146, 148, 152, 155, 158, 177-78
—and origin of CM, 70-77, 114
—political conjuncture and, 110-112
—role of, 119, 121
—types (Popular, Interclass, Elite), 3, 67-70
Social movements:
—manipulation of, 66, 67
—political parties and, 66
—spontaneity of, 66, 67
—theories of, 6-9, 66, 67, 118-123
—(see also urban social movements)
Social services:
—achievements, 91-92, 182-84, 198
—daycare, 26, 179-81, 182-84, 198
—demands, 26, 179-81
—state and reform, 40
Socialism:
—direct democracy and, 28-29
—Political Action Plan, 27-28
—(see also popular power; models of society; Guidelines Document)
Socialist Party:
—(see PS)
Spínola, António de: 15, 16, 19, 20, 21, 36
State:
—CMs and, 78
—housing agency (FFH), 45
—institutional reform, 40, 101, 103-105, 130-133
—internal conflict, 19, 40
—popular power and, 61, 131-133, 133-137
—social welfare agency (IFAS) strike, 46, 140, 152

—urban social movements and, 12, 102, 119, 130-133
—(see also local government)
Strikes:
—COPCON and, 32
—IFAS, 46
—strike law, 20, 21
—various, 15, 17, 141

Tilly, Charles:
—critique of, 7-8
—theories of collective movements, 7

Urban social movements:
—Castells' models of, 118-123
—characteristics (distinction from other movements), 2
—expansion of social base, 100-101
—government and, 12, 13
—international comparisons, 1, 135-136, 199, 200
—issues and, 9, 10, 118
—origins of, 113-118, 118-123
—political conjuncture and, 9, 10-11, 108-113
—relation to popular movement, 12
—social classes and, 9, 10, 11, 12, 13
—sources and dynamics of, 1-2, 10, 108-113, 123
—theories of, 1-2, 6-9, 113-117, 118-123
—(see also popular movements; social movements)

Workers commissions:
—coordination (see coordination bodies)
—demands, 35, 36, 102
—direct democracy and, 28
—(see also labor; workers control)
Workers control:
—demand, 28
—general, 22
—(see also workers commissions; labor; direct action)

Author Index

Ash, Roberta: 192

Bermeo, Nancy: 84
Borja, Jordi: 8, 9, 193
Botelho, A.: 195

Carvalho, Otelo Saraiva de: 193
Castells, Manuel: 8, 117, 118-123, 124, 125, 192
Cherki, Eddy: 125
Cloward, Richard: 7, 11, 13, 117, 192, 193

Downs, Charles: 41, 136, 195
Dunleavy, P.: 8, 192

Fainstein, Norman: 117, 130-131, 192
Fainstein, Susan: 117, 130-131, 192

Gamson, William: 192, 193
Gurr, Ted: 6, 192

Handelman, Howard: 115, 124
Harnecker, Marta: 200
Henig, Jeffrey: 114, 115, 117, 192, 193
Hibbs, Douglas: 6
Hobsbawn, Eric: 192

Johnson, Chalmers: 6

Katznelson, Ira: 8
Kornhauser, William: 6, 199
Kusnetzoff, Fernando: 193

Lefebvre, Henri: 7
Lipsky, Michael: 9, 192

Lowe, Stuart: 1, 8, 9, 118, 192, 199

Milkman, Margaret: 27

Nelson, Joan: 115, 124, 127, 193
Neves, Orlando: 28

Oliveira, D.: 127

Pastrana, E.: 127
Pickvance, Chris: 8, 9, 118, 193
Pinheiro, M.: 195
Piven, Francis: 7, 11, 13, 117, 192, 193
Poulantzas, Nicos: 193

Rodrigues, A.: 17, 19, 20, 22, 23, 193
Rude, George: 192

Santos, Maria de Lourdes Lima dos: 193
Schwartz, Michael: 192
Serra, Luis: 136
Skocpol, Theda: 193
Smelser, Neil: 6
Snyder, David: 6

Tilly, Charles: 6, 7, 192, 193
Topalov, Christian: 198
Threlfall, M.: 127

Useem, Michael: 9, 192

Vieira, M.: 127

Walton, John: 193
Wolf, Eric: 192

215